D1050579

The Trainee Secondary Teacher's Handbook

Also available from Continuum

100 Ideas for Trainee Teachers, Angella Cooze

Trainee Teacher's Survival Guide, Hazel Bennett

Getting the Buggers to Behave (3rd edition), Sue Cowley

How to Survive Your First Year in Teaching (2nd edition),
   Sue Cowley

The Trainee Secondary Teacher's Handbook

Gererd Dixie

WITHDRAWN

BOWLING GREEN STATE
UNIVERSITY LIBRARIES

continuum

Continuum International Publishing Group

The Tower Building   80 Maiden Lane
11 York Road   Suite 704
London   New York
SE1 7NX   NY 10038

www.continuumbooks.com

© Gererd Dixie 2009

All rights reserved. No part of this publication may be reproduced or transmitted in any form or by any means, electronic or mechanical, including photocopying, recording, or any information storage or retrieval system, without prior permission in writing from the publishers.

Gererd Dixie has asserted his right under the Copyright, Designs and Patents Act, 1988, to be identified as Author of this work.

Cartoons drawn by Peter Rennoldson | peter@bigcarrot.co.uk

British Library Cataloguing-in-Publication Data
A catalogue record for this book is available from the British Library.

ISBN: 978-1847-063090 (paperback)

Library of Congress Cataloguing-in-Publication Data
A catalog record for this book is available from the Library of Congress.

Typeset by Ben Cracknell Studios | www.benstudios.co.uk
Printed and bound in Great Britain by MPG Books Ltd, Bodmin, Cornwall

Contents

Introduction

Those who educate children well are more to be honoured than parents, for these only gave life, those the art of living well.

Aristotle

'Good morning Mr Dixie, I'm thinking about becoming a teacher but I am not exactly sure what the job entails, what qualifications I need or how I go about finding out which training route to take. To be honest, I'm not absolutely sure whether teaching is the right job for me but I am really interested in finding out. Can you help?'

As a longstanding professional tutor in a large comprehensive school, it has been my pleasure and privilege to have experienced countless conversations similar to the one described above. However, despite doing all that I can to support these potential trainees, I am always left feeling somewhat frustrated that a lack of time has simply not allowed me to do more. In situations such as these I would usually invite you to visit the school and have a chat with me about your hopes and aspirations and possible ways forward. I would also clarify that you hold the relevant qualifications (as outlined in Chapter 3). In order to provide a realistic perspective of a modern-day secondary school, I would probably arrange for you to take a tour of the school and then set you up with a lesson observation schedule for the day. In many cases this would be the sum total of preparation/thinking time formally afforded to you by the school. Many trainees apply to, and are accepted on, Initial Teacher Training (ITT) programmes without gaining an intimate understanding of what is in store for them during their training year.

The initial purpose of this book is to furnish you with the information, guidance and advice that you will need to make an informed decision about whether to teach or not. Then to explore the nature of your teacher training should you decide to apply for a course. If you are forewarned about the expectations and experiences that you are likely to encounter during your training year, you will be able to make the necessary practical, emotional and academic preparations which are so fundamental to you in being able to make a successful start to your course.

Although as a professional tutor, advanced skills teacher (AST) and experienced teacher trainer I feel well qualified to write a book such as this, it would be somewhat hubristic of me to do so without having canvassed the views of other relevant professionals and, more importantly, without having sought the opinions of current and past trainees. Therefore, much of the advice and guidance offered within this book has been fuelled by questionnaire research carried out with trainees on Postgraduate Certificate in Education (PGCE) courses, School Centred Initial Teacher Training (SCITT) programmes and the Graduate Teacher Training Programmes (GTTPs). In addition to this I have sought the views of numerous professional tutors and subject mentors as to what constitutes sound advice for trainees about to embark upon their ITT courses.

So, who exactly has this book been written for? The most obvious target audience is the members of that group of successful ITT applicants who simply want to make effective use of the six-month period prior to starting their course and who are likely to require a constant source of guidance throughout their training year. A less obvious, but nevertheless important, audience is the substantial number of people for whom teaching is merely one possibility among a whole host of career options. If, having explored the issues discussed in this book, you decide that teaching is simply not for you, you will have reached this decision in an informed and considered manner. Therefore, my aims will have been realized. Another significant audience for this book is the secondary school ITT tutor, who will be able to select specific chapters to inform the various training modules offered by his or her school. The book will provide these tutors with an excellent overview of a range of training issues and will sit extremely comfortably on the shelves of any professional development library.

This handbook is divided into seven parts, six of which represent your training needs at various points along a chronological continuum from the point at which you first started to think about teaching as a career right through to the end of your training year (see Figure 1.1).

It should be stressed at the very outset that the advice and guidance offered within this book is generic in nature and will not meet all your subject-specific needs. However, a chapter on how to gain, develop a subject and utilize your subject knowledge has been included in Part 5. I outline the various parts below in textual and diagrammatic form so

Your journey through this handbook

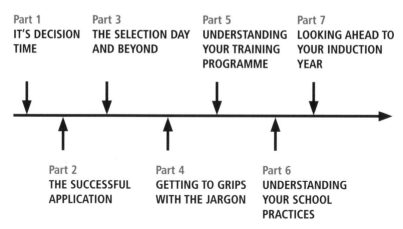

Figure 1.1 The teacher training continuum

that you gain an understanding of the sequential nature of the chapters in this handbook.

The three chapters in Part 1 have been written with those early decisions in mind. Chapter 1 explores your initial exploratory thoughts about teaching and offers guidance on how to find out whether your dreams of becoming a teacher meet the reality of life in a modern-day secondary school. Chapter 2 provides guidance on visiting schools and how to conduct additional research in an attempt to discover realistic scenarios about teaching. It is hoped that from these you will be able to make informed decisions about whether or not to go through with the application process. Chapter 3 takes the process one step further by furnishing you with a range of different routes into teacher training. This will be followed by an exploration of the pros and cons of each ITT programme. In doing this I hope to afford you the opportunity to match your ability, personality, personal background and/or dominant learning styles with an appropriate course. Some consideration will also be given to the pre-course requirements associated with each of these ITT programmes.

I have entitled Part 2 *The Successful Application* because the purpose of all three chapters is to provide advice and guidance about what to do once you have decided to apply for an ITT course. Having chosen your preferred teacher training route, you need to think about the nature of the application process itself. Chapter 4 offers advice on how to use your pre-course school visits to full effect in gaining a knowledge and understanding of the hidden curriculum before then going on to explain how to use this information to support your application. Chapter 5 provides detailed guidance on how to use your lesson observations to explore a range of teaching styles and how to gain a rudimentary understanding of the behaviour management strategies used in secondary schools today. A detailed exploration of the preparatory work required for a successful interview will then take place. In Chapter 6 I go on to show you how to successfully complete your application form and personal statement.

Two of the chapters in Part 3 provide guidance on how to perform well on the training course selection day. I use the term 'selection day' rather than 'interview day' because I need to make it clear to you that your assessment will not merely be confined to your performance in the formal interview. Chapter 7 focuses on the selection tasks you will have to complete before, during and/or after the selection day, while Chapter 8 provides you with detailed guidance about how to perform well in the interview itself. On the assumption that your application has been successful, Chapter 9 goes on to offer a full exploration of the pre-course preparations you are advised to make in order to enjoy a successful training year. In addition to this, Chapter 9 will also help you to gain a fuller understanding of the functions and roles of education, of the school and of the teacher.

One of the things you will be confronted with during the initial few days of your first school visit will be the amount of educational jargon used on a daily basis. What is meant by the terms SENCO, PAD, EAL, GNVQ? Who or what is ALICE? Part 4 consists of only one chapter (Chapter 10) and is selective in offering an exploration of some of the educational terms and issues that you are highly likely to come across during your training year. This chapter has been produced to enable you to become familiar with the language of teaching.

Part 5, which has been given the title of *Understanding Your Training Programme,* focuses on the principles of teacher training and on the requirements of your specific training programme. The part starts with Chapter 11 which describes many of the issues that could arise during what may possibly be an extremely turbulent year. This chapter affords you an opportunity to explore these issues and, in doing so, will provide an indication of the training journey ahead. Chapter 12 goes on to furnish you with advice and guidance, designed to help you get to know, and meet, the Professional Standards for QTS. Chapter 13 highlights the need for you to show an understanding of the principles of reflective practice and to be able to use this to inform your training and teaching. All teacher training providers will require you to complete academic work to support your professional practice. Chapters 14 and 15 have been designed to help you to get the most out of your presentations, workshops and lectures and to provide guidance on how to write good assignments and essays. Bearing in mind the high status afforded by the Training and Development Agency (TDA) to the importance of subject knowledge, Chapter 16 has been written to help you to improve and demonstrate your subject knowledge for teaching.

Finally the moment has arrived – you are ready to start your first school practice. Part 6, *Understanding Your School Practices,* consists of 14 chapters which explore a range of issues relating to your time in schools. These are as follows:

- different types of school practices
- acclimatizing yourself to the school
- preparing yourself psychologically for your practice
- understanding your development as a trainee
- understanding the roles of those supporting the training process
- making effective use of classroom teaching assistants
- working with parents
- getting to grips with your behaviour management
- lesson planning
- engaging your pupils
- using ICT to support your professional practice
- understanding the issue of inclusion
- gaining form tutor experience
- Ofsted inspections.

Part 7, *Looking Ahead to Your Induction Year,* comprises seven chapters all of which have been written to support your move towards NQT status. Chapter 31 explores some of the social, philosophical and practical issues you will have to think about when deciding which type of school you intend to apply to. Chapter 32 provides in-depth guidance on how to write a good letter of application and what you could do should you get towards the end of your training year and still not have a job. Chapter 33 provide some top tips to help to you 'stay one step ahead of the game' in the selection process and support a successful application for your first teaching post. As is pointed out in Chapter 3, making an impression on pupils and staff is a requisite ingredient of any successful job application. Chapter 34 explores the ways in which you can use your personality and interpersonal skills to make an impression on those involved in the selection process. Bearing in mind that it is highly likely that you will have to teach a specimen lesson on your selection day, Chapter 35 provides you with a range of top tips to consider when planning this lesson. And then there is the interview itself. In the same format as that presented to you in your ITT interview guidance, Chapter 36 provides a range of advice on how to perform well at interview. This is supported by a menu of potential interview questions and model answers. Finally, to prepare you for what is likely to be one of you final tasks as an ITT trainee, Chapter 37 explores the role of the Career Entry and Development Profile, and offers you guidance on how to complete this in an effective and productive manner.

How you choose to use this book is entirely up to you. You might, for example, prefer to read it from cover to cover in order to gain an overall picture of the themes, issues and practices relevant to your training year. Alternatively, you may wish to focus on the specific chapters that are most representative of your needs at any given point along the training continuum. However you decide to use this book, I am hopeful and confident that it will fulfil its role as originally envisaged when I first put pen to paper – that of acting as a supportive, informative and critical friend throughout your training year. With this in mind I would like to wish you all the very best for the journey ahead.

Part One
IT'S DECISION TIME

Early thoughts

It is true to say that teachers start their career journeys in very different ways. For a small number of those who took part in a survey I undertook, the process of thinking about becoming a teacher was almost revelatory: a 'light bulb' moment that helped to illuminate the new career path ahead of them. However, for the vast majority of people, the process started with an initial germ of a thought which grew exponentially until it eventually became all-consuming in nature. Many of these teachers explained that they first started to think about teaching as a career as a result of being extremely unhappy in their current jobs and/or because they were simply desperate for a new sense of direction. Others felt less strongly about their circumstances. They certainly did not experience a sense of dread when getting up for work in the morning but felt that they were simply coasting through life without any real sense of purpose.

If you find that so amusing, perhaps you can do better!

My conversations with numerous trainees and qualified teachers over the past 15 years have informed me of the importance of those early school days in influencing their decisions to become teachers. During this initial exploratory phase their thoughts often drifted back to their own school days to those teachers who had inspired them to greater things or conversely to those teachers who had demotivated them and/or humiliated them in front of their peers. Either way there is no doubt that the quality of teaching they experienced as pupils has had a dramatic effect upon their decision to become teachers.

In Dixie (2005) I devoted a chapter ('No One Forgets a Good Teacher') to exploring this very issue. Using the teaching staff of two large secondary schools as a target research population, I discovered that the memories of the respondents of their own school lives had played a significant role in their decision to become teachers. In deciding to take up the profession they had drawn upon these experiences, both positive and negative, to inform their decision as to what type of teacher they would like to aspire to be. In all cases an overwhelming desire to make a difference was displayed. I am sure that you will empathize with some of the feelings expressed in the quotes below.

> Geography was never really a subject that I would have said that I actually 'enjoyed' until I had this teacher. As a result of his lessons my perception was altered and I went on to do geography A level. (The subject I got my best A level grade in!) I always knew how hard the teacher worked for us and in return I always ensured I worked equally hard. The teacher's enthusiasm for the subject really inspired me and made me want to learn … this is the teacher that made me want to enter the profession – I hope that I am able to inspire pupils in the same way.

> Mr X was my history teacher for GCSE and A level. He was enthusiastic and knew a lot of stuff! He made the subject relevant and exciting to study … He made me see that history is the most important subject in the world – to understand human nature, decisions and events, and to make sense of the world in which we live. He *inspired* me to learn and to become a teacher.

> Mr X opened my eyes to media studies and I have always said that it is down to him that I now teach this subject. He had a passion for media, and most of the information he gave us had come from his own research, not textbooks, and I really admired him for that. He opened my eyes to new films and ideas, which I surprised myself by liking … I remember him today mostly because when I plan lessons for new topics I always think about how he'd do it. If I can imagine him teaching my lesson, I know it is right.

> My form teacher in Year 10 enjoyed inflicting punishment and took pleasure from his form watching the punishment being inflicted. I tend to recall those who failed rather than those who succeeded. Mr X (physics) said there was nobody capable of passing O level and refused to teach it. After much pressure, he agreed to let me take the exam but refused to teach me – he just gave me the books and told me to get on with it.

> (From Dixie, G., *Getting on With Kids in Secondary Schools*, 2005 with the kind permission of Peter Francis Publications.)

It is fair to say that at this early stage of their teaching journey many potential trainees have a rather idealistic view of their roles as future teachers. They are yet to realize that the skills and qualities demonstrated by their favourite teachers often involved a lot of soul-searching, a great deal of emotional turmoil and that these took many years to master. The very best teachers constantly strive to meet the highest of professional standards and attempt to hold the highest expectations of their pupils. It is fair to say, however, that in the 'hurly burly' of everyday school life, where teachers are often presented with scenarios that challenge this philosophy, it is often difficult to maintain such idealism. While I would never want you to totally lose this idealistic streak, I do feel that you will need to temper this perspective with a degree of realism. In this initial exploratory stage of your journey it is important for you to find out what life in the modern-day secondary school is really like. Before you make any decisions to apply for an ITT course you need to take the first steps to discover whether teaching really is for you. This chapter has been specifically written to help you to do just this.

So, what is teaching actually like? There is no doubt in my mind that teaching is a special calling. I have found it to be the most challenging and yet rewarding way to make a living and feel extremely privileged to have been part of the profession for the past 34 years. However, before you make any decisions about whether it is for you or not, you need to fully understand the demands of the job.

Teaching is a demanding career, physically, emotionally and intellectually. It calls for energy, dedication, patience and enthusiasm. This is all well and good when you are feeling physically well and emotionally strong, when you have had a good night's sleep and when you and/or your family are not experiencing personal problems that are likely to impinge on your preparation and planning time. I have felt for a long time that the teaching and acting professions have a great deal in common. It doesn't matter what you feel like on the day, you have simply got to get up there and perform. It is not like a routine office job where you can sit in the corner, nurse your hangover and get on with your paperwork without being disturbed. The pupils, quite rightly, will demand your full attention and commitment during their time with you and will not usually let you get away with an under-par performance. In order to teach effectively you must have enthusiasm for your subject and be able to deliver your lessons in a confident and effective manner. Classroom management skills are therefore essential. No matter how well you plan your lessons, things often go awry so you do need the ability to be able to think on your feet. If you have the perception that teaching is a nine-to-five job and that you will be able to get back home in time to watch your favourite quiz show on the television, then please think again. There will be a lot of preparation and marking to do in the evenings and weekends. All this calls for good time management, self-discipline, administration and organization as well as good supervisory and leadership skills. It sounds basic, but it is essential that you like and relate well to young people and that you are committed to opening up young minds. You'll also need excellent communication skills, a keen intellect, creativity and bags of energy. Perhaps one of the most important qualities you will require as a teacher is that of reflectivity. If you are highly sensitive to criticism, or if you have a tendency to be overconfident and to think that you know all the answers, then teaching is certainly not the profession for you. Throughout your training year you will receive a whole gamut of advice and guidance designed to improve your pedagogic practice. Even for the most experienced of us this process can be quite uncomfortable at times. This feeling of vulnerability, so vital to becoming a good teacher, is often exacerbated when the advice is being offered by someone who is younger than you. We will explore the reflective process in more detail in Chapter 13.

As indicated earlier, there are many rewards that come with this career. As a teacher you will be afforded the privilege and opportunity to unlock the potential of pupils in your classes. Although not every pupil will succeed academically, you should hold on to your beliefs that every one of them has the potential for success in one form or another. The onset of each new academic year presents new and exciting challenges and new potential successes, and I am sure that you can imagine the feeling of absolute euphoria when you have been instrumental in turning a challenging pupil around.

You will never learn a topic better than when you start teaching it. It is highly likely that even the most conscientious of university graduates will initially be uncomfortable in teaching everything in the department's curriculum. The research and planning stages, so necessary for good teaching, will help you to gain more intimate subject knowledge and, more importantly, will provide you with the skills with which to deliver this to your audience. I therefore fully support the old adage that it takes three years of teaching to truly master a subject.

Despite a whole host of government and school-based initiatives it is fair to say that once you qualify you will still be able to maintain a high degree of control over what goes on in your classroom. Very few jobs offer such a large scope for autonomy and creativity as teaching. Most teachers will tell you that it helps to have a sense of humour. I would go further than this by saying that a sense of humour is *absolutely essential* if you are going to be successful in establishing and maintaining good relationships with your pupils and in engaging them in the learning process. If you have a positive attitude and a sense of humour, you will find things to laugh about on an everyday basis. In 1998 I carried out exhaustive research into pupils' perceptions of what makes a good teacher. High on the list was a sense of humour. No matter how much they groan, pupils like the silly jokes you will make up as you teach especially if they are at the gentle expense of your colleagues. There is currently a television advert sponsored by the Training and Development Agency that encourages people to think about teaching and to work with some of funniest people in the world. They have got this absolutely right. Sometimes it will be jokes that kids share with you that give you the most pleasure but mostly the opportunity for humour will arise from the spontaneity of your pupils who will make the funniest statements without realizing what they have said. It is important in your darkest hours in teaching to keep your sense of humour.

Many of you reading this book will have children and it cannot have escaped your notice that, on the face of it, the school calendar will allow you to have the same school time commitments as them. There is no doubt that this is an added bonus to the job but please be aware that you will have numerous meetings after school and that you will probably have to work long into the evening. It is fair to say that this is likely to create stress and will certainly impinge on your personal and family time. Having said this, there are plenty of opportunities for you to work part time in the profession while you are bringing up your family. You may even wish to take up the opportunity to job-share in a school. It is possible to do this even during your newly qualified teacher (NQT) year although this will of course affect the length of your induction period. The following quote outlines one of the benefits of taking up such a flexible career:

> Ten years ago, single, no ties and highly ambitious, I became a teacher. I quickly realized that it was more than a profession, it was a lifestyle. Now, as the mother of two small boys, my family are my world. Although it is fair to say that I always put my family first, my teaching career has also continued apace. When the bell goes at the end of the school day, I am usually able to leave quickly and get to my son's school in time to meet him as his school day ends. However, once the children are in bed, I am able to get on with my work for the following day.
>
> (Katy Williams – Advanced Skills Teacher (AST) English)

The other thing you need to note is that much of the so-called holiday time will be used to prepare and/or mark pupils' work. Many teachers feel that the only real break they get is the five-week holiday afforded to them during the summer. Even then they say that it takes a couple of weeks to wind down and forget about school, albeit on a temporary basis. You also need to know that the holiday period is usually when many teachers often become unwell. Having been stoical in staving off illness during the course of term they start to relax during the holiday period and, as a result of doing so, often come down with coughs and colds and the like.

If your partner is not a teacher then you both need to be very clear about the possible impact of your new career on your relationship and on your lifestyle. Bearing in mind that you will have a great deal of marking and preparatory work to do, your partner had better get used to the idea that he or she might be seeing a lot less of you. You may also have to ask him or her to do more around the house. There are also financial implications associated with the stringent nature of your working conditions. No longer will you be able to choose the cheapest times to go on holiday. Be prepared for a substantial increase in travel and accommodation costs during the school breaks.

The Training and Development Agency is committed to promoting diversity in the teaching profession and is keen to make it more representative of society as a whole. It openly welcomes applications from under-represented groups that include, but which are not limited to, people from minority ethnic backgrounds, people with disabilities, men wanting to teach in primary schools and people able to teach through the medium of Welsh in Wales. In accordance with current legislation, all workers who have contact with children are asked to complete a self-disclosure questionnaire confirming their physical and mental fitness to teach. If you have a disability, ITT providers will look at how they can make reasonable adjustments for your needs. By law, you are also subject to a criminal records check. It is vital that you disclose any criminal convictions when you submit your application. A criminal record will only normally count against you if it affects your suitability to teach. Failure to make an accurate disclosure could have serious consequences for your training and/or teaching. I have been in a situation where one of my trainees was asked to leave the ITT course because they failed to disclose a criminal act from their past, so it is worth being totally upfront about any previous misdemeanours.

There is no doubt that job security and a decent pension is an important factor in any career decision. Pay has also improved in recent years. New research from the Training Development Agency (TDA) found that almost half of Britons (47 per cent) believe that newly qualified teachers start on less than £16,000. However, the reality of the situation is that in

September 2007 NQTs received an extremely healthy minimum salary of £20, 333 per annum in England or £24,168 in inner London, which compares very favourably with other professions. The pay scale for good, experienced classroom teachers who have 'crossed the threshold' rises to between £31,878 and £34,281 outside London and £37,809 to £40,100 in inner London. Additional allowances may be paid to teachers considered to be excellent, and to those who take on management and other responsibilities. There are plenty of opportunities to progress. You need to recognize that the figures quoted are correct at the time of writing. For up-to-date details of the pay-scale ladder please go to www.teachernet.gov.uk/pay where an outline of the current pay scales is provided.

In addition to your salary you will receive a competitive and generous occupational pension package. In England, teachers may be eligible for help with housing costs through the government's key worker living initiative. You may also qualify for additional recruitment and retention incentives and benefits.

I hope I have provided you with a balanced view of teaching and that you have enough information at this point to decide whether you would like to explore the issue further. The fact that many new teachers leave within the first 3–5 years of teaching indicates that teaching is certainly not a job for everyone. It also leads me to believe that these teachers did not carry out enough research before they entered the profession. Still interested? Then read on.

2 Is teaching the right job for you?

Arranging a school visit

It is all well and good to read up on joys and pitfalls of being a teacher but the only real way to discover whether teaching is for you is to get yourself into a school and find out. The first thing you need to do is to contact the professional tutor in a local secondary school and ask if you can spend a couple of days observing lessons and talking to both teaching and non-teaching staff. Although at this stage you may not feel totally confident in dictating the itinerary for this two-day visit, I would strongly advise that you to try to gain some ownership of the process. I certainly advise you to carry out a pupil-shadowing activity on one of these days. By doing this you will be able to obtain a full flavour of the diet provided to a typical pupil in the school and this will give you an indication as to whether you would be able to cope with the pace of life and noise levels characteristic of most secondary schools. The other thing I strongly advise you to do on the second day is to arrange to shadow a newly qualified teacher (NQT). The rationale behind suggesting this is that these teachers represent a point along the continuum not too distant from where you are now. In other words, should you be successful in your application to join an ITT programme, you would be in exactly this position in just over a year's time. I would also advise that you talk to a range of teachers about the pros and cons of the job but strongly urge you not to be too influenced by the cynics in the school. All schools have a group of teachers whose one remaining aim in the profession is to get out as soon as possible. Most schools have ITT trainees of one type or another, training in the school. You are advised to take every opportunity to seek these people out and get them to talk to you about their training experiences and their times in schools. They will certainly provide you with a different perspective to the one proffered by the TDA in its seductive glossy brochures. They will tell you how it really is. You will notice that at this stage I have deliberately avoided providing too much guidance and structure for your visit. If you like what you see and should you decide to take the process further and apply to an ITT programme, then you will need to read the detailed guidance on what to look for in schools as outlined in Chapters 4 and 5.

Choosing to teach is a life-changing decision and should not be taken lightly. In addition to your school visits I strongly advise you to carry out further primary research to ascertain whether you are really suited to the profession. The TDA website provides an absolute wealth of information from which to make an informed decision about your possible future career. This website provides video clips of teachers talking about life in the classroom and about their feelings towards teaching. In addition to this, the website provides a list of frequently asked questions, all of which are highly relevant at this stage of your teaching journey. I have summarized some of the excellent advice below.

Open Schools Programme

www.tda.gov.uk/
Tel.: 0845 6000 991

If you are unable to personally arrange a visit with a local school you could do this through the Open Schools Programme which is sponsored and organized by the Training and Development Agency (TDA) but which only applies to schools in England. If you are interested in visiting an open school for a day you are advised to contact the TDA, although you do need to bear in mind that, owing to high demand for places, these visits are subject to availability. The programme gives you the chance to:

- see at first hand what it's like to be a teacher in today's schools;
- find out if you like the school environment;
- talk to teachers about their profession;
- discuss topics such as managing pupils' behaviour.

Taster courses
If you are pretty sure that you want to be a teacher, you might like to enrol on a three-day taster course designed to give you an in-depth view of teaching today and the training options available. The following courses are run by the TDA and are available in England:

- secondary-level courses covering two or more of the following subjects: mathematics, science, modern languages, information and communication technology (ICT), music, religious education and Design and Technology (D&T);
- courses designed for people from ethnic minority backgrounds;

- courses designed for men who are interested in teaching in primary schools.

Teacher Advocate Programme

Tel.: 0845 6000 991

The Advocate Programme allows you to speak to a teacher by phone or email. If you are interested in a career in teaching but haven't yet made the final decision, you can talk things over with an experienced teacher before you finally make up your mind. The teaching advocate programme will:

- give you the opportunity to fully explore the issue with someone who will listen to you and who will more than likely mention things you had not thought of;
- allow you to hear at first hand what it's like to be a teacher today;
- allow you to ask about the curriculum and related subject knowledge;
- allow you to discuss issues that may be worrying you such as managing pupils' behaviour.

Face-to-face recruitment events

www.teach.gov.uk/events
Tel.: 0845 6000 991

The TDA runs regular recruitment events where you can talk to experienced teachers, mentors, trainers, current trainees and NQTs about teaching. Alternatively, if you know of any ITT providers in your area, a simple phone call will determine when the next recruitment event will be held.

Impartial careers advice

www.teach.gov.uk
0845 6000 991

If you are looking for impartial and objective advice then your local careers service can offer you advice about teaching. If you are a graduate considering a change of career, you can obtain impartial advice from the TDA's regional careers advisors. You might feel my assertion that the TDA will offer you impartial advice on the issue to be rather contradictory. After all, is it not in their interest to recruit new teachers? Of course it is, but I need to stress that this is not merely a numbers game. It is more important for the organization to recruit enthusiastic, motivated and skilled people who will be highly committed to their training and teaching roles. Failure by the TDA to sift and sort people at this early stage would result in great financial expense in terms of wasted training costs and would also be doing the trainees themselves a serious injustice. So, if you are thinking about changing your career to teaching and want to teach a priority subject such as maths, science, design and technology, information and communications technology, modern languages, music or religious education in a secondary school, then the regional careers advisers programme is for you. Alternatively, if you are from a diverse background this service could help. It will give you the chance to:

- use a career guidance specialist to help you explore teaching as a career;
- get impartial advice about a career change to teaching;
- find out about teacher training;
- explore the best routes into teaching.

The Student Associate Scheme

www.tda.gov.uk/sas
Tel.: 0845 6000 991

The 15-day student associate scheme has been designed for students interested in gaining classroom experience while still pursuing their studies. It gives them the chance to discover what teaching is like, to work alongside experienced teachers and develop new skills. While they are on the scheme, students are paid a bursary. The scheme is open to students registered on relevant HND, foundation degree, undergraduate degree and postgraduate programmes. I have first-hand knowledge of using this scheme in school and have known students who have used their visits to schools to further inform their option choices at university. The scheme gives you the chance to:

- explore teaching as a career;
- help raise the attainment and aspirations of young people in schools;
- work alongside experienced teachers;
- improve your CV by broadening your personal skills;
- bring your subject knowledge into the classroom to support teaching;
- do work aligned with the standards for qualified teacher status;
- receive a training bursary.

Another useful source of information in which you will find realistic teaching scenarios presented to you is the *Times Educational Supplement* (*TES*) and it is certainly worth obtaining copies of this on a fairly regular basis in order to keep up with contemporary issues. The 'New appointments' section of the newspaper will be of particular relevance to you because it covers a range of issues directly related to your roles as trainees and future NQTs.

The purpose behind your seeking advice and/or visiting a school is for you to gain a warts and all view of a typical school day and to use this to make a decision on whether to take the process further. However, if you'd like to understand what it's like to work with children, you are by no means limited to observing what goes on in a school. You could also volunteer to work in a youth club or as a Scout or Guide leader. This will give you just the kind of awareness and experience to make your teacher training application stand out from the crowd, should you decide to apply.

Those already working in schools

As an experienced teacher trainer I have noted an increase in the number of ITT trainees who have previously been employed in schools as teaching assistants (TAs) or learning support assistants (LSAs), cover supervisors and instructors. Many of these trainees used their time in schools to gain classroom experience before making their final decision to apply for an ITT course. ITT providers will certainly look favourably on those applicants who take it upon themselves to gain this level of experience before applying for their course. If you are interested in teaching and you have decided to take this route make sure that you log virtually everything you do and that you save and annotate every working document you use. This material will be extremely useful to you when you are putting together a portfolio for your interview and/or for when you eventually start a training course that is highly portfolio based. The qualified teacher status (QTS) standards have been provided in Appendix 1 to help you reference your log entries.

The aim of this chapter is twofold: to present you with a balanced view of teaching as a potential career; and to furnish you with a range of suggestions on how to find out more about life in a modern-day secondary school. I hope that both these aims have been realized. If you are still interested in exploring teaching as a career then you need to read and inwardly digest the information provided in the next chapter which focuses on the nature of teacher training in general and on the different training routes available.

Choosing the right training provider

Having made the decision to teach, you now need to move on to the next stage of your journey: that of exploring your possible routes into teaching. This chapter will initially provide a detailed description of each of these routes before then going on to explore some of the factors that you need to consider when choosing a specific course.

Gaining QTS

The first point to make about your training is that it should provide the conduit through which you eventually achieve your Qualified Teacher Status (QTS) or its equivalent if you are training in Scotland or Northern Ireland. QTS is required in England and Wales to become a teacher in the state mainstream and special education sectors. QTS, as such, does not exist in Scotland or Northern Ireland. However, as in England and Wales, all teachers in Scotland and Northern Ireland are required to register with either the General Teaching Council for Scotland or the General Teaching Council for Northern Ireland. The General Teaching Councils will only consider graduates with a PGCE (Postgraduate Certificate in Education) or a PGDE (Postgraduate Degree in Education).

Those holding English or Welsh QTS (or an equivalent from another country) must apply for registration with the relevant General Teaching Council. Each case is considered individually and even those with English or Welsh QTS are not guaranteed to be allowed to teach in Scotland or Northern Ireland.

A candidate must have completed and passed a teacher training course, such as a PGCE or a teaching degree (BEd).

QTS is technically only recognized in the country it was awarded (England or Wales), but teachers can normally apply for QTS in another country with relative ease. QTS is also recognized by many other countries once the relevant paperwork has been completed. Teachers trained outside England and Wales must also apply to be awarded QTS if they wish to teach in England and Wales.

Choosing the right course

There are so many different routes into teaching and hundreds of different initial teacher training (ITT) courses available in the UK. Choosing between them is a challenge in itself, but if you are going to find the course most suitable to your needs you need to be prepared to put in a lot of research. There is a number of things you need to think about before choosing an initial teacher training course.

The subject and age group you intend to teach

ITT courses and programmes are organized according to age groups and/or subjects. If, for example, you'd like to teach a subject to an advanced level, you may choose to teach at a secondary level, rather than primary. If your love of your subject is such that you would relish the challenge of teaching GCSE or sixth form students then you will need to seek out training courses that cover Key Stages 4 and 5. On the other hand, if you would prefer a 'mixed diet' that involves teaching younger secondary school pupils, while at the same time keeping your hand in with teaching GCSE, you may prefer to train over Key Stages 3 and 4. It should be noted here that failure to train at Key Stage 5 will not necessarily preclude you from teaching sixth-form classes. The decision to allow you to do this will be made by your school once you have qualified as a teacher.

Which ITT programme should you choose?

When choosing a teacher-training course it is important to consider and research all the possible pathways and opportunities available. It is essential to familiarize yourself with the structure of the course and with the training opportunities offered. When selecting an appropriate ITT course it is vital that you give full consideration to your prefered way of learning, to your personal circumstances and to your past experiences. It is also important that when finalizing your choice of provider and/or venue, you speak to past and present trainees about their experiences. Finally, it is essential that you choose a course which will offer you the best guidance and support during your training year.

Lee Jordan – SCITT trainee

Each and every one of us has a unique set of personal, emotional, academic and social characteristics and, although it would be impossible to provide an ITT course which has been completely tailor-made to your individual requirements, there are specific courses that will prove to be more or less suitable to your needs. I provide an overview of the various programmes in Figure 3.1.

Programme type	Course type	Abbreviation
Undergraduate	Bachelor of education	BEd
	Bachelor of arts/science with qualified teacher status	BA/BSc with QTS
Postgraduate	Postgraduate Certificate of Education	PGCE
	Teach First	Teach First
	School-centred initial teacher training	SCITT
Employment based	Graduate Teacher Training Programme	GTTP
	Registered Teacher Programme	RTP
Assessment only routes	Qualified teacher status only	QTS
Overseas trained teachers	Overseas trained teacher programme	OTTP

Figure 3.1 Summary of ITT courses available
Source: www.tda.gov.uk/Recruit/thetrainingprocess/typesofcourse.aspx

Baseline qualifications

Before you trawl through the range of information offered on the following ITT programmes it is important to note that to train as a secondary school teacher, on any programme, you must achieve a standard equivalent to grade C in GCSE English language and mathematics. Knowledge of this information is assumed when describing the additional qualifications required for all of the following courses.

Undergraduate courses

The Bachelor of Education Degree course (BEd)

The Bachelor of Education Degree course (BEd) is a four-year honours degree course in education which will eventually provide you with QTS. These university-based BEd courses enable you to study for your degree and complete your initial teacher training at the same time. The BEd is a particularly popular choice for those who are interested in teaching primary school children, but it is also an option for anyone wanting to teach in the secondary school sector.

How long does the course take?

Obtaining a BEd honours degree usually takes four years of full-time study; although, if your personal circumstances are as such, you do need to know that you can also complete the course on a part-time basis. If you decide to study part time, the course usually takes between four to six years to complete. If you have undergraduate credits from previous study you may be able to finish the course in two years.

Where can you do a BEd?

You can complete BEd degree courses at universities and colleges throughout the UK.

What qualifications do you need?

Although each university has its own specific course entry requirements, a minimum of two A levels or equivalent is usually required. You will need to contact your individual course providers to find out more details.

Is there any additional funding available?

The financial arrangements for these courses are the same as for all other undergraduate courses.

How do you apply?

Apply through the Universities and Colleges Admissions Service (UCAS), www.ucas.ac.uk/

When should you apply?

For most BEd courses starting in September or October, UCAS accepts applications between the preceding September and January. If you feel like taking a break before starting your training you need to rest assured that many universities are happy for a successful applicant to defer entry for a year.

What should you do next?

- Visit the UCAS website and search for BEd courses and find out more about the application process.

- Visit the National Academic Recognition Centre (NARIC) website www. naric.org.uk to find out whether your qualifications are of an equivalent level to UK GCSEs, A levels and an undergraduate degree.

BA/BSc with QTS

A BA or BSc with QTS is an honours degree that also incorporates teacher training. By taking a bachelor of arts (BA) or bachelor of science (BSc) degree with qualified teacher status (QTS), you can study for a degree and do your initial teacher training at the same time.

How long does a BA/BSc with QTS course take?

Courses generally take three or four years full-time or four to six years part time.

Where can you do a BA/BSc with QTS course?

You can complete BA/BSc with QTS degree courses at universities and colleges throughout the UK.

What qualifications do you need?

Entry requirements vary according to the specific course, although a minimum of two A levels or equivalent is usually required. You do need to check with individual course providers for details.

Is there any additional funding available?

The financial arrangements for these courses are the same as for all other undergraduate courses.

How do you apply?

Apply through the Universities and Colleges Admissions Service (UCAS), www.ucas.ac.uk/

When should you apply?

For most BA/BSc with QTS courses starting in September or October, UCAS accepts applications between the preceding September and January. It is often also possible to apply to defer entry for a year.

Next steps

- Visit the UCAS website.
- Search for BA/BSc courses and find out more about the application process.

- Visit the National Academic Recognition Centre (NARIC) website. Find out whether your qualifications are of an equivalent level to UK UCASs, A levels and an undergraduate degree.

Postgraduate courses

Postgraduate Certificate in Education (PGCE)

Alternatively you could could gain a university degree in a subject of your choice and then gain your QTS by doing a one-year PGCE at a university. Training is usually carried out over a 40-week period excluding the summer holiday. A PGCE course focuses primarily on the development of your teaching skills, and not on the subject you intend to teach. For this reason, you are expected to have a good understanding of your chosen subject(s) – usually to degree level – before you start training.

How long does a PGCE take?

Courses generally last for one year full-time or up to two years part time.

New bursaries for extended PGCE

From 2007 there has been funding available for extended postgraduate mathematics and science courses. These courses are aimed at people who want to teach mathematics or science but need some additional subject knowledge training. The length of these courses varies between 18 months and two years. Eligible trainees currently undertaking these courses will receive a supplementary bursary, details of which can be found by going to this website: www.teach.gov.uk/funding. You need to note that these bursaries are tax free. If you are interested you need to visit the website for more information about the eligibility criteria. To qualify, trainees must meet the normal conditions for initial teacher training (ITT) and be taking a course that will lead to them being qualified to teach mathematics, physics or chemistry to Key Stage 4 and Key Stage 3 or post-16.

Where can you do a PGCE?

PGCE courses are available at universities and colleges throughout the UK. You need to be aware that there are also university distance learning teacher training programmes available (e.g. Open University) but of course you would still have at least two placements in local schools during the year. You also need to note that the Open University does offer part-time PGCE placements. Visiting its website would provide you with further information: www.open.ac.uk/. In addition to the PGCE courses offered by univerities, it is also possible to gain PGCE by completing a programme of school-centred initial teacher training (SCITT). Details of the SCITT programme are given later in this chapter.

What qualifications do you need?

You must have a UK undergraduate degree or a recognized equivalent qualification. If your degree subject does not link closely to the subject you intend to teach, you have the opportunity to improve your chances of gaining a place on an ITT programme by following a pre-training course to boost your subject knowledge.

Is there any additional funding available?

Eligible trainees completing secondary PGCE courses in England are entitled to receive a tax-free training bursary. However, you need to be aware that the precise amount depends on the subject and course start date. Similar training bursaries are available in Wales, depending on the subject, and you can still also receive a tuition fee grant, meaning that the overall level of support in Wales is the same as in England. Visit the Student Finance Wales website to find out more: www. studentfinancewales.co.uk. Trainees who undertake secondary ITT through the medium of Welsh may be eligible for the Welsh Medium Incentive Supplement (a higher sum is available for trainees undertaking science and mathematics courses). This is aimed at trainees who need extra support to raise confidence in their ability to teach effectively through the medium of Welsh.

In addition to funding such as this, you may be eligible to receive taxable 'golden hello' payments (or teaching grants in Wales), depending on the subject you train for. Please be aware, however, that this payment depends upon you successfully completing your induction period as a NQT.

Funding arrangements from 1 August 2008

As from August 2008, English, dance and drama have been demoted to non-priority subjects and, as a result, the bursary has been reduced. Trainees on these courses will not be eligible for a golden hello.

How do you apply?

The majority of PGCE applications are made through the Graduate Teacher Training Registry (GTTR), www.gttr.ac.uk. However, some ITT providers require that you approach them directly. For secondary courses, you are able to apply to up to four different providers. If you are unsuccessful with your first choice, your application will be passed on to your second, and so on.

Next steps

- If you contact the Training and Development Agency (TDA) they will provide you with more detailed information about PGCE courses and other postgraduate routes into teaching, as well as regular news and updates from the ever-changing world of teaching and teacher training, www.tda.gov.uk
- Visit the GTTR website.
- Search for PGCE course vacancies and course entry profiles, find out more about the application process and complete an application online.
- Visit the National Academic Recognition Centre (NARIC) website. Find out whether your qualifications are of an equivalent level to UK GCSEs, A levels and an undergraduate degree.

Teach First

Teach First is a programme run by an independent organization enabling top graduates to spend two years working in challenging secondary schools in London, Manchester and the Midlands, qualifying as a teacher while completing leadership training and work experience with leading employers. Working with specially selected partner schools and businesses, Teach First aims to build the leaders of the future by providing high-quality teacher and leadership training, internships, coaching and networking.

Teach First has been designed for high-flying graduates who may not otherwise have considered teaching or aren't sure of it as a long-term career. It leads to qualified teacher status (QTS) but also provides the potential to develop a commercially oriented career.

Where can you do Teach First?

Teach First places teachers in challenging secondary schools in the Greater London, Greater Manchester and Midlands areas only.

What qualifications do you need?

Teach First aims to recruit *top graduates* who have shown high levels of ability in areas such as leadership and communication. As such, its entry requirements are strict. You will also appreciate that the interview plays an extremely important role in the selection process. You must have all of the following:

- a minimum of a 2.1 undergraduate degree;
- 300 UCAS tariff points (24 points using the old tariff, equivalent to BBB at A level);
- grade C or above in GCSE (or equivalent) mathematics and English;
- an ability to show high levels of competency in areas such as leadership, teamwork, resilience, critical thinking, communication skills, initiative and creativity, and respect, humility and empathy. What you studied at university is not important, provided at least 40 per cent of your degree relates to a national curriculum subject.

School-Centred Initial Teacher Training (SCITT)

You need to be aware that a number of Local Authorities (LAs) run their own School-Centred Inititial Teacher Training (SCITT) programmes which, like the university courses, also run over a 40-week period. If you're a graduate and want to complete your training in a school environment, consider school-centred initial teacher training (SCITT) programmes, which are designed and delivered by groups of neighbouring schools and colleges.

Taught by experienced, practising teachers and advisors, and often tailored towards local teaching needs, all SCITT courses lead to qualified teacher status (QTS). Many, although not all, will also award you the postgraduate certificate in education (PGCE) validated by a higher education institution.

If you prefer to spend more time training in the classroom, putting theory into practice and gaining confidence through increased contact with the school environment, then a SCITT programme is a good option for you.

How long does SCITT take?

SCITT training generally runs over a 40-weeek period between September to June. You need to be aware that some courses start earlier.

Where can you do SCITT?

There are consortia of schools and colleges running SCITT courses all over England. These groups provide all kinds of SCITT, covering primary, middle years and the full range of secondary subjects. Readers need to be aware that there are currently no SCITTs running solely within Wales. However, some consortia run on the English/Welsh border and may use Welsh schools as part of their programmes. Some SCITT providers locate themselves in the lead school from the consortium whilst others base their headquarters in separate LA buildings.

What qualifications do you need?

You need a UK degree or a recognized equivalent qualification. Your degree should relate to the subject you want to teach.

Is there any additional funding available?

Eligible trainees completing SCITT courses in England are entitled to receive a tax-free training bursary. The precise amount depends on the subject and course start date. In addition to funding such as this, you may be eligible to receive taxable 'golden hello' payments (or teaching grants in Wales), depending on the subject, after successfully completing your induction period as a NQT.

Funding arrangements from 1 August 2008

As with university based PGCE courses, trainees starting secondary postgraduate English, dance and drama ITT courses, will receive a reduced bursary. Trainees on these courses will not be eligible to receive a golden hello.

How do you apply?

In most cases, you need to apply for SCITT courses through the graduate teacher training registry (GTTR), although some SCITT providers require direct applications. You can apply to up to four different providers, in order of preference. You need to visit the GTTR website for full details of available courses and methods of application.

When should you apply?

SCITT courses follow the academic year, so you start your training in August, September or October depending on the provider. You generally need to apply through the GTTR or directly to the provider during the preceding academic year before.

What you should do next

- Visit the GTTR website.
- Search for SCITT course vacancies, find out more about the application process and complete an application online.
- Visit the National Academic Recognition Centre (NARIC) website to find out whether your overseas qualifications are of an equivalent level to UK GCSEs, A levels and an undergraduate degree.

Employment-based routes

Graduate Teacher Training Programme (GTTP)

If you are not too concerned about obtaining the PGCE and are quite happy with QTS certification on its own then you may want to think about applying for the Graduate Teacher Training Programme (GTTP). The programme is delivered by a designated recommending body which could take the form of a single school, a cluster of schools or a separate and distinct organization. The graduate teacher scheme is a programme of on-the-job training allowing graduates to qualify as a teacher while they work. It's a good choice for mature people who want to change to a teaching career but who need to continue earning while they train. Once on the programme your training will be tailored to your own individual needs and lead to qualified teacher status (QTS). Whilst in your school you will be employed as an unqualified teacher.

How long does the GTTP take?

Training usually takes up to one school year, full-time, depending on your previous teaching experience. In certain cases, where the trainee has substantial relevant experience, they may be 'fast-tracked' and can complete the course in as little as one term.

Where can you do the GTTP?

You can complete the GTTP in any English or Welsh maintained school, as long as it is prepared to employ you as an unqualified teacher for the duration of the programme. Independent schools can be involved in the GTTP, but these applications would have to be self-funded. Pupil-referral units cannot employ GTTP trainees, or have any involvement with the training. It is also not possible to train as a GT in a school that has had an Ofsted inspection and which has gone into special measures.

What qualifications do you need?

You need qualifications at least equivalent to a UK bachelor's degree in additon to the baseline qualifications described at the beginning of the chapter.

Is there any financial support available?

Your school will pay you on an unqualified or qualified teacher's salary which will be provided by the TDA in order to help meet your employment costs. The TDA also provides the school with a substantial grant towards your training. If the school does not receive this funding, there is also a self-funded option available, whereby the school will meet the costs of the GTTP. To find out whether this option is available to you, you will need to enquire at your local GTTP provider, known as an employment-based initial teacher training (EBITT) provider.

How do you apply?

To take part in the GTTP you can either respond to an advertisement for the GTTP programme, apply direct to a GTTP provider who may find you a school, or you will need to find a job in a school to support you through the programme. If you cannot find an advertisement for the GTTP to respond to, you should apply for a place through your local EBITT provider.

When should you apply?

GTP providers usually recruit well in advance of programme start dates. You need to speak to your local training provider about application deadlines.

Next steps

- You can get more information on the Graduate and Registered Teacher Programme by emailing grtp@tdainfo.co.uk
- You can also call the Teaching Information Line on:
  Tel.: 0845 6000 991 (0845 6000 992 for Welsh speakers)
  Fax: 0117 915 6578
- Some EBITT providers can help you find a post in a school – otherwise you can look for vacancies in the local and national press, as well as on local authority and recruitment websites. EBITT providers do not operate in Wales as all employment-based programmes are run by the Welsh Government.

Please bear in mind that competition for funded places on the GTTP is strong and any application you make is not guaranteed to be successful. The quality of the school, the candidate and the training plan are important factors in assessing applications, and places are offered to the strongest.

Registered Teacher Programme (RTP)

The Registered Teacher Programme (RTP) provides a blend of work-based teacher training and academic study, allowing non-graduates with some experience of higher education to complete their degree and qualify as a teacher at the same time. To take part, you first need to be working in a school as an unqualified teacher. This makes the RTP a good option for mature people who want to change to a teaching career but need to continue earning while they train.

Once on the programme your training will be tailored to your own individual needs and lead to qualified teacher status (QTS). Your training provider will also work with a local higher education institution to ensure that you receive suitable training to extend your subject knowledge to degree level. You need to be aware that this is an incredibly demanding way to train as a teacher and is certainly not for the 'faint-hearted'.

How long does the RTP take?

The programme normally takes two years. However, if you already have some teaching experience, it may take less time.

Where can you do the RTP?

You can complete the RTP in any English school, as long as it is prepared to employ you as an unqualified teacher for the duration of the programme. Independent schools can be involved in the GTTP, but these applications would have to be self-funded. Pupil-referral units cannot employ RTP trainees, or have any involvement with the training. Please note that the RTP is not now available in Wales.

What qualifications do you need?

You must have completed the equivalent of two years (240 Credit and Accumulation and Transfer scheme (CATS) points) of higher education. For example, you may have completed an HND, a DipHE or the first two years of a bachelor's degree. The recognition of 240 (CATS) points is at the discretion of the RTP provider. Again as with all teacher training courses you need the baseline qualifications in English and maths.

Is there any financial support available?

Your school will pay you an unqualified or qualified teacher's salary, which will depend on your responsibilities, experience and location. The TDA may also provide the school with a grant to cover the cost of your training.

If the school does not receive this funding, there is also a self-funded option available, whereby the school will meet the costs of the RTP. To find out whether this option is available to you, you will need to enquire at your local RTP provider (known as an employment-based initial teacher training (EBITT) provider).

How do you apply?

You must first find a school willing to employ you and support you through the programme. You then need to apply directly to your local EBITT provider, which will assess your application and establish what further training you would need to meet the standards for QTS. Some EBITT providers can help you find a post in a school – otherwise you can look for vacancies in the local and national press, as well as on local authority and recruitment websites.

When should you apply?

You can apply to join the RTP at any time. Keep in mind, however, that it is a challenging programme, requiring substantial effort and commitment. The RTP is not as widely available as the GTTP, and competition for places is high. You need to be sure that this programme is absolutely right for you before you apply.

Next steps

- Find an employment-based initial teacher training (EBITT) provider. Search for an EBITT provider offering the services you need in your area.
- Visit the National Academic Recognition Centre (NARIC) website. Find out whether your qualifications are of an equivalent level to UK GCSEs, A levels and an undergraduate degree.

Qualified teacher status only

If you already have a degree and substantial experience of working in a UK school as an instructor or unqualified teacher, or as a teacher in an independent school or further education institution, you may be able to qualify without undergoing any further teacher training.

The QTS only option, or assessment only as it is known, offers you an opportunity to demonstrate that you meet standards required to achieve QTS by compiling and submitting a portfolio of evidence of your abilities as a classroom teacher.

In addition to you providing this portfolio evidence you will undergo a rigorous day-long assessment visit to your school. You need to be aware that the 'assessment only' process can take up to a year to complete and that it can start and finish at any time.

The University of Gloucestershire administers this process for England; the scheme is not available in Wales. It is available to teachers of the following subjects:

- mathematics
- modern languages

- religious education
- science
- art and design
- geography
- history
- physical education.

How to apply

If you are interested in submitting yourself for QTS assessment only, please contact the University of Gloucestershire School of Education directly, www.glos.ac.uk/faculties/ehs/education/index.cfm

Next steps

- Register with the TDA.
- The university will provide you with more detailed information about qualifying to teach, as well as regular news and updates from the ever-changing world of teaching and teacher training.

Overseas Trained Teacher Programme (OTTP)

If you are qualified as a teacher overseas and outside the European Union, you may be eligible to work in England as a temporary teacher without qualified teacher status (QTS) for up to 4 years. This programme is currently available in England only.

Once you have found a teaching position in a school, the Overseas Trained Teacher Programme (OTTP) will provide you with your own individual training and assessment programme which will ultimately lead to your qualification to teach in England permanently.

What qualifications do you need?

You must first be qualified as a teacher overseas and working as an unqualified teacher in a school in England. In addition, if you qualified outside the European Union (EU), you will need a qualification equivalent to a UK bachelor's degree in additon to the baseline qualifications outlined earlier in the chapter.

How long does the OTTP take?

The length of the programme will depend on the extent of additional training you need. However, the longest you can spend on the programme is one year full-time. If you feel your skills and experience are sufficient to meet all the QTS standards without further training, you may apply for QTS assessment only.

Is there any additional funding available?

If you need to undertake a programme of additional training, the TDA will make a contribution towards the cost of this training and towards the cost of your final assessment. Your school will continue to pay your salary.

How do you apply?

Once you have a teaching post and you have established that you have all the necessary qualifications, you should apply directly to an EBITT provider in your area. It will assess and approve your application, discussing your training needs with you as necessary.

When should you apply?

There are no deadlines for the OTTP although it is up to EBITT providers to establish start dates for programmes.

OTTP four-year rule

The four-year rule for overseas trained teachers (OTTs) states that you can teach for up to four years before you have to be awarded QTS. The four years starts from the first day that you teach in a mainstream school in England, and includes any time out of service.

Next steps

- Visit the National Academic Recognition Centre (NARIC) website to find out whether your qualifications are of an equivalent level to UK GCSEs, A levels and an undergraduate degree.
- If you qualified as a teacher in Scotland, Wales, Northern Ireland, another country in the EU or Switzerland, you may be eligible for qualified teacher status (QTS) without further assessment. You will need to contact the General Teaching Council for England (GTCE) to have your qualifications assessed.
- If school are unable to fill a vacancy they may advertise the post as an instructor role. You may be able to use this need as a bargaining tool to get them to act as a conduit for your teacher training.

ITT course content

It is not possible to provide a detailed outline of the course content of all ITT providers in the UK. Having said this, however, it is fair to say that there are common elements with all of the ITT programmes and you need to be fully aware of what you can expect when you embark on your course. This may sound pretty basic but all teacher-training programmes have been designed to equip you with the skills and knowledge you will need to teach successfully. ITT programmes focus on a number of themes, all of which are linked to the qualified teacher status (QTS) standards. Whatever programme you choose, your initial teacher training will involve you being shown how to:

- gain a knowledge and understanding of the relevant national curriculum programmes of study for your subjects;
- plan and prepare lessons and how to set learning objectives;
- manage classes, promote good behaviour and minimize disruptions in your lessons;
- use information and communication technology effectively;
- become fully aware of the professional values expected of teachers, in their attitudes and behaviour towards pupils and colleagues.

Most trainee teachers (except for those on employment-based or assessment only routes) divide up their time between a university or other higher education institutions and a school, where they will undertake supervised teaching practice.

Assessment

Again it is not possible to delve into the assessment criteria for every single ITT provider in the UK. Suffice to say that the most common assessment tools are as follows:

- through lesson observations where your performance as a teacher will be assessed against the standards for QTS;
- through the completion of a professional portfolio which requires you provide evidence of having met all of the 33 QTS standards;
- through the completion of a school practice/training folder which requires you to keep records of your times in each practice school and of the training provided in your ITT programme;
- through the reflective process designed to move your professional practice on;
- through the completion of assignments which link theory to practice.

The institution you'd like to attend

No two courses of initial teacher training are the same – largely because no two ITT providers are the same. Universities, colleges and schools all display varying characteristics, strengths and entry requirements, not to mention course content and structure.

Things to consider when making your choice

- Bearing in mind that many postgraduates end up with serious debts after their courses finish, money might be an issue for you. If this were the case you would probably be better looking for a locally based ITT programme which uses local schools. By doing this you then have the option of living at home and will also be able to keep travel costs down. Unless you are lucky enough to have a university in your vicinity, the GTTP and SCITT courses would probably be your best bet in this situation.

- If you would prefer to study your subject in depth before then focusing on pedagogical issues, you would be advised to take a degree course and then enrol for a PGCE or GTTP course. If you would prefer to spend more time learning how to teach your subject then you may prefer to take the BEd degree course.

- It is important for you to have an understanding of your preferred learning style before you make such an important decision as this. If you are fully at ease in exploring the social, philosophical and theoretical side of teaching in detail you may prefer the BEd course. If you are a more kinaesthetic learner, who learns quickly from practical experience, you may prefer the PGCE or GTTP option.

- Are you the sort of person who does not work particularly well under pressure? There is no doubt that the four-year BEd degree course is a more stress-free route through the teacher training process compared to the one-year programme offered by the PGCE and GTTP courses which usually involves a steeper learning curve for trainees.

- The willingness to make mistakes and to learn from them is a fundamental requirement of any good teacher. Having said this, some trainees are more comfortable with this principle than others. There is no doubt that a BEd course will afford you the most time and space to make your mistakes and to learn from these. Some BEd courses offer trainees up to four practices, which in essence represent four opportunities to start afresh and have another go at 'getting things right'. It is fair to say that the PGCE option offers fewer opportunities for trainees to 'start afresh'. Although most PGCE courses offer trainees two school practices, there is a number of courses that do ask their trainees to undergo three school placements. This is something you need to look into when applying for your course. There is no doubt whatsoever that the GTTP route is the most robust form of teacher training available. With the exception of a brief second practice, you will spend the whole of the academic year in one school. Therefore, if you make mistakes in the early stages of your practice you will either have to rectify these, or simply live with the situation for the complete academic year. This is certainly the course for the fast learners among you. Trainees who embark on a GTTP course are contracted to the school for their training year and thus should be treated as bona fide members of staff. Many trainees are very happy about this and like to feel part of a real team but you need to be aware that there can be a downside to this. I have experienced situations where GTTP trainees have been thrown in at the deep end and left to get on with the job as if they were qualified experienced teachers. Luckily this doesn't happen very often but it is an issue that is worth giving some thought to. It is certainly worth finding about the ethos and culture of the school and about it attitude towards ITT. Visit the school and/or log on to the school's website to get a flavour of the school as a conduit for your training.

If you rise to the surface, you've qualified.

- The level of your life experience is also an important factor in helping you to decide upon your training route. The GTTP is often a preferred route for graduates who have done something else before deciding to join the teaching profession. A GTTP provider will go out of its way to help you to identify and utilize the skills and qualities you have amassed during your previous working lives to support your training and teaching. The fact that these skills and qualities are formally audited and given full credit at the beginning of the training year has attracted many older candidates to the GTTP route. Although the GTTP does provide opportunities to study the theoretical elements of teaching, the dominant learning tool for trainees is the time spent in the classroom.

Comparing training providers

It is absolutely vital when you are deciding on which type of ITT training you are going to embark, that you make a rational and informed decision. One of the things you could do to find out more about each of the ITT providers available to you is to visit the TDA's Performance Profiles website to search for and compare universities, colleges and schools.

This dedicated database will allow you to search through and define your ITT options, and will provide you with the Performance Profiles of the various ITT providers, thus making it easier to find providers that meet your specific requirements. The Performance Profiles database contains yearly data on all the universities, colleges or school-centred initial teacher training (SCITT) providers in England. Each ITT providers' records include contact details, the courses offered and the characteristics of its trainees and details of their qualifications on entry to the course. These records also provide information, based on Ofsted inspection evidence, about the quality of providers' ITT courses, the proportion of their trainees gaining qualified teacher status (QTS) on completion of their training, and how many enter a teaching job within six months of successfully completing the course.

In addition to enabling you to review and compare the detailed characteristics of ITT providers, the TDA Performance Profiles website also allows you to search for a provider or group of providers according to a range of different criteria, including:

- location
- subject
- age group
- provider
- TDA quality category
- training route.

By using these criteria, individually or together, you can generate a shortlist of ITT providers that match your preferences. You can then compare providers using the reports provided and narrow down your options further still.

If you want to train as a teacher in Wales

The TDA Performance Profiles cover ITT providers in England only. For information about providers of initial teacher training in Wales, you should visit the TDA website for Education and Learning Wales, http://new.wales.gov.uk/. You can also view information about provider performance in Wales on the Higher Education Funding Council for Wales website. In addition, the Teacher Education and Training in Wales website (www.hefcw.ac.uk/) provides details of all the initial teacher training providers in Wales and the courses it runs.

Funding and finances

Let's face it, this has got to be one of the major factors in deciding which ITT provider to choose or indeed whether to embark on a teacher training course in the first place. Unless you are fortunate to have sufficient funds to get you through the training year, it is highly likely that you will experience some debt during this period. Even if you embark on an employment-based route into teaching, you are either highly likely to have run up debts at university or, if you have moved directly from paid employment onto the teacher training course you are probably going to experience a significant drop in income.

Paying fees

For most teacher-training courses, the university or college fees will be fully or partially paid for by the Local Authority (LA). It is therefore, absolutely vital that you apply to your LA in plenty of time to see if you are eligible. It is important to note that once the LA has agreed to pay your fees, the agreement is binding and lasts for the whole time you are at university even if you move to a different area.

Those postgraduate students who are thinking about applying for SCITT training courses should be aware that a number of them have started charging fees, although even these are partly paid by the LA. This is, of course, providing that you have completed the appropriate pro forma and the appropriate time during the course.

Living expenses

Most undergraduates embarking on a four-year training journey will probably take on holiday jobs to support themselves during this period. Even so, most of them will take out a low-interest loan from the Student Loan Company www.slc.co.uk/ which is a government-sponsored company set up to financially support all students irrespective of their courses. You need to be aware that this money does not have to be paid back until you start earning.

Additional financial advice

- You may be able to gain some financial assistance with childcare, travel and other course-related costs by contacting the DfES information line on 0800 731 9133.
- Welsh trainees need to ask their providers about the Welsh Language Incentive.
- If you intend to apply for a Welsh undergraduate course you may be eligible for means-tested grants, a further financial award for secondary undergraduates to support them through their school placement if they are teaching priority subjects and a lesser figure if they are teaching non-priority subjects.

Bennett (2006) offers the following useful contact information:

- www.tda.gov.uk/fundingfortrainees
- DfES Student Support free information line 0800 731 9133
- Teaching Information Line 0845 6000 991 or 0845 600 992 for Welsh Speakers
- Your own LA. Ask for the department for student support for student teachers.

Part Two
THE SUCCESSFUL APPLICATION

Understanding your school visit 4

Understanding the hidden curriculum

Virtually all teacher training providers will require you to have visited at least one school before you make your application. In Chapter 1 we discussed the importance of you gaining experience in schools and I stressed how unwise it would be for you to submit an application 'blind' without ever having determined whether the hurly burly of life in a secondary school is really for you. I realize that time may be an issue for a number of you, especially if you are busy working and/or if you have a hectic and demanding family life. However, in order to prepare yourself for the interview, you need to spend some time in different types of secondary schools. Ideally I would suggest that you visit a small rural state school, a large urban state school and, if you are able to, you could perhaps spend some time in an independent school. Having said this, it is important to stress that merely spending a token amount of time in a school is not enough on its own to prepare you for your interview, nor is it sufficient to provide you with the required background knowledge to fully inform your training or teaching. In short, you need to know what you are looking for. Therefore, I have provided structured guidance on how to use your visit(s) in such a way as to fully prepare you for the interview and for your first school practice.

If you get the chance to visit more than one secondary school you will notice that each school has a very different feel about it. Every school has its own distinct culture, ethos and atmosphere which together provide the visitor, and more importantly the pupils, teachers and corporate staff, with a strong signal as to the norms, values and expectations of the institution. We call this the school's hidden curriculum.

The hidden curriculum is a combined set of values, attitudes and knowledge frames which are embodied in the organization and processes of schooling and which are implicitly conveyed to pupils. Although all schools have a formal curriculum comprising areas of the academic knowledge which pupils are expected to acquire, it is the form of schooling and the messages transmitted as a result of its organization and practices, which are more powerful than the content of its subjects. It promotes social control and an acceptance of the school's, and hence society's, authority structure.

When you visit a school it is very important that you focus your attention on its hidden curriculum. Although you may understand the term as a generic principle, you may not yet be fully aware of what this actually means in practice. Bearing this in mind, therefore, I have provided you with a number of sub-headings describing the areas you will need to explore during your visit. I strongly suggest that you arm yourself with a pen and notebook and that you carry out a rudimentary enquiry into these aspects of school life. By doing this you will be well able to discuss your school visits in a highly critical and informed fashion at your interview. The experience will also prove to be invaluable when it comes to you gaining a full understanding of your practice schools, and of the schools you will work in during the course of your career.

How the school day and the curriculum are organized

The way in which a school organizes its teaching time can have significant effects upon pupil behaviour and upon the quality of teaching and learning that takes place. Some schools follow a two-week timetable and divide up their teaching day into three discrete lesson blocks. The rationale behind this decision is threefold: first, because doing so means that there is far less pupil movement around the school thus reducing the opportunities for friction between pupils and/or for pupil indiscipline in the corridors; second, a longer block of learning time means that teachers are able to plan for greater variety in lessons; third, pupils get the opportunity to have a break and 'let off steam' at the end of each lesson. On the other hand, some schools divide their teaching day into as many as six or seven lesson blocks on the premise that by doing so they are able to cater more successfully for the limited concentration spans of their pupils. In short, they deem numerous 'short, sharp' learning experiences to be preferable to the three-period day. The net result of this decision, however, means that there is significant pupil movement around the school as youngsters trek from one lesson to another. Obviously there are numerous permutations of these models but, whatever timetabling pattern is prevalent within the school you are visiting, you need to think carefully about the repercussions of these planning decisions on the culture and ethos of the institution.

You also need to ask yourself a number of questions about the issue of accessibility. Has the timetable been constructed in such a way as to allow pupils to opt for the subjects of their choice? To what degree is there flexibility in the sixth form timetable? Are popular subject options blocked against each other? These types of decisions are made by members of the senior management team and can have a dramatic effect upon the culture and ethos of the school.

With this aspect of the hidden curriculum in mind, I have provided you with a list of prompt questions that might help to provide you with an initial focus when you visit your schools.

- How much pupil traffic is there around the school at change of lessons? What effect does this have on the 'feel' of the place?
- Have you witnessed conflict between pupils caused by overcrowding in the corridors?
- How easy is it for pupils to gain quick and easy access to their classrooms?
- Are pupils happy with the structure of their school day? Are there times when they start to 'flag'?
- Are pupils happy with the range of option subjects presented to them at GCSE and A Level?
- Do pupils feel these subjects are accessible to them?

Relationships within the school

Few could argue that teacher–pupil relationships lie at the very heart of the learning equation. While you are visiting your schools keep a watchful eye out for the way in which pupils interact with their teachers during their lessons and in out-of-lesson contexts. Although it is important for you to note the degree to which pupils display respect for their teachers, it is equally important for you to explore the extent to which this respect is reciprocated by teachers, especially when they are admonishing pupils. Keep a particular look-out to see whether 'labelling' is occurring. In Dixie (2005) I refer to the work of Rist (1970), Keddie (1976) and Mitzos and Browne (1998) who describe the labelling process in some detail and whose work has greatly influenced my teaching over the past 20 years or so. So, what exactly is labelling? Basically, labelling is the way in which pupils are encouraged and/or taught to see themselves by their teachers. It is highly probable that you will have witnessed many situations where positive labelling has occurred and where the self-belief of pupils has been fully enhanced by the teacher through the use of praise and positive motivational language. However, all teachers need to be very careful about labelling pupils in a negative way. Negative labelling is often carried out in an overt way by referring to pupils as being nasty, evil, thick, trouble-makers, etc. However, be aware that negative labelling can also be carried out in a more subtle manner by ignoring or not challenging specific pupils or groups of pupils within the class. In making an assessment of the hidden curriculum you will no doubt pick up on the nuances of pupil–teacher relationships in your host school(s).

Most schools promote the corporate nature of their establishments, stressing that all staff share the norms and values of their institution and that each and every person in the school is fully valued and 'singing from the same hymn sheet'. While you are at the school, make an assessment of the quality of relationships between teaching and non-teaching staff as these can often indicate whether the school acts as a corporate body or whether there is any divisiveness in the system. In order to help you to do this I have listed a few questions below for your consideration:

- Is there a them and us situation in the staffroom?
- Are non-teaching personnel invited to staff meetings?
- Are non-teaching personnel offered full opportunities for professional development?
- Are non-teaching personnel afforded the same status when implementing the school's behaviour management policy?
- Do teachers share their lesson plans and learning objective with teaching assistants?

School policies

It is a legal requirement that all schools produce their own policy documents on such issues as special educational needs, pupil behaviour, pupil inclusion, equal opportunities, anti-bullying, health and safety, etc. You may very well be impressed by the fact that you have been presented with a pile of these policies when you arrive on your first school visit. However, the sign of a good school is when staff actually put these policies into practice on a daily basis. I have been in a number of schools where the paperwork looks mighty impressive but where the actions of the staff do not always match the high ideals laid out on the written page. While on your visit, keep a particular look-out for consistency of approach from all staff on such things as managing pupil behaviour, health and safety issues in science, technology, drama and PE lessons. Find out what happens when there is a racist incident in the school. Do the actions of the school match the recommendations laid out in the policy? Explore the extent to which opportunities for pupils with special educational needs (SEN) are congruous with those laid out in the SEN policy. In short, adopt a critical stance when reviewing the paperwork presented to you. In order to help you to do this I have provided you with yet another set of questions for you to ponder on.

- How accessible are these policies to teaching and non-teaching personnel? Have posters and/or summary documents been posted around the school?
- To what extent do the aims and objectives laid out in these policies reflect the reality of school life?
- To what degree are the teaching and non-teaching personnel aware of, and intimate with, the details of these policies? For example, do they know what to do in the event of a pupil making a disclosure to them? Do they know the procedure for reporting a racist incident? Do they know what to do if they suspect that a child is suffering some form of abuse?
- To what degree are the pupils aware of, and intimate with, the details of these policies? For example, do they know what to do if they are being bullied? Do they know the procedure for reporting a racist incident? Are they fully aware of the details of the school's behaviour policy?

Extra-curricular activities

A really good way to assess the commitment and drive of the teaching staff in your host school is to choose a day when there are no after-school meetings, and then pay a visit to the school car park about half an hour after the end of the teaching day. At this point simply note the number of cars still in the car park. Of course, there will always be those teachers who cannot get out of the school gates fast enough, but the majority of staff stay behind at the end of the teaching day to prepare for the next day or to catch up with their marking. There are, however, also a significant number of teachers who use this time to referee or umpire sports matches, to run training sessions, to run drama rehearsals or to run extra-curricular clubs. Most schools will be able to provide an audit of the extra-curricular activities that occur at lunchtime or after school, so it is worth having a look at this in order to make an assessment of the level of commitment of the staff and/or to see whether there is anything you feel you could get involved in. You could use the questions laid out below to help your enquiry into this aspect of school life.

- What extra-curricular activities and school trips does the school provide?
- Are these activities and trips available and accessible to all pupils?

- How aware are the pupils of these activities and trips? Are they publicized?
- Do these extra curricular activities and trips help to improve the quality of the relationships between teachers and pupils? If so, how?

Assemblies

Functionalist sociologists such as Durkheim and Parsons have argued strongly that schools can be seen as microcosms of society and that the social conditions prevalent with the workplace and within society in general, are often deliberately replicated within the school environment. The extent to which this should be the case can be debated at a later date, but what is important for you to realize is that one of the functions of the school is to prepare its pupils for life in the outside world. Nowhere is this preparation more obvious than in school assemblies. I strongly advise you to attend the assemblies aimed at a range of year groups and to make a careful note of the types of messages being imparted and of the standard of behaviour exhibited by the pupils. Assemblies are often used as a strategy to transmit strong corporate messages to pupils and to engender a sense of 'togetherness' in the school. You need to decide the degree to which your host school is successful in doing this. The following questions might help you to arrive at your decision.

- Are whole-school assemblies delivered?
- How many assemblies does each year group have?
- What strategies are used to establish and maintain social order?
- How well do the pupils behave in assemblies? How attentive are they?
- To what extent are the assemblies used to deliver religious messages?
- To what extent are the assemblies used to deliver humanist messages?
- How successful are the assemblies in helping to transmit the norms and values of the school?

Quality of classroom and corridor displays

In Dixie (2005) I give a lot of attention to the positive messages that can be transmitted to pupils through the medium of effective classroom and corridor displays. Bearing in mind that we know the hidden curriculum is a set of values, attitudes and knowledge frames which are embodied in the organization and processes of schooling, then you will appreciate that the classroom and corridors are the perfect scenarios in which to do this. Again, I am confident that you will understand the general principle outlined to you above but you may need more guidance as to the specific questions you need to ask yourself when exploring this particular aspect of the hidden curriculum. To this effect I have provided a number of questions for you to consider while you are making your tour of the school.

- What *academic skills* are being transmitted through the medium of classroom/corridor display?
- What *personal qualities* are being transmitted through the medium of classroom/corridor display?
- How do classroom/corridor displays encourage a positive attitude towards work?
- How do classroom/corridor displays encourage a positive attitude towards authority and the school rules?
- How do classroom/corridor displays encourage hard work and productivity?
- How do classroom/corridor displays encourage a respect for others?

Careers and work experience opportunities

It is true to say that a number of schools provide opportunities for careers education through the formal curriculum, often through the medium of personal social and health education (PSHE). However, in a substantial number of schools, advice and guidance offered on vocational issues may be transmitted in an informal manner through the hidden curriculum. While you are in your schools, take an opportunity to talk to some sixth formers about the quality of career's guidance offered. Make sure that you visit the careers room to have a look at the wall displays and to ascertain the quality of the resources offered to the pupils. Talk to the work experience coordinator about the whole-school opportunities offered to pupils and about the vocational opportunities provided for 'challenging' pupils lower down the school. My final list of questions can be used to ascertain the degree to which the school caters for the vocational needs of its pupils.

- Does vocational education form part of the school's timetable? If so, how many hours per week are allocated to careers-related issues?
- To what extent are vocational issues promoted around the school through the medium of wall displays?
- Does the school have a careers advisor?
- Does the school have a careers room? How comprehensive is the information provided?

- Does the school have a work experience programme? Is this available to all pupils?
- Does the school have links with the vocational departments in local colleges? To what extent do they work together to provide opportunities for the pupils in the school?

Making the most of your lesson observations

5

Any school worth its salt should provide you with a lesson observation schedule for the duration of your visit. Having carried out and organized hundreds of lesson observations, I am fully aware of the pitfalls of the observation process. While the first few lesson observations prove to be quite interesting to the visitor, there does come a point where the experience starts to become less meaningful and where the observer, no matter how well meaning, begins to switch off. It is also fair to say that at this point along the continuum, most observers are not fully aware of what they should be looking for. In other words, they don't know what they don't know. Therefore, I have provided you with two observation pro forma that have been designed to offer you a focus for this task and to help you to get the most out of your lesson observations. Having worked with hundreds of teacher trainees over the past 15 years or so, I am fully aware that behaviour management is one of their biggest concerns. With this in mind I am suggesting that you initially use observation sheet A (following) to focus on this issue when observing classes. You will notice the various elements of behaviour management have been broken down in an attempt to help you articulate the good or bad practice that you see happening before you.

Observation pro forma A

OBSERVATION FOCUS: EFFECTIVE CLASSROOM MANAGEMENT	
DATE & LESSON:	**SUBJECT:**
Indicators	Evidence-based judgements
START AND END OF THE LESSON	
Pupil entry to room and initial behaviour	
Teacher activity at the start of the lesson	
Settling up/issuing/collection of resources	
Knowledge of pupils' names	
Lay-out of furniture	
Tidiness of classroom	
Orderly ending of lesson	
COMMUNICATION WITH PUPILS	
Tone, volume and pace of voice	
Effective questioning technique	
Clarity of explanation	
Awareness of individual pupils	
Use of black/whiteboard	
Use of audio-visual aids	
LESSON STRUCTURE	
Appropriate timing and phasing of lesson	
Suited to class ability and previous work	
Tasks broken down into small steps	
Maintain pupils' attention	

PUPIL BEHAVIOUR	
Clear consistent ground rules identified	
Pupils follow ground rules	
Watchfulness maintained on all parts of classroom	
Acts to pre-empt inappropriate behaviour	
Avoids confrontation	
Uses praise to promote positive attitudes	
Pupils sustain concentration	
Pupils are courteous	
Pupils work collaboratively	
REFLECTIVE COMMENTS – What are the implications of this observation for my teaching?	

Reproduced from *Managing Your Classroom*, by G. Dixie, 2007, by kind permission of Continuum International Publishing Group Ltd.

Although I have stressed the importance of good behaviour management in lessons, it is important for you not to be seduced into thinking that an orderly and well-behaved class is necessarily a learning class. I have witnessed many situations where a teacher's behaviour management has been superb but where very little learning has taken place. Therefore, I have provided you with a second observation sheet which focuses entirely on the issue of effective learning (Observation pro forma B). You may like to use this pro forma in conjunction with the behaviour management observation sheet, or you may prefer to start using this particular sheet towards the latter part of your school visit.

Observation pro forma B

OBSERVATION FOCUS: EFFECTIVE PUPIL LEARNING	
DATE & LESSON:	**SUBJECT:**
Indicators	Evidence- based judgements
INDIVIDUAL PUPIL DIFFERENCES	
Shows knowledge of ways pupils learn best	
Matches subject matter and tasks to individual's ability	
Creates opportunities to raise individual self-esteem	
LEARNING OPPORTUNITIES, GOALS AND TASKS	
Defines learning goals	
Offers learning activities relevant to learning goals	
Uses differentiated learning activities relevant to learning for groups and individuals	
Challenges pupils' thinking	
Provides opportunities for pupil interaction	
Assesses whether pupils have met learning goals and provide constructive feedback	
Teaches individual and collaborative study skills	
WORK ENVIRONMENT	
Pupil seating/workplace matched to learning activity	
Resources well organized and accessible	
Makes use of ICT	

EFFECTIVE COMMUNICATION	
Communicates learning objectives clearly and links to pupil activities	
Relates activities to previous/future learning	
Stimulates curiosity and enthusiasm for learning	
Communicates clear, sequenced instructions and expectations	
Makes effective use of questioning technique to provide pace and direction	
Listens to, analyses and responds to pupils	
REFLECTIVE COMMENTS – What are the implications of this observation for my teaching?	

Reproduced from *Managing Your Classroom*, by G. Dixie, 2007, by kind permission of Continuum International Publishing Group Ltd.

Having carried out your observations, I would strongly advise that you start to collate and synthesize your findings in order to come up with a set of generalized learning points. By doing this you will be in a better position to share your new-found expertise, and articulate these experiences during your teacher training interview. I have provided you with an example of this, as follows.

Lesson Observation Summary focusing on: Effective behaviour management

- My observations taught me that it is imperative for teachers to set out their rules, routines, expectations and sanctions when they first meet their classes and to revisit these during the course of the year. This practice was most effective when teachers provided the rationale behind their rules, routines and sanctions. I now understand my need to make my expectations clear to pupils from the very outset.

- I noted that the most effective learning environments occurred in classes where the teachers obviously knew a lot about the backgrounds of the pupils within their charge. These teachers showed a high level of respect to their pupils, even in situations where they had to reprimand them for their misbehaviour. They also took a lot of trouble to learn and use their pupils' names. I will make it my business to research the background of my pupils before I start teaching my classes.

- It was interesting to note that the best-behaved classes were those in which a 'Can do' culture had been engendered by the teacher. This was often done pictorially through the use of motivational posters and/or through the display of pupils' work on classroom walls. In many lessons good behaviour was achieved through the teacher's use of positive and supportive language when responding to pupils' contributions in class discussions and question/answer sessions. I was also interested to note how good teachers made meaningful use of praise as a behaviour management tool. I intend to emulate the practice of some of these by creating my own reward system for my classes.

- At the end of each lesson I asked the teacher whether he/she had constructed a seating plan for their pupils. It was interesting to note that pupils' behaviour was far better in classes where youngsters had been placed in seating plans for their lessons. I will make sure that I produce seating plans for my classes and show the class teacher these before I start teaching.

- What absolutely 'shouted out' at me while I was carrying out these observations was how pupils responded so positively to teachers who demonstrated 'teacher warmth' and who showed a sense of humour in their lessons. I will endeavour to keep my sense of humour even if things go badly in my lessons.

Lesson Observation Summary focusing on: Effective pupil learning

- The best lessons occurred when teachers provided the pupils with a variety of activities and tasks. Some teachers overtly set up activities that catered for the various learning styles of their pupils. By doing this the teacher was able to successfully fully engage the visual, auditory and kinesthetic learners within their classes. I will find out how the pupils in my classes learn best.
- I discovered that pupils learn best when the teacher has made the learning objectives transparent and when these are revisited on a regular basis during the lesson. I will make sure that I ask my pupils whether they understand the purpose of each lesson.
- I found out that pupils also learned best when their teachers issued clear sequential instructions. I will write my instructions down and show these to my class teacher before I start teaching my lessons.
- The most positive learning environments were created where pupils felt comfortable in making mistakes and where it was 'OK to be wrong'. I will try to build up a climate of trust in my classroom. By doing this, my pupils will realize that making mistakes is just part of the learning process.
- The most effective lessons were those that had an effective 'starter', 'core' and 'plenary'. I will make sure that my lessons are well structured and that I provide that initial 'hook' which will get my pupils 'on board'.
- I was really impressed by the way in which some teachers managed to involve every pupil in their discussions and/or question/answer sessions. In these classes no pupil was 'marginalized'. I will try to ask a question of every pupil during the course of each lesson.
- In some lessons pupils were given the opportunity to assess their own work as well as the work of their peers. I felt that this increased pupil ownership of their learning and kept the youngsters on task. I will try to get pupils to evaluate their own work and to feed back their findings to the rest of the class.
- In some lessons I witnessed an excellent use of ICT in lessons. Some teachers made good use of PowerPoint to cater for the visual learners in their classes, while others made superb use of the interactive whiteboard to fully involve their pupils. Other teachers used ICT to run quizzes in the 'starter' phase of their lessons. I now fully realize the need to become ICT proficient.

If you use your pre-interview school visits in this way, I am certain that you will feel more confident when completing your personal statement and you will also be more likely to perform well at interview. In short, you will have made your school visit work for you.

6 Preparing to make your application

Bearing in mind that you already are, or soon will be, of graduate status, it is assumed that you will be able to complete most of the application form without too much trouble. With this in mind most of the advice offered to you on this issue will be confined to helping you write your personal statement. However, you do need to take this very important point on board. The application form is a conduit through which you are expected to provide evidence of your social and communication skills, and to show how you can organize your information in a clear and accessible manner. It is therefore vital that you take every opportunity to get the spelling and grammar on your application form thoroughly checked. You are also strongly advised to make a copy of your application form and take it along to the interview. This will provide you with a last-minute reminder of the issues that may be brought up by the interview panel.

Having spoken to a number of current and potential trainees about the application process, I have arrived at the conclusion that the personal statement is the section of the application form that most candidates find difficult to complete. Many current trainees felt that in hindsight they did not do themselves justice fully in demonstrating their skills, experience and enthusiasm for teaching young people, and for teaching their subject. I am sure that they would have appreciated the advice offered in this chapter.

Although it is very important that you use the application process to display your individuality and your uniqueness as a person, I would advise that you keep within specific parameters. To help you to do this I have provided a number of questions for you to consider when completing your personal statement.

- Why do you want to be a teacher? Who or what has influenced your decision to apply to join the profession?

- Why do you think you will enjoy working with young people? What previous experiences of working with young people can you bring to your training and to the profession in general?
- What relevant skills and personal qualities are you able to bring to the teaching profession?
- How have you developed your subject knowledge and how will you use your expertise to enthuse, motivate and inform your pupils?
- How have your experiences in schools or other educational environments informed your view about teaching?
- What else can you offer the profession in addition to your own specialist subject?

It is important that you give your personal statement a great deal of thought and that you complete this as comprehensively as you are able. Although I have provided some exemplar responses in the following pages, it is vital that you emphasize your own individual experiences and that your statement does not appear to be too formulaic. Remember that training places are limited, so try to make your personal statement as original and appealing as possible.

I would also strongly endorse the advice proffered by the Training and Development Agency (TDA) which warns applicants not to over-claim. ITT providers are highly likely to explore the statements you make in more depth. If you are found to have made a false claim it is almost certain to seriously jeopardize your chances of getting onto your course. I have been in the embarrassing situation where a trainee has given false information and has been asked to leave the course. It is always best to be upfront when making your application. Let us now explore these questions in more detail.

Why do you want to be a teacher? Who or what has influenced your decision to apply to join the profession?

The responses to this set of questions will provide the opening sentences to your statement; therefore it is very important that you get this right. In the introductory chapter we explored some of the reasons why people wanted to become teachers. If there was a specific time when you decided to become a teacher, then you need to describe how you came by this realization. Between the years 2000 and 2001, the Teacher Training Agency ran an inspirational campaign entitled 'No one forgets a good teacher!' This recruiting message was conveyed extensively on cinema and television screens and on billboards across the country, and was a resounding recruiting success. If you were inspired by particular teachers when you were at school, then you could briefly describe the effect of these teachers on your decision to apply for a teacher training course. Examples of possible openers from the TDA website include:

'What attracts me to teaching is …'
'I am interested in teaching because …'
'Teaching appeals to me as a career because …'

I have also provided an example of an introductory paragraph below.

As a youngster who struggled greatly with the academic side of school life, I know what it is like to fail. I am interested in becoming a teacher because it will afford me the opportunity to raise the expectations and achievement of late developers such as me. I am convinced that my ability to empathize with the plight of the less able will help me to establish and maintain good relationships with my pupils. However, I am fully aware that a good teacher needs to embrace the needs of *all* the pupils in his/her class, and I relish the opportunity to provide learning scenarios that will stretch and motivate youngsters right across the ability range.

The next question for you to consider when writing your personal statement requires you to relate your experiences of working with young people to your application to become a teacher.

Why do you think you will enjoy working with young people? What previous experiences of working with young people can you bring to your training and to the profession in general?

You need to link the skills used in these situations to your potential role in the classroom. I have provided you with three exemplar statements below.

Example A

While I was at university I carried out some voluntary work in a local primary school. One of my reasons for doing this was to see whether teaching really was for me, and to also get an idea of what it might feel like to be an adult in a classroom. I also intended to use this experience to ascertain whether my personality was more suited to teaching primary rather than secondary age pupils. While at the school, I was allocated the role of 'Right to Read Tutor'. This role involved me assisting pupils who were experiencing difficulties with reading and required me to work on a one-to-one basis with these youngsters over a 5-week period. I found the whole experience extremely rewarding and thoroughly enjoyed my time in the school. To further support this experience I spent some time in a secondary school helping teachers to run the Young Enterprise Scheme. This scheme gave me the opportunity to work with Year 9 pupils on English-related issues over a 5-week block of time. At the end of the five weeks I was asked to stand up in assembly and present these youngsters with their certificates. Although I was extremely nervous at the time, both experiences proved to be thoroughly enjoyable and helped me to make the decision to apply to teach in the secondary sector. I feel that my passion for English and my ability to relate really well to older children means that I would be well suited to teaching in a secondary school.

Example B

In order to find out about my suitability for secondary school teaching, I became a Classroom Teaching Assistant (CTA) in my local secondary school. While carrying out this role I learned a great deal about children with special needs and was pleased to discover that I was able to strike up good working relationships with even the most challenging of pupils. As my role required me to work with individual pupils across the curriculum, I was fortunate enough to observe a whole range of teaching and learning styles. I was also able to witness teachers carrying out their classroom management strategies with varying degrees of success. In making this decision to apply to train as a secondary school teacher, I do so having gained a full and realistic view of classroom life.

Example C

Although I have had no formal teaching experience, I feel that my work with the Scouts over the past 5 years has stood me in good stead when making this application. In addition to helping to run the regular weekly meetings and activities, I have also been involved in helping to organize and run summer camps in the Lake District and the Norfolk Broads. My role involved me working on a one-to-one basis with young people on their 'personal targets' and in helping groups of youngsters to set up camp and to organize the competitive activities that took place during our stay at the site. I would certainly welcome the opportunity to use my organizational and interpersonal qualities in a classroom situation.

The next question for you to consider when completing your personal statement relates to the skills and qualities you have amassed throughout your lifetime. According to the TDA website there are many qualities that can be attributed to good teachers. They suggest that a good teacher should demonstrate:

- an ability to relate to young people, good interpersonal and listening skills;

- the capacity to be alert, creative, imaginative, energetic and enthusiastic;
- an ability to be adaptable and versatile;
- a sense of responsibility and reliability;
- good time-management and organizational skills;
- resilience, motivation, tenacity; and
- a desire for self-development.

The question set out below requires you to focus on the attributes that match your own strengths and to identify a specific time when you have demonstrated those qualities. I have provided you with three examples.

What relevant skills and personal qualities are you able to bring to the teaching profession?

Example A

I am a good team worker and have particularly demonstrated this skill playing football for my local team over the last 6 years. I was appointed team captain and have represented our side in local, county and national competitions. I have recently trained as a children's football coach and now run an under 15s side that competes in the Sunday morning league. I am keen to develop my coaching skills further and to use these to help young people to improve their performances. I believe these skills and qualities to be fully transferable to a classroom situation, and am hopeful of being given the opportunity to show what I can do.

Example B

After leaving university in 2007 I spent a year in Zambia as a voluntary aid worker for the Save the Children charity organization. During my stay in the country I lived in a small village just north of Lusaka. Some of my time was spent helping the villagers and other aid workers to build wells in the villages in the area. At other times I helped experienced teachers in the teaching of English in the local primary school. Not only did this extremely rewarding experience allow me to get my own life into perspective, but it stimulated my desire to give something back to the world. Teaching technology would be my way of doing this.

Example C

On leaving university I accepted a post at a local insurance company. Within a year I was appointed a section supervisor with responsibility for ten staff. On getting the job I was informed by my own supervisor that, among my other skills and qualities, it was the high quality of my organizational and interpersonal skills that had specifically led to me landing the job. I feel that these two qualities are of vital importance both to the training year and to the teaching profession in general.

There is no doubt that good subject knowledge is high on the TDA's list of priorities for teacher trainees. When writing your personal statement, you need to make sure that you include something about the way in which you have developed your subject knowledge over your training year and how it may be relevant to the national curriculum. You can look at the Curriculum Online website to see what topics are taught at Key Stages 3 and 4. I have again provided you with two exemplar responses to the key question set out below.

How have you developed your subject knowledge and how will you use your expertise to enthuse, motivate and inform your pupils?

Example A

Having studied drama to both BA and MA level, I decided to develop my skills further by attending two 'Circus Space' courses in the summer of 2005 where I learned how to juggle and perform as a clown. Since this time I have used these newly acquired skills, along with the more traditional skills gained on my degree courses, to run drama workshops in some of my local secondary schools. I really enjoyed these experiences and soon realized that working with young people and supporting colleagues were excellent ways to use my skills and fulfil my desire to work with, and support, children in a learning environment.

Example B

Throughout my academic career, history has always been a subject that has excited and challenged me. In order to meet the demands of my degree course I have developed such skills as analytical thinking, persuasive writing and the ability to communicate orally. Taking history to degree level has greatly improved my research skills as well as my ability to interpret primary and secondary sources. I used these skills to gain a first class honours grade for my dissertation which focused on the role of women during the First World War. Having taken steps to become intimate with the content of Key Stages 4 and 5 of the national curriculum, and the specifications for the AQA and EXCEL examination syllabuses, I am confident that I have the necessary background to bring history alive in the classroom and beyond. While I was in my second year at university I was fortunate to accompany a Year 7 class to the town's castle and its immediate surroundings. This experience provided me with real insight into how the teachers used pupils' previous knowledge and experience to help them explore and interpret the rationale behind the construction of a number of local historical buildings and monuments. This has made me really keen to develop my own pedagogic skills in such a way as to inspire my pupils and to engender a similar love of history within them.

You will remember the advice given to you at the beginning of this chapter about your need to visit a range of schools and to take full advantage of your experiences. Hopefully when you see the question laid out below you will fully appreciate the rationale behind the guidance offered. This really is your chance to reflect upon your school experiences and show how perceptive and astute you have been during your school visits. You should identify and comment on particular aspects of your experience and demonstrate how these affected the teaching and learning process. Some examples include:

- the layout of tables and chairs, different tasks and teaching methods;
- the individual teacher's personality or behaviour management techniques;
- the way the teacher assessed work and gave feedback to pupils; and
- how the teacher worked with other adults in the classroom.

How have your experiences in schools or other educational environments informed your view about teaching?

Again, I have provided two exemplar statements for your perusal.

Example A

As I had not been in a school since I left full-time education at the age of 16, I felt the need to spend a couple of weeks in a local secondary school. The rationale behind this was that I needed to gain a realistic perspective of a modern-day secondary school before I decided whether to apply for this teacher training course. While at the school I was provided with numerous opportunities to observe classes and to discuss the observation notes I had taken in lessons. I observed some excellent lessons particularly in maths, English and science. I am now far clearer about the necessity to provide pupils with clear learning objectives, and about the need to cater for the learning styles of all the pupils in the class. Because I had mentioned my concerns about behaviour management, I was also provided with the opportunity to reflect on this aspect of my observations with the professional tutor. Although I realize that I have a long way to go, I am now more confident about stepping into a classroom as a teacher for the first time.

Example B

In preparation for my application to join this course, I spent a week in my local comprehensive school where I was given numerous opportunities to observe a range of teachers at work. However, the most useful part of my visit occurred on the first day when I was given a tour of the school. This gave me an opportunity to explore the school's hidden curriculum. Armed with pen and paper, I visited a number of classrooms, attended the Years 7 and 10 assemblies, and spent some time walking around the corridors and school grounds with the duty staff. Having already carried out some work on the role of the hidden curriculum in creating the culture and ethos of a school, I found the whole experience fascinating. I was impressed by the quality of pupil/teacher relationships, the learning conditions in the classrooms and also with the way that teaching and non-teaching staff seemed to work together with one common aim. This is certainly a school I would like to work in.

The final question requires you to think beyond your immediate remit as a trainee. When selecting applicants, all ITT providers will look beyond the training year to the time when most of you will be employed in schools on a full-time basis. Through the medium of your personal statement, they will seek to find out what additional contributions you will be able to make to the schools in which you will eventually be employed.

What else can you offer the profession in addition to your own specialist subject?

Here, you should focus on other skills you have that would be of benefit to a school. These could be:

- language skills, including community languages such as Urdu or Punjabi;
- your interests, such as photography, ICT, sport, drama or music; or
- training experience or management skills that you have gained in other employment.

I have provided you with three exemplar statements below.

Example A

As a native Bengali speaker I can use my linguistic skills and cultural understanding to offer support to pupils in the school for whom English is a second language.

Example B

Although I do not intend to train in business studies, I would be more than happy to share my experiences of running my own business with pupils on the GCSE and/or A level business studies courses.

Example C

I was a junior downhill skiing medallist for Great Britain and would love the opportunity to help coach pupils, should the school organize a skiing trip.

By now you will have realized the importance of the application form and, in particular, the personal statement in the 'sifting and sorting' process carried out by ITT providers. I would like to end this chapter by offering the following piece of advice. Having completed your application form to the best of your ability, you are strongly advised to find a friendly ITT tutor and/or English teacher in a local school and ask him/her to read it through before sending it off. Providing you have followed the advice offered in this chapter, and your application has been written in efficient and coherent English, I am confident that you can look forward to being called to interview by at least one ITT provider. Chapter 8 offers guidance on how to prepare for your interview and perform well on the big day!

Part Three
PREPARING FOR
THE SELECTION DAY
AND BEYOND

Completing the selection tasks

Bearing in mind that the reputation of ITT providers depends very much on having a small drop-out rate, they will do absolutely everything they can to select appropriate candidates for their courses. Before being accepted on an initial teacher training (ITT) programme, you will be asked to attend an assessment interview which will usually take place over a full day but may take as little as one hour. When you receive the call to attend an interview, it is very important that you read the letter and/or information sheets very carefully. A number of ITT providers require you to carry out a pre-interview task, so be careful not to miss this among the paperwork. You may be asked to read a book or an educational article of your choice and to be prepared to discuss this on the day. On the other hand, you may find that you have been prescribed a specific text to explore prior to your interview day. Whichever scenario applies, if you want to earn Brownie points from the interview panel, make sure you use the information gained from your reading to *identify* the potential implications of this material on your teaching. For example, if you have read an article on managing challenging classes from the *Times Educational Supplement* (*TES*), then you need to identify and describe some of the things you would need to do in order to manage your classes effectively. If you have chosen to read up on the recent changes in the 14 to 19 curriculum, then you need to know how you might deliver a vocational element to the teaching of your subject. Being able to identify implications from our own practice, or from our observations of others, is a vital reflective skill and one which we need to be able to use throughout our career.

Alternatively, you may be required to carry out a piece of small-scale school-based research which will then be discussed at your interview. Again, the need for you to identify the implications of your findings on your potential practice as a teacher is paramount. You could, for example, be asked to find out how pupils' preferred learning styles have been catered for and/or challenged in your specialized subject area in your host school. I can assure you that any interview panel would be extremely impressed if you were able to identify examples of observed good practice, and if you then went on to show them how you would use or adapt these ideas for your own teaching purposes.

There are some ITT providers that will require you to sit tests and/or carry out tasks on the day of the interview. This process could take on the form of a comprehension exercise which will require you to respond articulately to an educational article or extract presented to you on the day. In effect, the providers are simply checking to see whether you are able to comprehend the sophisticated nature of the text in front of you, and whether you possess the ability to communicate your thoughts efficiently and effectively using the written word. Alternatively, you may be advised to keep yourself up to date with any current educational initiatives or news stories, with a view to being set a question to answer on the interview day.

I also know of some ITT providers who require potential trainees to work with pupils for a part of the interview day. To all intents and purposes, when this happens, the interview day takes on a different slant and becomes more of a *selection* day. Potential trainees are asked to prepare a 5-minute presentation to a select group of pupils and to then hold a 5- to 10-minute discussion on the topic. This having been done, pupils are then asked what they think about each candidate. This will either be done by interviewing the pupils, or by giving them a questionnaire to complete. As you can see in Figure 7.1, I have included (on the following pages)) a copy of an observation questionnaire given to pupils in my school to fill in while potential GT candidates are making their presentations to the Year Council committee. While it is highly unlikely that you will come across such a rigorous form of assessment on your interview day, you should find this questionnaire useful in helping you to identify the areas of focus for the interviewers and/or pupils when making their judgements on your performance.

If you are presented with a scenario such as this, my advice would be to choose a topic that is relevant, close to pupils' hearts and one which is likely to invoke strong opinions. Choosing the right topic is absolutely vital if you want to get the pupils talking and interacting with you. Examples of such topics could be:

- teenage pregnancy
- the role of the media in helping to cause eating disorders
- the role of sport in keeping youngsters away from crime
- an element of youth culture
- heroes
- reality TV programmes.

Candidate: Observer: Tutor group:

The candidate was able to make appropriate eye contact with the pupils.

Strongly agree	Agree	Disagree	Strongly disagree

Evidence

The candidate adopted a positive and assertive body posture when standing in front of the class.

Strongly agree	Agree	Disagree	Strongly disagree

Evidence

The candidate was able to use an appropriately effective tone of voice when talking to the class.

Strongly agree	Agree	Disagree	Strongly disagree

Evidence

The candidate was able to gain the full attention of the pupils when required.

Strongly agree	Agree	Disagree	Strongly disagree

Evidence

The candidate was able to give clear, transparent instructions to the pupils.

Strongly agree	Agree	Disagree	Strongly disagree

Evidence

The candidate was able to use good scanning techniques during the session.

Strongly agree	Agree	Disagree	Strongly disagree

Evidence

The candidate showed the potential to forge good relationships with pupils.

Strongly agree	Agree	Disagree	Strongly disagree

Evidence

The candidate displayed an ability to think on his/her feet and to use his/her initiative.

Strongly agree	Agree	Disagree	Strongly disagree

Evidence

The candidate displayed the ability to stem pupil indiscipline in the session.

Strongly agree	Agree	Disagree	Strongly disagree

Evidence

The candidate displayed a good sense of presence.

Strongly agree	Agree	Disagree	Strongly disagree

Evidence

Additional comments

Figure 7.1 ITT Candidate assessment form

It is very important when launching your session, to make the objectives transparent to the pupils. In doing so they will be able to see where your train of thought is leading and it will make it easier for them to contribute to the discussion.

The other strong piece of advice I would like to offer you is to make your presentation as dynamic as possible – include audio and visual input if you can, and try to get the pupils actively involved in discussions and/or question/answer sessions. Most schools will have LCD projectors should you wish to use PowerPoint to deliver your presentation. If you can get pupils up and moving about in a meaningful manner then do so. You may also consider bringing relevant artefacts into your session. I have seen a number of potential trainees use items of clothing, jewellery and pottery to successfully stimulate discussion.

I appreciate that this can be quite a daunting experience for you, especially if you have only made one visit to a secondary school since you left school at the age of 16 or 18. However, just thank your lucky stars that you are not being made to teach a complete lesson, as is the case with many trainees who attend selection days at the end of their training year. Now, that really *is* stressful!

It is also highly possible that this sifting and sorting process will continue to occur *after* your interview has taken place. Some ITT providers require you to participate in further recruitment exercises, which may include any of the following:

- a group task, discussion or presentation
- a further individual interview and/or
- a written test.

8 The interview

Then there is the interview itself. The format of the interview can vary greatly between ITT providers and subjects. Your interview could take place on a one-on-one basis, or it could simply be a panel interview. In some interview scenarios the process will be extremely formal with you sitting opposite a small panel of lecturers and/or senior staff. Alternatively, your interview may be far more informal and relaxed than this. My experience tells me that in situations where interviews take place in schools, rather than in Higher Educational Institutions (HEIs), candidates are far more likely to encounter a more informal approach to the process. Whichever stance the panel adopts, you need to remember that they are trying to get to know you, and to ascertain whether their ITT programme and, indeed, whether teaching in general, is really for you. With this in mind, I suggest that you are highly proactive in offering the appropriate amount of personal/professional information to the panel. You will note that I used the term 'appropriate'. It is fair to say that you need to take every opportunity to elaborate on the information provided in your personal statement, and that your responses should be sufficiently detailed to have answered the question, but you need to be very careful not to waffle. This is why it is important that you rehearse your responses beforehand.

'Okay, then, perhaps one of you could have a guess at today's date.'

There is absolutely no doubt that you will be asked about your experience of working with young people, about your commitment to teaching, and about your relevant knowledge and skills. The providers are also looking for applicants to show evidence of their full commitment to the profession. A proficiency in, and an enthusiasm for, the subject you wish to teach is obviously an important element of your application. However, providers are looking for far more than this. They require you to provide evidence to show that you have demonstrated a full commitment to the social and academic well-being of children, and are far more likely to offer a place to someone who can discuss concrete examples of situations where this has occurred. As an experienced ITT interviewer, one of the things I tend to focus on during the interview process is how much passion and enthusiasm candidates display when talking about their experiences of working with young children. My advice to you, therefore, would be for you to talk enthusiastically about your experiences but to be very careful not to lose focus. The panel will require you to offer specific examples of the relevant experiences you have had before attending this interview. Below I have provided a list of prompts to help you, although I do need to stress that this list is by no means exhaustive:

- organizing or helping with trips
- working with and/or supporting parents
- helping children to resolve conflicts
- managing challenging children
- preparing children for tests and examinations
- coaching children
- supporting the learning of children
- supervising children at work.

During your interview, the panel will be looking to see whether you fully understand the qualities required to be an effective teacher, and whether in fact you possess some or all of these. In preparation for your interview, you would be well advised to think about the ways in which you can you show that you do have what it takes to join the profession. As you will see in Figure 8.1, I have displayed the qualities required to be an effective teacher in diagrammatic form. To do so in list form would give the impression that these qualities are hierarchical in value. You need to show that you recognize the value of all these qualities, and that you understand how they interact with each other to produce the successful teacher.

It is up to you to use the time allocated to you during your interview to convince the interview panel that you understand the need for, and that you possess, many of these qualities.

Figure 8.1 Qualities needed to make an effective teacher

As your interviewer(s) will be looking for you to demonstrate the qualities displayed in Figure 8.1, you need to tailor your answers and contributions to reflect them when responding to their questions. An additional prompt list is offered below:

- a commitment to, and understanding of secondary education and of the role of the teacher;
- good personal, intellectual and communication skills;
- a positive attitude towards children and working with children;
- an enthusiasm for, and understanding of, your subject(s) and teaching in general;
- the ability to express yourself in clear and accurate spoken English.

The panel will not only be listening very carefully to the quality of your responses, but they will also be keeping a close watch on *how* you deliver these responses and whether you possess the potential to command the attention of pupils in a classroom. Therefore, you are advised to take the following guidance on board:

- ensure that you are dressed appropriately for the interview;
- make a confident (but not arrogant) entrance into the interview room. Shake the hands of each member of the interview panel and make good eye contact with them;
- ensure that you adopt an confident (but not over-confident) body posture; that you hold your head up and that you keep your shoulders back. Ensure that you make eye contact with the interviewer(s) when they ask you a question;
- no matter how nervous you are, try to look as self-assured as possible;
- do not to mumble – speak clearly, assertively and with authority;
- under no circumstances should you fabricate or exaggerate your experiences. As is the case with making false claims on your application form, if you are found out you will be refused entry onto the course.

It is absolutely vital that you fully prepare and rehearse for your interview, as a failure to do so will result in a great deal of frustration on your part when you realize that you have not done yourself full justice on the day. You need to think very carefully about the types of questions you are likely to be asked by the interview panel. If you know any current trainees or NQTs who could advise you on the interview process, you need to sit down and go through the potential questions with them. You are strongly advised to make notes of your responses to these questions and to scrutinize them in the hours leading up to the interview. Whereas it is virtually impossible to identify every question you may be asked by an interview panel, experience allows me to suggest a number of fairly predictable areas of enquiry. To help you to prepare for your interview, I have provided you with a list of questions and married them with some suggested responses.

Q: What made you want to become a teacher?

A. I want a job that makes a difference to people's lives. I believe that teaching will allow me the opportunity to do this.

I was inspired to make this application by my sixth form English teacher. He showed me how rewarding it could be to challenge, enthuse and motivate young people.

Both my parents are teachers and, although they do mention some of the drawbacks to the job, they constantly talk about how rewarding the profession is.

Q: What qualities do you think make a good teacher?

A. I think it is very important to be able to communicate clearly with young people. I also feel that it is important to show imagination and creativity when planning lessons. Teachers also need to be resilient, patient and highly organized. When all else fails, it is important to hold onto your sense of humour.

Q: What experience do you have of working with young people, and how could you utilize this in the classroom?

A. As you can see from my application form, I have worked extensively in the youth service, and have had many dealings with teenagers in an informal context. I feel that I know how young people think and what they feel about school in particular, and feel confident that I can use this knowledge and experience to introduce relevance to my lessons.

I have worked as a teaching assistant for the past two years and have gained a 'warts and all' picture of teaching. I have witnessed some excellent classroom practice and would welcome an opportunity to use the ideas gained from my observations in the classroom.

Q: What skills and qualities could you bring to the teaching profession?

A. I feel that I am quite a creative person and am confident that I will be able to find new ways to introduce potentially dry topics to pupils, and to keep them on task during my lessons. I also feel that I am a good communicator and that I will be able to transfer the concepts and content covered in my lessons into language that my pupils will be able to understand. Because I was not particularly successful at school myself, I have a great deal of empathy for those pupils who might experience difficulties in my lessons. I also think that teachers need to be highly organized if they are going to be able teach effectively. I feel that my good organizational skills will allow me to plan effectively, to keep on top of the marking and to meet any deadlines issued by the school.

Q: How could you motivate and inspire pupils who do not share your love of your subject?

A. I often feel that when pupils express a dislike for a particular subject, what they are really saying is that 'I don't like the teacher', or 'I don't like the way it is being taught'. The most important thing for me to do, therefore, would be for me to build up positive relationships with these youngsters. I would then set about introducing a high degree of relevance to my lessons by showing them exactly how the topic content is related to their own lives. I would do this through the use of newspaper clips, video, popular music, stories, etc. In addition to this I would include as much active learning as possible. I would also try to 'lead by example' by displaying a passion and enthusiasm for the subject during my lessons.

Q: Can you identify one topic within your subject area that you feel might be difficult for pupils to understand? How could you deliver this topic in an accessible manner?

A. Pupils are likely to find topic X difficult because it requires them to understand a number of challenging concepts. In order to make these concepts accessible to my pupils, I would break them down and link them with their own experiences. (At this point you would need to explain how you could do this for your own specific subject.)

Q: How do you feel about the National Curriculum? Is it help or hindrance to pupil progress?

A. There are obvious benefits to having the National Curriculum. It provides a degree of uniformity within the school system so that pupils entering secondary schools in different parts of the country do so having had a similar educational experience. This makes it easier for secondary teachers to build upon a high degree of presumed knowledge. It also makes it easier for pupils to transfer from one school to another without their progress suffering too much. Having said this, there is a significant disadvantage to our National Curriculum. Many teachers feel that because it is so content-led, they do not have time to be creative or to introduce process-based learning. I would be concerned that I could not provide pupils with enough time to find out things for themselves, and/or to learn through their mistakes. This is where good planning comes in.

Q: Describe how the contents of an article/book/extract you have read recently might impact upon your professional practice.

A. I recently read a very interesting article about parents' consultation evenings which highlighted my need to be thoroughly prepared for these meetings. Having read this article, I will now make sure that I have prepared detailed notes on each pupil; that I have the pupils' books marked and placed in appointment order on the desk, ready to show the parents; that I have produced a running script which allows me to structure the meeting and to meet the 5 minutes allocated to the process.

Q: How might you deal with pupils who constantly talk over you while you are trying to deliver your lesson?

A. The first thing I would do would be to ask myself whether I had established my rules, routines and expectations firmly enough in the initial stages of my practice. I would then set about reinforcing my expectations and sanctions in a robust manner with the whole class. Having done this, I would then take these pupils out of the room separately, and talk to them on an individual basis. I would adopt a pleasant but assertive manner and warn them that should they continue to act in this way I would be keeping them back after school to repeat the part of the lesson they missed.

Q: How will you ensure that you show respect and include pupils of all backgrounds in your teaching?

A. Bearing in mind that we live in a multi-cultural and multi-faith society, and that we have an extremely diverse pupil population, I am aware of my need to provide opportunities for my pupils to learn more about the cultures and beliefs of other people. I would make it my business to integrate different cultural and religious perspectives into my lesson planning, and I would ensure that the views of every pupil are treated with respect. I would make certain that I have read the school's equal opportunities policy and that I have identified ways in which I can deliver this policy through my everyday professional practice.

I have spoken at some length about your need to rehearse your interview. To help you to do this, the TDA has produced an excellent interactive interview for you to use. This can be found at the following web address: www.tda.gov.uk/Recruit/thetrainingprocess/makingyourapplication/theinteractiveinterview.aspx

Preparing for your training course 9

On the assumption that you have been successful in your interview, you now need to consider what you can usefully do to prepare for your training course which will commence about six months after you have received your acceptance letter. My first suggestion would be for you to arrange further visits to as many different types of schools as possible. Although you have been accepted on the course, this does not mean that your career is necessarily carved in stone. You may find that having had these additional experiences in schools, the job is simply not for you. It is far better to withdraw from the course at this point rather than waiting until later.

Having read the previous chapter you now know what to look for in a school. Focus your attention on the hidden curriculum and try to observe as many classes as possible. At no other time in your career will you be afforded as many opportunities to observe a range of teachers at work. However, can I remind you to undergo this process with tact and sensitivity? No matter how competent or experienced a teacher is, he/she is still likely to experience a degree of self-consciousness and discomfort when being observed, even if it is only by an inexperienced pre-course trainee. Try to put the teacher's mind at ease by making positive comments about the wall displays or about the quality of his/her relationships with the pupils. Make it clear that you want to learn from him/her and that you are not there to judge performances. It really is worth keeping notes of all the things that might prove useful to you later on in your career, but be very careful not to appear like an Ofsted inspector. Share your findings with your host teacher and thank them for the good ideas that you have gained from watching his/her lessons. If you are able to go one step further by taking on some temporary work as a learning support assistant or cover supervisor, then take every opportunity to do so. This experience, especially if it is supported by considered reflection, will be invaluable to your training and to your future teaching career.

One thing I would strongly recommend you do is to visit your first practice school and spend some time getting to know your mentor. By doing this you will be able to find out how he/she works, what makes him/her tick and what he/she expects from you. Hopefully you will have a tour of the school, be introduced to members of your department and be provided with a list of things to do before commencing your practice. If you feel able to do so, ask your mentor for his/her contact details, so if you think of something after your visit, you can email or telephone him/her.

Many secondary school ITT providers insist that you visit a primary school for a minimum of a week before you start the course in August/ September. Even if your provider does not insist upon this, I would strongly advise that you take every opportunity to arrange a placement. Gaining primary school experience is a good idea because it will:

- give you an idea of children's experiences prior to their moving up to secondary school;
- allow you to explore the issue of transition and will give you an idea of how your subject is taught in Key Stages 1 and 2;
- provide you with a range of teaching ideas which you will be able to transfer to a secondary school scenario;
- give you an idea of the level of maturity of the pupils at the top end of a primary school.

In addition to my role as professional tutor at a large comprehensive school, I have carried out a lot of developmental work into the role of the school ITT mentor. This work has led to me producing mentor training courses for ITT mentors in the east of England. When planning the sessions for these mentoring modules, I have placed a great deal of emphasis on the need for mentors to have an intimate understanding of their own roles as teachers; the notion behind this being that it is only when we understand our roles as teachers that we really begin to become effective mentors. To support this work, I have relied heavily on an article written by Zimpher and Howey entitled 'Adapting supervisory practices to different orientations of teaching competence' (1987), in which they categorize a teacher's role into four domains or competences. These four competences are: technical, clinical, critical and personal. The details of each of these are outlined below:

Teachers display *technical competence* when they:

- determine *what* is to be learned;
- determine *how* it is to be learned;
- employ the criteria by which success is to be measured;

- show mastery of methods of instruction, for example specific skills such as how to ask good questions;
- apply appropriate teaching strategies;
- select and organize appropriate resources;
- structure the classroom for learning;
- employ techniques that are successful in helping to establish and maintain good classroom discipline.

Teachers display *clinical competence* when they:

- adopt the role of a problem solver and clinician who is able to frame and solve practical problems through the process of reflective action and inquiry;
- set up and test hypotheses in the classroom, and solve such problems as what should be done about disruptive pupil behaviour, or what the best format for group work should be;
- take on the role of action researcher, exploring the extent to which the various learning theories match the realities of classroom life.

Teachers display *critical* competence when they:

- adopt a critical role of the education system by looking at such issues as the social conditions of schooling, and the influence of the 'hidden curriculum';
- explore the power and authority bases both within and outside the school;
- ask questions about the basic ideology of schools, about the nature of society in general, and about the effects of negative socialization on the teaching process;
- ask other questions that present a more critical and radical notion of the structures of schools.

Teachers display *personal* competence when they:

- use themselves as effective and humane instruments of classroom instruction;
- use their intra-personal skills to confront themselves critically and develop their levels of self-awareness;
- fully understand the interactive nature of teaching by showing an awareness of the role of verbal and non-verbal symbols in the teaching process;
- understand how small group processes work;
- use their good inter-personal skills to create a warm and supportive learning environment.

So, how exactly can the above information help to support you in your training year? As potential trainees and eventual teachers, you need to be aware that all of these competences are important and that you should not be over-reliant on one particular domain. It is vital, therefore, for you to adopt a considered and balanced approach towards your role as a teacher. For example, it is not enough for you simply to rely on your personality and good relationships with your pupils (personal domain) to get you through the school day. You need to make sure that your behaviour management strategies are in place (technical domain), and that you have planned your lessons to cater for all pupils in your class irrespective of creed, culture and ability levels (clinical domain). In addition to this, you need to be clear in your own mind what your teaching philosophy is, and what your overall aims are as a teacher within the British educational system (critical domain). It is also important for you to note that these four competences do not exist in isolation. A teacher has many roles in a school, most of which overlap. However, I do feel the classification offered by Zimpher and Howey (1987) provides us with a basic framework from which to work. In Dixie (2005) I describe some of the research I carried out with pupils on what makes a good teacher. I feel that the following quote summarizs our need to work on all aspects of our teaching personality:

> Although most pupils are not fully able to articulate the prerequisites of a good teacher, I am convinced that they do ask a number of quite searching internal questions about the person standing in front of them. (page 3)

I go on to describe my research findings which showed me that pupils *do* see good teachers as being able to: control their classes; make their teaching spaces purposeful; and create effective scenarios for learning. My research further informed me that pupils *do* want their teachers to reflect on the things that do and do not work in the classroom; they *do* want their teachers to understand how their home backgrounds and family situations affect their work in school. With this pupil shopping list in mind, you need to do everything you can to make sure that you adopt a balanced approach to your professional practice. Using the teaching domains as guidelines will help you to do this. In addition to providing you with a useful insight into your roles as a potential teacher, I hope I have gone some way to whetting your appetite for further reading on pedagogical issues such as this. With this in mind, the following is a list of publications which you might want to read before you embark on your teacher training course.

Preparatory reading list

Battersby, J. and Gordon, J. (eds) (2006) *Preparing to Teach: Learning from Experience*, Routledge: London

Capel, S., Leask, M. and Turner, T. (2001) *Learning to Teach in the Secondary School*, Routledge: London

Cohen, L., Manion, L. and Morrrison, K. (1996) *A Guide to Teaching Practice*, Routledge: London

Cowley, S. (2006) *Getting the Buggers to Behave*, Continuum: London

Cowley, S. (2006) *Getting the Buggers to Learn*, Continuum: London

Dixie, G. (2005) *Getting on With Kids in Secondary Schools*, Peter Francis: Dereham

Dixie, G. (2007) *Managing Your Classroom*, Continuum: London

Ellis, V. (2002) *Learning and Teaching in Secondary Schools*, Learning Matters: Exeter

Kyriacou, C. (1998) *Essential Teaching Skills*, Nelson Thornes: Cheltenham

McManus, M. (1989*) Troublesome Behaviour in the Classroom*, Routledge: London

Moon, B. and Mayes, A.S. (eds) (1994) *Teaching and Learning in the Secondary School*, Open University Press: Milton Keynes

Rogers, B. (1998) *You Know the Fair Rule*, Pitman: London

Scott Baumann, A., Bloomfiel, A. and Roughton, I. (1997) *Becoming a Secondary School Teacher*, Hodder & Stoughton: Milton Keynes

Wragg, E. (1994) *An Introduction to Classroom Observation*, Routledge: London

For those of you who wish to extend your reading to explore educational research literature I recommend the following publications:

Elliott, J. (1992) *Action Research for Educational Change*, Open University Press: Milton Keynes

Thomas, G. and Pring, R. (eds) (2004)*Evidence-Based Practices in Education*, Open University Press: Maidenhead

It is also essential that you familiarize yourself with the National Curriculum documentation, both in terms of its overall structure and in relation to the subject you intend to teach. You can access the internet to obtain a general guide to the National Curriculum produced by the Department for Children, Schools and Families (DfCSF) at the following website address: www.nc.uk.net/home.html

In addition to this you can download schemes of work from the Qualifications and Curriculum Authority (QCA) by logging on to the following website address: www.qca.org.uk/nq/

Earlier in the chapter I advised you to acquaint yourself with current educational issues as a means of preparing for your interview. I strongly suggest that you continue to do this by making a point of reading the quality press. The *Times Educational Supplement* is published every Friday and is the main source of educational news. Other newspapers such as the *Guardian* (Tuesday), *The Times* (Monday), the *Daily Telegraph* (Wednesday) and the *Independent* (Thursday) have educational supplements which are all well worth reading.

One of the things that you are bound to notice while you are carrying out these initial reading tasks is the substantial use of acronyms and educational jargon included in the text. Education, like every other profession, has its own specialized language and, as trainees, it is important that you become accustomed to using this in your everyday professional life. Therefore, I have dedicated the next chapter to exploring some of the key educational terms that you are likely to encounter during your training year.

Part Four
GETTING TO GRIPS WITH THE JARGON

10 Understanding key educational terms and issues

Understanding key educational terms and issues

Anybody starting work in a new business or entering a new profession is highly likely to undertake induction training that has been designed to familiarize new entrants with the norms, values and culture of that organization. An integral part of this culture is the language used to communicate efficiently with people across the various components of the organization. In short, if they are to function efficiently in these organizational roles they need to learn the jargon and understand the issues associated with the terminology. Teaching is no exception to this. From the very early of stages of your teacher training, you will be bombarded with a code of educational shorthand that you will simply have to get to grips with if you want to function efficiently within the world of education. My role as a professional tutor over the past 15 years has shown me that this can be a bewildering experience for beginning teachers.

'Yes, I have a question. What do you mean by CATs, CRB, EAZs, EWO/ESW, IEP, LSU, NRA, PANDA, PAT, SENCO, SATs and SEN?'

You need to know that I have been highly selective in my choice of the key terms presented to you in this chapter and that I have only focused on the terminology that you are likely to encounter in your training year. You will also note that, alongside the description of some of these key terms, I have added brief guidance notes to help you to apply this new information to your professional scenarios.

A levels

An A level is simply an Advanced Level General Certificate of Education qualification. A levels are now made up of A/S units, which are typically taken in Year 12, and A2 units in Year 13, or at college. However, there is enough flexibility in the system for pupils to pick and mix their courses and it is not unusual for Year 13 pupils to study for their AS examinations along with Year 12 pupils. The new A level format was adopted in 1993, out of concern for the high drop-out rate in A level courses, where the examination system required pupils to take their exams in Year 13. The structure of the A level course is as follows:

- A level is taken to mean an A2 level which is the final school or college qualification which is usually sat by pupils aged 18.
- A/S level now stands for Advanced Subsidiary level. The notion behind the introduction of the A/S level was to provide pupils with the opportunity to study four subjects or more in the first year of their advanced level study and, by doing so, to gain a broader and more balanced education.
- A2 level courses follow some A/S courses in greater depth, but pupils are usually advised to reduce the number of subjects studied from four to three.

Attention-deficit disorder (ADD)

Attention-deficit disorder is similar to ADHD but without the hyperactive tendency. ADD is more common in females than in males and is often overlooked because of the absence of the disruptive behaviour that is usually associated with ADHD and which affects the learning of other pupils in the class. Pupils suffering from ADD are often extremely quiet and insular, and have a tendency to withdraw from other children. As is the case with ADHD, pupils find it difficult to focus in lessons, and this lack of concentration tends to have a negative effect upon their academic performances. However, unlike ADHD pupils, who are quite robust in demonstrating their failure, ADD pupils often fail quietly.

Attention-deficit hyperactivity disorder (ADHD)

Attention-deficit hyperactivity disorder has been recognized as a medical condition as well as a behavioural disorder. According to Leibling and Prior (2005) ADHD affects around 2 per cent of the population and is more prevalent among males than it is among females. There is a substantial body of research that suggests the condition is genetic, and you as teachers will probably find that it has affected more than one member of the same family. ADHD results from an imbalance of dopamine and noradrenalin, which are both required to transmit messages between brain cells during tasks. You will find that many of your ADHD pupils are given the drug Ritalin, which is often prescribed to reduce this imbalance. Symptoms of ADHD include:

- lack of attention – short attention spans which result in pupils failing to grasp the main thrust of the lesson even though they are not without academic ability;
- hyperactivity – inability to sit still in one place for very long;
- impulsiveness – pupils act spontaneously and fail to think about the consequences of their actions.

Bearing in mind the antisocial nature of this disorder, it is not surprising that pupils with ADHD are often rejected by their peers and find it difficult to make friends easily. This sense of isolation can often lead to a lack of self-esteem, to depression and to anxiety, and can lead to the pupil self-harming or taking drugs. In an effort to feel wanted, many of these youngsters get in with the wrong crowd and often become involved in acts of delinquency and crime. At home, their behaviour is often seen as destructive; their hyperactivity means that they usually need less sleep than other members of the family and often keep them awake at night. In addition, youngsters with ADHD can also have other disorders such as autistic spectrum disorder. Research carried out in the USA suggests that most pupils with ADHD underachieve especially when it comes to reading and writing. As teachers, it is very important for us to be fully aware of this condition and not to label pupils as being unintelligent and/or deliberately disruptive. To support you in your dealings with ADHD pupils I have provided you with a brief indication of some of the strategies you could employ to keep them on task in your lessons:

- Be explicit in describing the exact type of behaviour you expect from the pupil.

- Be explicit in outlining the consequences of any negative behaviour to the pupil.
- Help the pupil to recognize the danger signals and to plan ahead.
- Discuss the scenarios in which the ADHD pupil is likely to lose control and rehearse some possible solutions with them.
- Explain the benefits of the pupil behaving appropriately and support good behaviour with rewards.
- Reinforce pupils' success and/or effort.
- Ensure that the pupil is sitting close to you in the classroom.

Advanced skills teacher (AST)

An advanced skills teacher post provides an excellent opportunity for a high-quality teacher who wants to progress up the career and salary ladder, but who doesn't want to relinquish his/her work in the classroom. Although most ASTs do not have managerial experience, a large number of them are heads of department or heads of year. ASTs can take on specialist roles in their subject areas or can assume responsibility for initial teacher training. They can be appointed by individual schools or by the Local Education Authority. The fundamental tenet behind the appointment of ASTs is that they should be responsible for cascading good practice to teachers in schools other than their own. This work is known as outreach work. It is highly likely that you will come across ASTs either in a mentoring role and/or at the training sessions organized and run by your ITT provider. You would be well advised to cultivate relationships with these teachers because they can often be an important source of advice on subject-related or generic matters.

Anger management

Anger management sessions are designed to help pupils handle their anger in such a way as to minimize the negative effects on themselves, their families, their peers and the school in general. The general idea behind this approach is to take a child's anger and turn this into a positive force, and then use this to engender self-control and raise achievement.

It would be extremely unrealistic to expect you as a trainee teacher to be able to take prime responsibility for the anger management of the more challenging pupils in your classes. In fact, to assume this responsibility would be extremely unwise and dangerous. Having said this, providing you liaise with the class teacher and/or the head of year, there are things you can do to support a pupil with anger management issues. One of the first things you need to do is to make yourself aware of some of the things that could make a pupil angry. If you try to change a pupil's behaviour without understanding the reasons behind their actions and reactions, you could badly escalate the situation. In attempting to ascertain these reasons, you need to be aware that there are boundaries which you as a trainee should not cross. To this effect you are always advised to seek guidance from experienced colleagues and to run your ideas past those who have a more intimate knowledge of the pupils concerned. It is essential that you treat every pupil as an individual and that you spend time ascertaining their needs. I have listed some of the common reasons for pupils' anger below:

- family breakup – divorce, separation
- physical or sexual abuse
- lack of self-esteem
- frustration at not being able to understand the work
- frustration at not being provided with the opportunity to show what they can do (teacher not catering for pupil's learning style)
- feeling deprived or victimized by pupils or by teachers
- physiological and/or hormonal changes causing mood changes.

To further support you in your dealings with pupils who experience anger management issues I have provided you with brief guidance notes below:

- Offer the pupil opportunities to talk and let him/her know that it is normal for people to experience anger. When you are doing this, you need to try to show empathy for the pupil's situation.
- Model the type of behaviour you wish to engender within the pupil, rather than demonstrate your own anger by retaliating.
- Help the pupil to find goals and positive objectives in life.
- Help to raise the pupil's self-esteem by getting him/her to produce a 'can do' list of things they are good at both in and out of school.
- Make the pupil aware of the impact of his/her anger on others.
- Make it absolutely clear that hurting people or damaging other people's property is simply not acceptable behaviour.
- Help the pupil identify the cause of his/her anger and recognize and deal with the trigger points that occur along the way.
- Help the pupil release his/her energy in a more constructive way, e.g. sport, yoga, etc.
- Find out what the root cause of the pupil's anger is.
- Find a way of getting the pupil to redefine his/her anger so that it becomes a positive force and a catalyst for success.

Assertive discipline

This form of behaviour management is based on the presumption that the teacher has the right to determine the behavioural rules in the classroom, and that he/she has the right to expect pupils to comply with these. Assertive discipline in schools was developed in the 1970s by Lee and Marlene Canter in the belief that poor behaviour in classrooms should not be allowed to impinge on the learning of others. The main characteristics of assertive discipline are laid out below:

- Teachers should take responsibility for outlining their expectations, and for establishing the rules that define acceptable and unacceptable behaviour.
- Teachers should teach their pupils to follow their rules.
- Teachers should make pupils aware of the sanctions that might be imposed should pupils not follow their rules.
- Teachers should show consistency in the imposition of their sanctions.
- Teachers should expect participation and support from parents and colleagues.
- Pupils should expect to have a teacher who sets limits and who motivates and respects them.
- Teachers should give pupils opportunities to manage their own behaviours.

Assertive discipline requires a teacher to be assertive and confident in applying his/her learning rules. If the teacher is tentative, unclear and inconsistent in his/her approach to classroom management, then pupils can often become anxious, confused and even hostile. Teachers who practise assertive discipline provide feedback to pupils about their positive behaviours and usually employ their own rewards system. Bearing in mind that, at this stage of your pedagogic development, many of you will not yet be confident and assertive teachers, you need to remember that teaching is a journey and not a destination. Making yourself aware of the characteristics of assertive discipline and practising to be confident and assertive, will go some way to improving your behaviour management. One way you can do this it to carry out some reciprocal peer observations using the pro forma provided in Chapter 5 and use the observation notes to feed back to your colleagues. This really is a case of 'practice makes perfect'.

Assessment

In the past, the assessment of pupils' work tended to be mainly summative (i.e. assessment *of* learning). Traditionally, parents and carers were furnished with annual reports of their children's academic performances, and this brief overview provided them with a snapshot of their progress. In 1998 the Assessment Reform Group concluded that there was a fundamental need for teachers to use *formative assessment* (assessment *for* learning) in their lessons as a means of raising pupil achievement.

Summative assessment is a snapshot of each pupil's achievements. This can take a number of forms: as an annual or termly report, or in the form of the published *Standard Attainment Test (SATs)* results. Summative assessment is often used to keep parents informed of their children's progress. It is also a useful tool for informing the teachers of the progress and achievements of pupils new to the school. It provides an indication of the pupils' strengths as well as of their weaknesses and gaps in their knowledge and understanding.

Formative assessment of a pupil's work is usually carried out by the teacher on an ongoing basis throughout a course or project and is used to aid learning. Formative assessment might also involve the learner and/ or his/her peers in providing feedback on work, and is not necessarily used for grading purposes.

Assessment for Learning (AfL)

Assessment for Learning (AfL) is an evidenced-based process which is used to determine:

- exactly where pupils are in their learning;
- where pupils need to be in relation to targets and learning goals;
- how pupils might best meet these goals and targets.

The aim of Assessment for Learning is to raise achievement through the use of a clear plan of action designed to realize achievable and desirable goals. There are three ways to assess pupils' work:

- *criterion referencing* assesses achievement in absolute terms and simply measures whether a pupil knows X or can do Y;
- *norm referencing* assesses a pupil's achievement in relation to a group, rather than in absolute terms, e.g. is this pupil in the top 10 per cent of the assessed population group? If so, we will award them an A grade at GCSE or A level;

- oral assessments test the learning and understanding of pupils through a face-to-face conversation or question/answer session. Oral assessment is a particularly useful tool for assessing pupils with special educational needs (SEN). Some examinations still have an oral element to them, but standardization and moderation of results can be difficult to achieve.

You need to be fully aware that Assessment for Learning is a key issue in teaching today and that this will provide a focus for many a lesson observation on your school practices. It is worth getting to grips with this topic and spending some time exploring the various AfL strategies you could deploy in your lessons.

Autistic spectrum disorders (ASDs)

Autistic spectrum disorders, of which Asperger's syndrome and autism are examples, are brain-based disabilities that affect language, communication and/or information gathering. These disorders mainly affect the male population. Because their social and communication skills are particularly challenging, people with ASDs often experience difficulties in understanding how to behave. Their use of language is often pedantic and they often have a tendency to take things literally. I remember one incident from my teaching career when I was extremely cross with one particular child's behaviour and I instructed him to leave the classroom by telling him to 'take a walk'. When I went out into the corridor to talk to him I found that was exactly what he had done. I eventually found him walking around the school grounds. It is important to note that some, but not all, ASD pupils experience learning difficulties. In order to prepare you for teaching ASD pupils, I have provided you with some broad characteristics of the disorder below. However, it is vital that you do not jump to conclusions about pupils without seeking expert advice.

ASD pupils find it extremely difficult to:

- interpret the meanings behind normal everyday conversations;
- know what to say;
- have a meaningful conversation;
- form social relationships with adults and their peers;
- show empathy or concern for other people;
- behave appropriately;
- participate in group activities;
- hide their feelings;
- use their imagination;
- accept novelty or changes to their routines.

Bloom's taxonomy of the cognitive domain

Benjamin Bloom published his taxonomy in 1956. This taxonomy is a commonly used hierarchy of thinking skills and learning abilities, starting with the easiest skills and working through to the most cognitively challenging 'high order' skills (see Leibling and Prior, 2005). I have laid these skills out in order of difficulty as follows:

1 *Knowledge* – requires pupils simply to recall information and facts from memory. This could take on the form of biographical material about a famous person, historical dates, capital cities of the world, etc. Questions testing this basic skill would begin with: *inform me, describe, tell me, list, define, who, when, where*, etc.

2 *Comprehension* – requires pupils to show their understanding of the meaning of a specific element of knowledge by explaining things in their own words. It also requires them to be able to understand the implications of this knowledge. This is normally assessed by asking questions beginning with: *explain how or why, tell me in your own words, compare x with y, discuss*, etc.

3 *Application* – requires pupils to apply a concept to a novel situation. This could take the form of asking them to solve a new problem with existing knowledge. Questions testing application would start with: *apply, solve, experiment, discover*, etc.

4 *Analysis* – requires pupils to dissect a complete entity or problem into parts and recognize the patterns of parts that make up a totality. This could take on the form of troubleshooting a specific situation or ascertaining where things started to go awry in any given system. Questions that test analysis would begin with: *analyse, find, identify, sort out, deconstruct*, etc.

5 *Synthesis* – requires pupils to construct something new from existing parts. For example, this skill is tested in technology where pupils are required to design and produce something that achieves specific objectives, or when they have to rearrange what already exists in order to satisfy new needs. This skill is normally assessed by asking the pupils questions beginning with: *synthesize, create, design, invent, devise, what if?*, etc.

6 *Evaluation* – requires pupils to weigh up the evidence presented to them and make decisions about the value of something, e.g. from a range of possibilities select the most suitable solution. This skill is normally assessed by asking questions starting with: *evaluate, judge, compare, select*, etc.

So why is knowledge of Bloom's taxonomy so important to the teacher? The fundamental reason why you need to understand this skills/learning framework is so that you can *differentiate* your questions in your class discussions and question/answer sessions. By targeting your questions at the right level to specific pupils within a class, you can afford them the opportunity to show what they understand and, ultimately, what they can do. An intimate knowledge of Bloom's taxonomy is therefore an essential ingredient of personalized learning.

Brain structure

It is important for you as trainees and future teachers to have a basic knowledge of the structure of the brain and know how it affects learning. The simplest explanation is that offered by the Triune model (see Figure 10.1).

The *reptilian brain* is the area at the base of the brain which controls our survival instincts when we are put under threat. When a pupil feels insecure, unsafe or threatened, this part of the brain dominates and sets up mechanisms designed to protect the individual. In situations

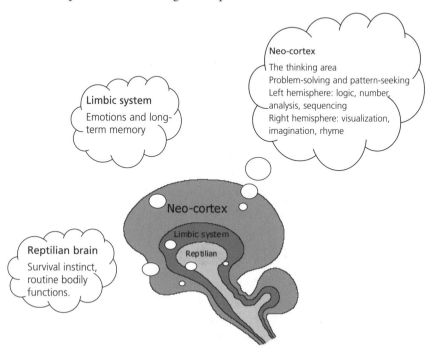

Figure 10.1 The structure of the brain (adapted from Dixie, 2005, page 71)

such as these, pupils often become hostile or simply turn tail and run. This is why the reptilian brain is often called the fight or flight part of the brain. Making sure that you deal with pupils' misdemeanours in an assertive rather than an aggressive manner will provide pupils with an opportunity to calm down and also maintain their dignity in front of their peers. As this part of the brain also controls our basic bodily functions, it is also important to make sure the classroom is well ventilated and that pupils have access to plenty of water. This part of the brain acts rather like a handbrake in a car. It is said that 80 per cent of learning problems are caused by stress-related issues (Shaw and Hawes, 1998), so if the needs of the reptilian brain have not been met, then the handbrake will remain on and learning will not take place.

The *limbic system* can be found in the middle of the brain and is thought to control our emotions and long-term memory. Bearing in mind that positive emotions produce endorphins that help to speed up learning, it is in the pupils' best interests that you create a positive can do culture within your classroom, and that you provide them with an opportunity to have some fun in your lessons.

The *neo-cortex* is positioned at the top of the brain and is thought to be the thinking or cognitive area where problem-solving and pattern-seeking occur. The neo-cortex itself is divided into two distinct hemispheres, each with a different learning function. The left hemisphere is thought to be the verbal and analytical side of the brain that controls facts, language and logic, whereas the right hemisphere focuses on the non-verbal, creative and intuitive element of our personalities, as well as controlling our movements. As trainees and future teachers, I would advise you to find out the hemisphere dominance of your pupils, so that you can set appropriate work that will both cater for, and challenge, their learning styles.

Catchment area

The school catchment area is a geographical area that provides a feeder population for the school. Even though a family may live within the catchment area, they must still apply to the school for a place for their child. Any parent may apply to a school outside their own catchment area, but their success in gaining a place for their child will depend upon a number of factors such as the capacity of the school and whether they have siblings already there.

Differentiation

One of the biggest lessons that you as trainees need to learn, is that all pupils are different. This may sound pretty obvious, yet when I make my observations of teacher trainees at work in the classroom, I note that they often adopt a one size fits all approach to their lessons. It is important to note that pupils have different abilities, different methods of working and different *learning styles*, and you should remember this when planning your lessons. I see differentiation as the means by which pupils can show what they understand, and demonstrate what they can do. The four common types of differentiation are listed below:

- *Differentiation by outcome* – this is the most commonly practised form of differentiation by trainees, and simply involves setting a common task or asking a common question of the class, and then awaiting a verbal or written response from the pupils.
- *Differentiation by source* – this is where a common task has been set, but where pupils have been given sources appropriate to their reading ages and levels of understanding to help them carry out the task
- *Differentiation by task* – this is where more than one task has been set in a lesson and where pupils have been allocated an activity that is appropriate to their ability level.
- *Differentiation by questioning* – this is where teachers ask questions at a level appropriate to the ability of the pupil(s) (see *Bloom's taxonomy*).

The more experienced you become as a teacher, the better you will be able to differentiate your work. By the end of your second practice, you may even feel confident to differentiate your pupils' activities according to their *sensory learning styles*.

Dyslexia

Dyslexia is a complex learning disability that mainly affects spelling and reading, although the disorder can also cause pupils to experience difficulties with writing and number work. Many people go through their lives without having had their dyslexia diagnosed, but they have simply devised their own coping strategies to get by. Many pupils, previously labelled as thick, stupid, backward or lazy, are extremely relieved to be diagnosed as having dyslexia. The important thing for us to note as teachers, is that dyslexia is not linked to intelligence. I remember one particular lad in my geography class who received support from a Learning Support Assistant (LSA) for the two years of his Geography GCSE course, and then went on to gain an 'A' grade in his examination. I have provided a list of common symptoms below:

- *Sequencing* – pupils with dyslexia get very confused with the sequences of numbers or letters that make up a date or that spell a word.
- *Speech* – pupils with dyslexia are often able to demonstrate their intelligence orally with some success, but this is not matched by their use of the written word. Poor spelling is often a big issue with these pupils.
- *Late development* – many youngsters with dyslexia are slow to learn speech, tell the time, tie shoelaces and may get confused between right and left. They may also experience difficulties with their motor skills such as catching, throwing, skipping and jumping, all of which require some degree of sequential thought.
- *Reading* – pupils with dyslexia really struggle with reading, often complaining of letters being jumbled up. They often get their letters mixed up when reading text, e.g. mistaking bs for ds and vice versa. Pupils with dyslexia will often do everything they can to avoid reading in class, especially out loud.
- *Concentration and memory* – pupils with dyslexia often have difficulty in concentrating for long periods of time. It is also true to say that their short-term memory may also be poorer than their peers. As a result of this, they may be very slow to complete the tasks you set them in class and may have to give up without finishing.
- *Achievement* – in most, but not every, case, pupils with dyslexia will underachieve.

Bearing in mind the large number of pupils with dyslexia in our schools, it seems apposite for me to offer some guidance on how to get the best out of these pupils:

- Make sure that you headline the main points of the lesson before you start teaching it. Constantly check the pupils' understanding of what you have told them. Provide a verbal summary of what you have taught them before, then ask them what they have understood and not understood. Make sure that you praise, reinforce and correct where necessary.
- Do not refer to people with dyslexia as 'dyslexics'. Using this term creates a master label for a pupil that does not do justice to the qualities and characteristics of the whole person.
- Provide regular breaks for these pupils, especially if the activities require them to concentrate for long periods of time.
- Integrate these pupils with the rest of the class wherever possible.

- Take full account of their condition when marking their work, and do everything you can to promote a positive attitude towards their learning and self image.
- Use mind maps with these pupils when you can.
- Make sure that you constantly repeat your instructions, but do so in a patient manner.
- Adopt a positive attitude towards dyslexia. Avoid using terms such as 'overcoming', 'disability', 'handicap' or 'drawback'.
- Always write down the homework and other instructions you might expect other pupils in the class to remember.
- Provide them with scaffolding when helping them to organize their work.
- Never ask them to read out loud, or ask them to read a form or to sign something on the spot.
- *Always* liaise with the special needs coordinator (SENCO) about these pupils.

Dyspraxia

Dyspraxia is a coordination disorder which manifests itself in clumsiness and disorganization of thoughts and movements. Pupils with this disorder may have difficulty with their fine motor skills, thus making it difficult to produce legible handwriting. They may also find it difficult to use a computer mouse in a coordinated and effective manner. Their gross motor skills may also be affected and they may experience difficulties in PE lessons where they are required to catch a ball or maintain their balance. Pupils with dyspraxia also have problems with sequencing movements and thoughts, so would find it difficult to imitate other people's actions. Getting organized for school is likely to be a problem. As is the case with dyslexia, it is thought that the signals from the brain are not correctly received by the parts of the body that need to act on the signals.

General Certificate of Secondary Education (GCSE)

The GCSE was introduced in 1988 as a replacement for GCE O levels.

General Teaching Council (GTC)

The General Teaching Council (GTC) was founded in 2000 as an independent non-profit making professional body for qualified teachers. It has been afforded statutory powers to advise the Secretary of State for Children, Schools and Families on matters relating to teaching and learning. You are now required by law to join the GTC irrespective of whether you work in a maintained, non-maintained, special school or pupil-referral unit. As a teacher trainee you do not have to join the GTC, but when you gain QTS your name will be put onto the teaching register and you will soon be asked to make arrangements to pay the annual fee.

Governors and governing bodies

Governing bodies exist for every maintained school. The role of the board of governors is to ensure high educational standards, take general responsibility for the conduct of the school's affairs, and oversee the budget, the curriculum and the appointment of personnel to the school. The governing body also has a responsibility to respond to Ofsted reports. The board of governors consists of the headteacher, Local Authority (LA) appointees, support staff representatives, elected parents, elected teachers and members of the local community. It is the duty of the governors to read all the relevant material, to keep up to date with current educational practice and to meet on a regular basis.

Individual Education Plan (IEP)

An Individual Education Plan (IEP) is used for all pupils in special schools and for pupils with specific learning difficulties in mainstream schools. It typically covers language, literacy, mathematics, behaviour and social skills. An IEP provides information that indicates:

- what type of help has been given to the pupil;
- how often the child receives this help;
- who has provided this support;
- what the current targets are for the pupil;
- how and when the pupil's progress will be monitored;
- what help the parents are giving their child;
- what the next moves are as far as providing additional support for the pupil.

In-service training day (INSET – also known as professional development days)

These training days are organized on a whole school basis and are usually timed to occur at the beginning or the end of term when disruption of school life can be kept to a minimum. Some schools disaggregate one or more of these days and carry out the INSET in twilight sessions after school. There are usually five in-service training days per year. As trainees you are highly likely to be required to attend the INSET days, especially the ones at the start of your practice, since they will provide you with an opportunity to meet the staff and to become acclimatized to the school.

Key skills

The key skills programme forms part of the post-16 curriculum and has been designed to help training providers, schools and colleges to improve the core skills of pupils beyond GCSE. It is funded by the Department of Children, Schools and Families. The key skills comprise the following:

- communication (both verbal and written);
- application of number (how to carry out calculations, interpret results and present findings);
- the use of information technology (IT) which requires pupils to find, explore, develop and present information using IT;
- improving one's own learning and performance (learning how to learn);
- problem solving;
- working with others.

Key Stage 3 Strategy

The Key Stage 3 Strategy was launched in 2001 to consolidate the national literacy and numeracy strategies in Key Stage 2. This has led to improvements in mathematics and English results for 11 year olds. The idea behind this strategy is to raise standards for pupils aged 11–14, by:

- providing continuity of progression between Key Stage 2 and Key Stage 3;
- establishing high expectations and challenging targets for pupils;

- encouraging and promoting more interactive approaches to teaching and learning;
- developing teachers' skills through a programme of professional development and support.

Key Stages

A Key Stage is a stage of the state education system in the UK setting out the educational knowledge and understanding expected of students at various ages. These stages have been outlined below:

- Key Stage 0: Nursery and reception years (3–5 years old). More commonly known as the 'Foundation Stage'
- Key Stage 1: Years 1 to 2 (5–7 years old)
- Key Stage 2: Years 3 to 6 (7–11 years old)
- Key Stage 3: Years 7 to 9 (11–14 years old)
- Key Stage 4: Years 10 to 11 (14–16 years old). The exams at the end of this Key Stage are typically of the GCSE level
- Key Stage 5 (more commonly referred to as sixth form): Years 12 to 13 (16–18 years old). The exams at the end are typically A levels, A/S levels, NVQs or HNDs.

League tables

League tables are sometimes known as school performance tables and are based on pupils' attainment in School Attainment Tests (SATs), GCSEs and A levels. The better the results, the higher up the league table the school is placed. There is a great deal of debate about the value of league tables. The purpose of league tables was to offer information to parents which would allow them to make choices about which schools their children should attend. However, the degree to which parents can exercise this choice is variable. Whereas the current system does allow parents to show their preferences for which schools their children attend, their choices are often extremely limited because very often the 'best' schools are full. In short, catchment areas often override choice and parents are forced to send their children to schools which they know to be 'poor' performers. In recent years, and in reaction to severe criticism, the DfCSF has introduced a value-added component to the formula to show how a school has improved the performance of its pupils. It is interesting to note that although Scotland, Wales and Northern Ireland still publish the results of individual schools, they have abolished league tables.

Learning styles

The move towards catering for the individualized learning styles of pupils originated in the 1970s and has gained popularity in recent years. The assumption behind this initiative is that a person's preferred or dominant learning style is the method by which he/she is able to learn best. We all collect and process information through our five senses but in very different ways, and it has been proposed that teachers should assess the learning styles of their pupils and adapt their classroom methods to best fit each pupil's learning style. By doing this they are more likely to become engaged in the learning process and fully motivated to achieve. As it is totally impractical to explore the vast range of learning-style models available to educationalists in this book, I have chosen to describe the model which you are most likely to come across in your training year – the Sensory Preference Model.

This model describes the three ways we use to absorb information and express ourselves. Our preferences may be visual, auditory or kinesthetic in nature. *Auditory* learning occurs through hearing the spoken word. You need to make sure that you provide opportunities for your pupils to listen and respond to such stimuli as sound-effect CDs, radio broadcasts, talking books, song lyrics, etc. *Kinesthetic* learning occurs through doing and interacting, so you need to plan opportunties in your lessons for pupils to do such things as role play, card sorting, attitudinal exercises and sequencing activities. *Visual* learning occurs through looking at images, mind maps, demonstrations and body language. You need to provide opportunties for pupils to produce their work in a visual manner through such things as impact posters, newspaper frontispieces, creative drawing, etc. In order to find out about the preferred learning styles of the pupils in your classes, it will be necessary for you to issue them with a questionnaire. There are numerous visual auditory and kinesthetic (VAK) questionnaires to be found online but you need care in selecting the right one for your pupils. To give you a basic idea of what these questionnaires are like I have provided you with the following website addresses:

www.businessballs.com/vaklearningstylestest.htm
www.vark-learn.com/english/page.asp?p=questionnaire

Finally, below is a list of additional guidance on learning styles which will further inform your practice:

- If you notice that there are pupils who are not fully engaged in the learning process ask them what you need to do to stimulate and motivate them.

- Although it is very important to cater for the preferred learning styles of the pupils in your classes, it is also very important to *challenge* them. Explain the three sensory terms and outline the purpose of the activity. Inform the class whether the activity has been designed to *cater for*, or *challenge* their learning styles.
- You need to be aware that most teachers teach their lessons in sympathy with their own preferred learning styles. This can severely limit the breadth and balance of opportunities presented to their pupils. My advice to you is to have a go at one of the VAK quizzes yourself, and challenge yourself to deliver your lessons in an unfamiliar style.

Multiple intelligences

The concept of multiple intelligences was introduced in 1983 by Howard Gardner who theorized that there was not just one intelligence but possibly seven. A description of these intelligences is outlined below using information from the following web address www.infed.org/thinkers/gardner.htm (reproduced from the encyclopaedia of informal education [www.infed.org]):

Linguistic intelligence which involves sensitivity to spoken and written language, the ability to learn languages, and the capacity to use language to accomplish certain goals. This intelligence includes the ability to use language effectively to express oneself rhetorically or poetically; and language as a means to remember information. Writers, poets, lawyers and speakers are among those that Howard Gardner sees as having high linguistic intelligence.

Logical-mathematical intelligence consists of the capacity to analyse problems logically, carry out mathematical operations and investigate issues scientifically. In Howard Gardner's words, it entails the ability to detect patterns, reason deductively and think logically. This intelligence is most often associated with scientific and mathematical thinking.

Musical intelligence involves skill in the performance, composition and appreciation of musical patterns. It encompasses the capacity to recognize and compose musical pitches, tones, and rhythms. According to Howard Gardner, musical intelligence runs in an almost structural parallel to linguistic intelligence.

Bodily-kinesthetic intelligence entails the potential of using one's whole body or parts of the body to solve problems. It is the ability to use mental abilities to coordinate bodily movements. Howard Gardner sees mental and physical activity as related.

Spatial intelligence involves the potential to recognize and use the patterns of wide space and more confined areas.

Interpersonal intelligence is concerned with the capacity to understand the intentions, motivations and desires of other people. It allows people to work effectively with others. Educators, salespeople, religious and political leaders and counsellors all need a well-developed interpersonal intelligence.

Intrapersonal intelligence entails the capacity to understand oneself, to appreciate one's feelings, fears and motivations. In Howard Gardner's view it involves having an effective working model of ourselves, and being able to use such information to regulate our lives.

The implications of the theory of multiple intelligences for your teaching are vast, but too many to take all on board now. Below are a few suggestions on how to improve your practice:

- Find out about the dominant intelligences of your pupils by asking them to fill in a simple questionnaire. There are numerous examples of these to be found on the web. You might like to have a look at the following website address for an example, but you may need to trawl through a number of sites to select the most appropriate questionnaire for your pupils: http://www.bgfl.org/bgfl/custom/resources_ftp/client_ftp/ks3/ict/multiple_int/questions/questions.cfm?lang=en
- Have a go at completing the questionnaire yourself. As is the case with *learning styles*, teachers tend to teach according to their dominant intelligence and it is important that you challenge yourself as well as challenging the pupils.
- Use the information gathered from these questionnaires to plan activities which both cater for, and challenge, the dominant intelligences of your pupils.
- Make a point of giving status and credibility to the dominant intelligences of your pupils especially the less able among them. Instead of asking yourself *whether* the pupils are intelligent, you need to ask yourself *how* they are intelligent. By doing this you will see the jokers the carers and the pupils with ants in their pants in a very different way.

National Curriculum

The National Curriculum was introduced into the educational system in 1988 as part of the Education Reform Act. The general directive of this initiative is that there should be uniformity in what is being learned by pupils in schools at the different stages of their development. Independent schools are not required to follow the National Curriculum. There are two principal aims to the National Curriculum:

- The school curriculum should aim to provide opportunities for all pupils

to learn and to achieve.
- The school curriculum should aim to promote pupils' spiritual, moral, social and cultural development and prepare all pupils for the opportunities, responsibilities and experiences of life.

Bearing in mind that this book is aimed at secondary school trainees, I have confined the information provided to that relating to Key Stage 3 and Key Stage 4.

At Key Stage 3 (ages 11–14) all students in state education are required to study:

- English
- mathematics
- science
- ICT
- geography
- history
- art and design
- design technology
- modern foreign language
- music
- physical education
- citizenship
- careers education.

A programme of sex education should also be provided in accordance with local policy. In Wales, pupils are additionally required to study Welsh.

At Key Stage 4 (ages 14–16) all students in state education are required to study:

- English
- mathematics
- science
- ICT (England and Northern Ireland only)
- physical education
- citizenship
- religious education
- sex education
- careers education.

All Key Stage 4 pupils are also required to undertake a programme of work-related learning. Schools must provide religious education for all pupils, although parents can choose to withdraw their children from lessons. Again, as in Key Stage 3, in Wales pupils are additionally required to study Welsh.

Newly qualified teacher (NQT)

Newly qualified teachers are entitled to a teaching load that is 10 per cent lighter than other teachers in their schools. A reduced timetable has been ensured to allow e.g.:

- regular meetings with their induction tutor;
- progress reviews on a half-termly basis;
- progress reviews with both the induction tutor and head teacher on a termly basis.

When you become an NQT, you need to make sure that you have been set targets that will help you to meet your induction standards and that you have been given a clear indication of your progress.

Office for Standards in Education (Ofsted)

Ofsted is a non-ministerial government department set up from the school's inspectorate in 1992 to help improve the quality and standards of education. The mechanism through which this monitoring process occurs, is through the independent inspections of schools and through the provision of advice by the department to the Secretary of State for Children, Schools and Families. Although its original function was to manage the system for inspecting state-run schools in England, its role has expanded. It is now responsible for reviewing the standards of Local Authorities (LAs), sixth form and further education colleges, initial teacher training courses, early years of childcare and education. and some independent schools and youth services.

The job of the Ofsted inspectors is to gather the information required to assess the educational perfomance of the school. This process involves collecting and analyzing data, observing lessons, interviewing teachers and pupils, analyzing pupils' work and meeting with parents and governors. Their findings are published in a written report which by law must be made accessible to the parents of the pupils in the school. If a school is felt to be underperfoming, it will be declared as having 'serious weaknesses' and any lack of improvement might put the school into special measures. If improvements do not follow, then the school may be closed down under the Fresh Start programme.

As teacher trainees, your performances will not be subject to inspection by an Ofsted inspector. However, you need to be aware that it is a very stressful time for teachers and that this might affect the level of support you receive during the period of the inspection. You also need to be aware that some pupils pick up on the anxiety felt by teachers and other staff, and you need to reassure them that it is not they who are being assessed.

Performance Assessment and National Contextual Data (PANDA)

These data come from Ofsted, the DfCSF and the Qualifications and Curriculum Council (QCA), which is used to help schools develop plans to raise standards. However, unlike league tables and Ofsted reports, these data are not made accessible to the public.

Pupil Referral Unit (PRU)

Pupil Referral Units (PRUs) are designed for pupils who, for a variety of reasons (perhaps behavioural or emotional issues), have been excluded and who cannot now attend a mainstream school. PRUs work closely with schools, parents, social services and other agencies in an attempt to help the pupil re-enter mainstream education.

Qualifications and Curriculum Authority (QCA)

The QCA was established in 1997 and is responsible for standards in education, training and qualifications in schools, colleges and work.

Scaffolding

In the same way that scaffolding is constructed around a building in order to allow a builder to complete his tasks, learning is scaffolded when the teacher provides an infrastructure of support that allows pupils to complete the activities set before them. As a trainee teacher you may need to help your pupils get themselves organized, support and encourage them when they experience difficulties with their work, suggest the resources they might use, help to refocus them when they stray off task and/or provide key words and/or pictures as hints to support their learning. However, what you must not do is to actually complete the task for the pupils yourself.

Teaching assistant (TA)

Teaching assistants are also known as classroom teaching assistants (CTAs) or learning support assistants (LSAs), and work under the direction of the class teacher. Many teaching assistants use their classroom experiences to support their applications to train as teachers. Teaching assistants may have general roles, or they may be allocated the responsibility of helping specific pupils with learning difficulties. Some TAs are given organizational responsibilities such as preparing resources and getting the classroom ready for learning. If you are fortunate enough to be allocated a TA in one of your school practices, you need to make every effort to cultivate an effective working relationship with them. Make sure that you share your expectations of the class with them and clarify whether you want them to have a disciplinary role in lessons. It is also important that you share your lesson plans with them and generally engage them in dialogue about the pupils' learning and social issues.

Truancy

One of the most frustrating aspects of teaching is where the continuity of learning is interrupted by regular bouts of pupil truancy. Leibling and Prior (2005) report that one in five of England's secondary school pupils is truant for 15½ days a year on average. With staggering figures such as this, it is our duty to look at the reasons why this high rate of truancy exists in our secondary schools. Below are listed some of the reasons why these pupils may not want to go to school:

- The pupil sees no value in attending school.
- The school is not engaging the pupil.
- The pupil has few or no aspirations.
- The pupil receives no parental authority or support.
- The peer pressure not to attend school is a stronger influence than the culture of the school.
- Some pupils find themselves with family responsibilities, e.g. carers, childminders, etc.

If you suspect that one of your pupils is truanting from school, make sure you notify his/her form tutor and/or head of year. You could also look for patterns of non-attendance which might help to explain his/her absence.

Work experience

All secondary schools are required to provide some form of work experience opportunities for their Key Stage 4 pupils. These vocational programmes see pupils working in businesses and organizations for a period of time, usually a week or a fortnight. The placements provide valuable experience for the pupils who get to find out what the world of work is really like. Although schools themselves often cultivate close contact with local employers, it is very often the family or friends of the pupils who find work experience placements for them. It is fair to say that the quality of these placements varies greatly. Some youngsters are both nurtured and challenged and receive a comprehensive training programme. As a result of this they leave their placement more confident and competent than when they first arrived. However, in some scenarios, no training schedule is provided, and pupils are merely seen as an extra pair of hands spending most of their time photocopying, sweeping up or making the tea. Good schools make time for their pupils to feed back their experiences and to evaluate the whole process. As trainees, you may be asked to make a work experience visit so make sure that you read up on the relevant protocol before you make your first appointment with an employer.

Part Five
UNDERSTANDING YOUR
TRAINING PROGRAMME

Understanding your training year 11

So, you've done it – you've got onto your course – congratulations. Now the hard work begins. The main purpose of this chapter is twofold: to provide you with a broad overview of the nature and requirements of your training programme; and to provide you with an opportunity to familiarize yourself with the QTS standards. However, before I do this I feel I ought to offer you a few preliminary words of warning about the training year ahead of you.

As a teacher of some considerable experience, I can tell you that teaching is an all-consuming career. You must be willing and prepared to fully immerse yourself in your training for the duration of the course. If you have a non-teaching partner, then warn him/her that there may be a rocky ride ahead and that you may not always be there to support him/her as you may have done in the past. In fact, if a significant other is around, the decision to enter the teaching profession needs to be made jointly, as the workload and commitment required to do the job can often impinge on the time spent with your partner. Take the trouble to explain your commitments to your partner and make time for him/her whenever you can.

Having said how demanding your training is likely to be, you must be very careful that you do not become a workaholic. You do need to have an escape activity that will help you to reduce the stress and pressure of the job. If you can, I would suggest that you take up some form of physical activity. As a young teacher, I often found that playing a game of football or going for a run went a long way to exorcising many of the frustrations of the day.

My next piece of advice relates to the approach you make towards your training. The fact that you have taken the trouble to acquire and read this book probably means that you intend to be highly proactive in your attempts to become a successful trainee teacher. Please be aware that people enrol on courses for a host of reasons, and that there will be trainees who will not be as positive as you in their attitude towards the guidance and advice proffered to them, or towards the tasks/activities they are required to carry out. Just as is the case in the classroom, peer pressure is a powerful thing. I suggest that you steer well clear of these negative influences.

In any training group, you will always get people who make it their business to criticize their trainers and/or the training opportunities provided for them. Whereas I am not suggesting that you adopt a non-critical approach towards the course, I am asking you to err on the side of trusting the judgement of your training provider until circumstances prove otherwise. As an experienced trainer, I am fully aware that even the most critical of trainees don't know what they don't know and I am asking you to accept that on most occasions, providers will have a clear overview of your journey from trainee to teacher. In this situation teacher probably does know best.

Understanding and working towards the Professional Standards for QTS

12

Not only is it reasonable to expect your training provider to show an understanding of your needs as a trainee but they are also expected to comply with the legal requirements associated with the assessment process. The following section has been written to clarify exactly what you need to do in order to gain qualified teacher status (QTS).

In order to gain QTS you are required to demonstrate full competence in all of the 33 Qualified Teacher Standards as prescribed by the Training and Development Agency (TDA). These standards are laid out in Appendix 1. In your quest to realize these standards you are required by the TDA and/or your training provider to spend a specific number of days in school over the training year. In addition, you must have at least two school placements. The number of days required for you to spend in school depends upon the specific course you are undertaking. Details of these requirements can be seen below:

- A four-year undergraduate QTS programme   160 days (32 weeks)
- A two- or three-year QTS undergraduate programme 120 days (24 weeks)
- A secondary graduate QTS programme   120 days (24 weeks)
- An employment-based scheme   Determined by the training provider

Although this is not the place to go into too much detail on this issue, you do need to know that these QTS standards form part of the framework of professional standards for teachers. This in turn forms part of a wider framework of standards for the whole school workforce. This framework includes the TDA's review of the national occupational standards for teaching/classroom assistants and the professional standards for higher-level teaching assistants. It is important for you to know about this contextual information because there will be times when you will feel absolutely fed up to the back teeth with having to yet again meet your professional standards. However, the reality of the situation is that this mode of teacher assessment is prevalent from trainee and NQT level right through to headteacher, so you need to get used to it.

Evidence to show that you have realized competence in these standards is demonstrated in your teaching, through your portfolio, training practice file, reflective log and School Practice Reports. Some providers also make use of a viva to assess the trainee's competence to meet the QTS standards. I will go into more detail about these later in the chapter. As a teacher trainer for two ITT providers, I often have occasion to chat informally with trainees at all key stages. Unfortunately, I have found that in each training cohort there is a hard core of trainees who flippantly dismiss their need to provide evidence to support their quest for QTS as being merely a paper exercise. Sadly, I feel these trainees have missed the point. The QTS standards have been designed by experienced professionals, many of them teachers, in order to make sure that a range of potential experiences is made available to trainees throughout their training year. There have been countless occasions where, having just signed off a trainee's QTS standard in his/her portfolio, I have asked him/her whether they would have made the effort to explore this issue had it not been compulsory to do so. Because of the heavy workload and high levels of stress during the course, the answer is invariably 'no'. In response to those trainees who say; 'you know I can teach, what do you need the paperwork for?', my response is to ask them to imagine a teaching scenario in which one of their GCSE pupils reacts in a similar fashion to a request for a piece of coursework. How would they react to this? Will they simply allow this pupil to pass the examination on the basis of a nod and a wink? I doubt it. I feel strongly that qualifying as a teacher is a privilege which should be earned and it is up to the trainee to prove his/her competence in the various QTS standards beyond question: a teaching certificate needs to be earned.

Whether I have persuaded you or not about the intrinsic importance of the QTS standards, it is absolutely vital that you gain an intimate understanding of these at the onset of your training year. Professional standards at QTS level and at every subsequent level are divided into three main categories. These are:

- professional attributes
- professional knowledge and understanding
- professional skills.

These standards provide clarity of the required expectations at each career stage. Before I offer an exploration of the QTS standards, it is important to make the terms used transparent:

- The term *'learners'* is used instead of 'children and young people' when learning per se is the main focus of the standard. It refers to all children and young people, including those with particular needs, for example those with special educational needs, looked-after children, those for whom English is an additional language, those who are not reaching their potential, or those who are gifted and talented.

- The term 'colleagues' is used for all those professionals with whom a teacher might work. It encompasses teaching colleagues, the wider workforce within an educational establishment, and also those from outside with whom teachers may be expected to have professional working relationships, for example early years and health professionals and colleagues working in children's services.

- The term 'classroom' is used to encompass all the settings within and beyond the workplace where teaching and learning take place.

- The term 'workplace' refers to the range of educational establishments, contexts and settings (both in and outside the classroom) where teaching takes place.

- The term 'subjects/curriculum areas' is used to cover all forms of organized learning experienced across the curriculum. For example, areas of learning in the foundation stage, broad areas of curricular experience and learning through play in the early years, thematically structured work in the primary phase, single subjects, vocational subjects and cross-curricular work in the aged 14 to19 phase.

- The terms 'lessons' or 'sequences of lessons' are used to cover teaching and learning activities wherever they take place, whatever their nature and length and however they might be organized, and are applicable to all educational phases and contexts.

- Where the phrase 'parents and carers' is used, it is understood that the term 'parents' includes both mothers and fathers.

- The term 'well-being' refers to the rights of children and young people (as set out and consulted upon in *Every Child Matters* (Green Paper) and subsequently set out in the Children Act 2004), in relation to:
  - physical and mental health and emotional well-being;
  - protection from harm and neglect;
  - education, training and recreation;
  - the contribution made by them to society;
  - social and economic well-being.
  - The term 'personalized learning' means maintaining a focus on individual progress, in order to maximize all learners' capacity to learn, achieve and participate. This means supporting and challenging each learner to achieve national standards and gain the skills they need to thrive and succeed throughout their lives. 'Personalizing learning' is not about individual lesson plans or individualization (where learners are taught separately or largely through a one-to-one approach).

Rather than present a list of QTS standards and then leave you wondering exactly what you should do with these, I provide you with detailed guidance to help you understand what each of the standards mean and to find the supporting evidence for your portfolio. You need to be aware that different training providers make variable use of the portfolio as an assessment tool. Your own provider may have its own idiosyncrasies as far as the role of the portfolio is concerned. You should also note that not all the QTS standards are observable and that you need to start collecting this non-classroom-based evidence as soon as possible. What I offer in Figure 12.2 is a set of generalized guidance that will allow you to start collecting evidence early on in your training course. You do need to be aware that this menu of evidence is not exhaustive and there are bound to be numerous occasions when you will be able to come up with your own ideas on how to support your portfolio.

It is at this point that I need to stress the importance of how you present this portfolio evidence to your training provider. It is not sufficient simply to place your documentation into your file without providing a context, rationale and reflective comment to accompany your evidence. Whoever is responsible for checking and/or moderating the portfolio will need to see the background information that supports the evidence, how and why it meets a particular standard, what you have learned from gathering this evidence and most important of all – *how this new found knowledge has impacted upon your professional practice.* Although all ITT providers vary in their expectations of how the portfolio should be presented, the general principles described above will certainly be acceptable to all. Many training providers ask that a completed frontispiece be used to support each of the standards. An annotated example of one of these is shown in Figure 12.1. If the training provider has not been prescriptive in the way you present your portfolio standards you might like to consider this as a model.

QTS achieved	Q11: Know the assessment requirements for the subjects/ curriculum areas in the age ranges they are trained to teach, including those relating to public examinations and qualifications.

Evidence to support the Standard

Annotated Year 7 PE interim documents, including the rationale of how and why this process is used to record pupils' achievements and attainment levels.
Highlighted and annotated QCA core tasks showing the links between these and the QCA assessment criteria.

Highlighted and annotated PE National Curriculum core strand attainment levels and assessment criteria.

Highlighted and annotated pupil versions of relevant assessment criteria.

Explanation of how the evidence supports the Standard

This first piece of evidence supports the standard by showing that I am not only aware of the relevant assessment requirements for my subject, but that I am also aware of the relevant arrangements. My documentation shows that I understand how the National Curriculum levels have been used to assess PE core tasks and how the results of these have been used to feed into the reporting process in my first practice school.

The highlighted and annotated QCA core task information sheets show that I have a secure knowledge and understanding of the Key Stage 3 and 4 assessment requirements and arrangements in PE.

The highlighted and annotated PE National Curriculum core strand attainment levels show that I have a secure knowledge and understanding of the assessment requirements of my subject. I have also provided annotated evidence to show how I have used my knowledge of the assessment process to plan my lessons and to assess my pupils' work.

By translating the National Curriculum assessment levels into 'pupil-speak', I have displayed a secure knowledge and understanding of the assessment criteria.

You may wish to add to this initial reflection at a later date, in order to demonstrate progress throughout the course. If so, please complete a second copy of this sheet and get it signed by your professional tutor or your subject tutor.

(Continues overleaf)

Critically evaluate how this Standard has impacted on your teaching/ professional development
Having to read through and become intimate with the Key Stage 3 and 4 assessment criteria of my subject, has allowed me to become more proficient in assessing the performances of my pupils. This has resulted in me adopting a more confident approach towards my lessons. I feel that I am able to convey to the pupils that I know what I am talking about.   Becoming familiar with the assessment criteria and arrangements has helped me to match up pupil performance with the appropriate level. Having done this, I have then used the results to inform my planning and to set individual targets for my pupils. Examples of how this has informed my lesson planning can be seen in section Q26 while my pupil target setting can be see in section Q28.   The true test of my understanding of the assessment process in PE came when I decided to abandon the formal language of the National Curriculum and translate the levels into language that is accessible to pupils. The response to this has been extremely positive. I have overheard pupils talking about their attainment levels, what this means to them and what they have got to do to improve upon their performance. This signifies to me that my efforts have paid off.

Date of reflection	
Signed	
Professional Tutor/Subject Tutor (delete as applicable)	

This page should be placed in the portfolio as explanation of the evidence collected.

Figure 12.1 Overview of QTS standard

1. Professional attributes

Those recommended for the award of QTS should:

	QTS standards	Suggested source of portfolio evidence	Support notes where appropriate
Q1	Have high expectations of children and young people including a commitment to ensuring that they can achieve their full educational potential and to establishing fair, respectful, trusting, supportive and constructive relationships with them.	Lesson planning demonstrating use of prior attainment and special educational needs (SEN) data to set challenging learning and teaching objectives. Lesson planning demonstrating how individuals' or groups' needs have been catered for. Lesson planning with evidence of differentiated learning objectives being communicated to pupils. Lesson observation feedback and evaluations. Evidence in marking and feedback to pupils. Lesson evaluations in which reflection on specific issues/children takes place. Use of information in pupil reports and progress checks to set pupil targets. Records of conversations with parents/carers/pupils and reflective comments. Detention slips (for lack of work, etc.) and reflective comments.	This standard requires you to provide evidence to show that you hold high expectations of your pupils as far as their behaviour, attitudes and work rate are concerned. Competence in this standard also means that you have demonstrated your understanding of the need to establish and maintain good working relationships with your pupils.

| Q2 | Demonstrate the positive values, attitudes and behaviour they expect from children and young people. | Lesson planning and observation feedback which highlights learning, behaviour and relationship issues.

Evaluations showing how conflicts are resolved.

Observation feedback showing respect for all pupils, good relationships with classes and consistency in the way they deal with learning and discipline issues.

Observation feedback showing creation of a can-do culture through questioning, praise, posters, etc.

Use of school and personal rewards/sanctions systems.

Photographs of classroom displays.

Efficient turnover of marking.

Evidence of punctuality, time management, personal organization and reliability.

Testimonials, letters or cards from parents or pupils. | This Standard requires you to show how you have acted as a role model for your pupils. It could be realized in situations where you have demonstrated sensitive and effective ways to deal with conflict, or where you have helped to solve bullying or other personal issues. You may want to cite situations where you have used personal anecdotes or stories to highlight specific moral issues. You will easily be able to demonstrate this Standard if you adopt an organized, caring and professional approach in your role as a teacher. |
| Q3 (a) | Be aware of the professional duties of teachers and the statutory framework within which they work. | Annotation of school policies (e.g. health and safety, equal opportunities, SEN).

Reflective and personalized notes on child protection/safeguarding, anti-bullying) and issues of disclosure.

Reflective and personalized notes on restraint and/or medication issues.

Out of school trip organization procedure. Risk assessment.

Awareness of role of the governing body.

Reflective and personalized annotations on the various documentation. | You will note that this Standard simply requires you to 'be aware' of these professional issues. Although the Standard does not require you to provide evidence of how you have used this knowledge to actually carry out the duties, you are advised wherever possible to identify the potential implications on your professional practice. If you are able to personalize your annotation with examples from your own practice and/or experience, then so much the better. |

Communicating and working with others

| Q3 (b) | Be aware of the policies and practices of the workplace and share in collective responsibility for their implementation. | Contributions to concerts, presentations, extra-curricular activities, work experience visits.

Annotation and implementation of school policies (e.g. health and safety, equal opportunities, SEN, child protection/safeguarding, anti-bullying) and reflective notes.

Personal, social and health education (PSHE) work on stereotyping, bullying and harassment.

Lesson planning, observation feedback and evaluation.

Testimonial from appropriate staff. | Again, you need to show awareness of the content of the various planning and policy documents as well as providing evidence to show how you have worked with colleagues to implement some of these initiatives. |

Q4	Communicate effectively with children, young people, colleagues, parents and carers.	Lesson observation feedback highlighting effective use of language to secure learning.	You are advised to find at least one piece of evidence for each of these target groups to show how you communicate effectively with them.
		Notes home to parents via log books, letters home and logs of telephone conversations.	
		Notes from observing/contributing to parents' evening, review meeting or consultation meeting.	
		Contributions to report writing and progress checks.	
		Evidence of working with TAs, CTAs (see Chapter 5), technicians, librarians, teaching staff, contact with social workers, educational welfare officers, school nurse, educational psychologist and other children's services professionals.	
		Work with visiting speakers.	
Q5	Recognize and respect the contribution that colleagues, parents and carers can make to the development and well-being of children and young people and to raising their levels of attainment	Knowledge of statutory rights of parents and carers (Bristol Guide).	This standard is very similar to Q4, although in this case you simply have to find evidence to show that you recognize and respect the contribution of these three groups to the educational process. This is a find out all you can exercise. However, if you can personalize your annotations to illustrate how this new-found knowledge has impacted upon your practice and on the learning of pupils then so much the better.
		Notes home to parents via log books, letters home, logs of telephone conversations.	
		Notes from observing/contributing to parents' evening, review meeting or consultation meeting.	
		Understanding of the roles and evidence of working with TAs, HLTAs, technicians, librarians, teaching staff, social workers, educational welfare officers, school nurse, educational psychologist and other children's services professionals.	

| Q6 | Have a commitment to collaboration and cooperative working. | Testimonial from mentor, head of department, TA, etc. to show good working relationships with colleagues.

Preparation of resources/units of work with colleagues.

Contributions to work experience visits.

Team teaching.

Contributions to concerts, presentations, extra-curricular activities.

Minutes of a meeting (e.g. department, year group and/or house) describing your specific contributions and how you have collaborated with colleagues. | There is no reason why you cannot create your own pro forma with a description of the Q6 standard on and list all the things you do to support and work with colleagues. Get each of them to add a comment and a signature. |

Personal professional development

| Q7 (a) | Reflect on and improve their practice, and take responsibility for identifying and meeting their developing professional needs | Lesson evaluations, observation feedback sheets, tutor meeting logs.

Reflections from discussions with colleagues.

Extracts from your reflective log.

Examples of research or resources from, e.g., subject associations, e.g. Qualification and Curriculum Authority (QCA), *Times Educational Supplement* (*TES*), etc. to help improve teaching and learning.

Research carried out for assignments and/or completed assignments.

Subject knowledge audit and action plans.

Notes and reflections from involvement in school PD/INSET activities.

Reflective comments on Trainee Practice Report.

Relevant emails from head of department (HoD), subject mentor or professional tutor or external ITT tutor commenting upon your reflectivity. | This is perhaps the most important of all the Standards because the ability to critically reflect and act upon these reflections lies at the very heart of good teaching. You are required to demonstrate your ability to make judgements about the effectiveness of your teaching and to identify ways to bring about an improvement to your practice. If you are carrying out all the tasks set for you by your training provider properly you will have an overwhelming amount of evidence for this standard. Your reflective log should provide much of the evidence here. |

Q7 (b)	Identify priorities for their early professional development in the context of induction.	Career Entry and Development Profile completed at Transition Point 1 towards the end of final placement.	All you have to do here is complete and submit a copy of your Career Entry and Development Profile at Transition Point 1 document.
Q8	Have a creative and constructively critical approach towards innovation, being prepared to adapt their practice where benefits and improvements are identified.	Reflective journal entries. Lesson evaluations, observation feedback sheets, tutor meeting logs. Notes and reflections from discussions with colleagues. Examples of research from, e.g., subject associations, QCA, *TES*, etc. to help improve teaching and learning. Research for assignments and completed assignments. Notes and reflections from involvement in school PD/INSET activities. Reflective comments on Trainee Practice Report.	You need to be able to demonstrate that you are open to new ideas and that you have used these to support your practice.
Q9	Act upon advice and feedback and be open to coaching and mentoring.	Reflective journal entries. Lesson evaluations, observation feedback sheets, tutor meeting logs. Notes and reflections from discussions with colleagues. Trainee Practice Reports. Testimonial from mentors.	The key thing to note here is that it is all well and good your listening to advice and guidance from your colleagues but if you do not act upon this then the process has been in vain. You need to show how you have used this advice/guidance offered by your colleagues to support your practice.

2. Professional knowledge and understanding

Those recommended for the award of QTS should:

	QTS	Source of portfolio evidence	Supporting notes where appropriate
Teaching and Learning			
Q10	Have a knowledge and understanding of a range of teaching, learning and behaviour management strategies and know how to use and adapt them, including how to personalize learning and provide opportunities for all learners to achieve their potential.	Lesson planning, evaluation and observation feedback. Effective questioning technique as demonstrated in lesson observations. Effective use of praise. Selection and delivery of appropriate curriculum content and differentiated tasks. Assignments. Use of behaviour policy and behaviour plans for individual pupils. Evidence of implementation of behaviour management training session materials. Personalized annotations and notations to presentation/ workshop training on behaviour management handouts. Pupil seating plans with evaluation and justification. Effective use of different organizational strategies in lessons to support learning. Exploration of pupils' learning styles/intelligences and implementation of this information in lesson planning.	This Standard is pretty straightforward but I would advise you to provide evidence that covers each of the three elements: teaching, learning and behaviour management. You need to ensure that you demonstrate a knowledge and understanding of the ways in which you can personalize learning.

Assessment and monitoring			
Q11	Know the assessment requirements and arrangements for the subjects/curriculum areas in the age ranges they are trained to teach, including those relating to public examinations and qualifications.	Annotated National Curriculum subject handbook. Annotated syllabuses (e.g. GCSE and other public examinations) to show assessment requirements. Assessment criteria produced in pupil-speak. Contributions to moderation of coursework. Evidence of use of level descriptors at KS3. Annotated GCSE assessment grids. Marking of Standard Attainment Tests. Benchmarking of work against departmental mark schemes.	For this standard you are required to demonstrate a secure understanding of the assessment frameworks in which your pupils are working. You can demonstrate this in a number of ways; by presenting and annotating any research you have conducted or by demonstrating your proficiency in working to these assessment criteria.
Q12	Know a range of approaches to assessment, including the importance of formative assessment.	Lesson planning, evaluation and observation feedback. Evidence of use of Assessment for Learning (AfL) techniques. Formative marking of pupils' work. Evidence of oral assessment and feedback. Coursework marking and moderation. Marked tests and feedback. Peer assessment opportunities in lesson plan/observation. Target setting. Assignments.	Again, this standard is quite straightforward but you are strongly advised to present a range of assessment techniques in your portfolio. You also need to demonstrate an ability to monitor the progress of pupils and to use your judgement to intervene in order to enable your learners to succeed.

| Q13 | Know how to use local and national statistical information to evaluate the effectiveness of their teaching, to monitor the progress of those they teach and to raise levels of attainment. | Lesson planning, evaluation and observation feedback. Use of prior attainment data in lesson planning (SATs' results, reading and maths scores, pupils' learning styles). Use of targets for pupils/groups. Records of assessment in mark book. Use of academic flight paths to monitor pupil progress. | In order to realize this particular standard you need to do three things: first, research and present your data; second, show how you have used these to plan for differentiation in your lessons; third, show how you have used these data to evaluate your pupils' achievement and progress. |

Subjects and curriculum

| Q14 | Have a secure knowledge and understanding of their subjects/curriculum areas and related pedagogy to enable them to teach effectively across the age and ability range for which they are trained. | Subject knowledge audit and action plans. Lesson planning, observation feedback, evaluations. Evidence from question and answer sessions, extension tasks. Marking of pupils' work and feedback. Appropriate use of ICT. Long- and medium-term planning. Examples of marked examination papers for KS3, GCSE and A level, completed by trainee. Annotated handouts from training courses. Subject-specific qualification certificates. Evidence of awareness and use of the National Strategy approaches in teaching. Assignments Testimonials from key staff. | You need to know that subject knowledge is an absolute priority of the TDA and you should do everything you can to show progression in this aspect of your training and how you have identified specific areas for development. You then need to take this a stage further by demonstrating how these specific weaknesses have been successfully addressed. I need to stress that this standard is not just about how much subject knowledge you have personally, but how well you can impart this to your pupils. |

Literacy, numeracy and ICT

Q15	Know and understand the relevant statutory and non-statutory curricula, frameworks, including those provided through the National Strategies, for their subjects/ curriculum areas, and other relevant initiatives applicable to the age and ability range for which they are trained.	Lesson planning, observation feedback, evaluations. Evidence in planning of National Curriculum general teaching requirements (inclusion, use of language, use of ICT, health and safety). Evidence in planning to show how National Strategy approaches, materials and resources are used in subject teaching. Assignments Annotated citizenship programme of study and PSHE framework.	When planning your lessons you are strongly advised to provide links with such initiatives as the Key Stage 3 strategy, PSHE and citizenship.
Q16	Have passed the professional skills tests in numeracy, literacy and information and communication technology (ICT).	Copies of certificates obtained from test centre when tests are passed.	You are strongly advised to book up early for these tests. You can practise these tests online by logging on to the following web addresses Literacy: www.tda.gov.uk/skillstests/practicematerials/literacy/litbenchmark/literacybenchmark.aspx Numeracy: /www.tda.gov.uk/skillstests/practicematerials/numeracy/numbenchmark/numeracybenchmark2.aspx ICT Skills: www.tda.gov.uk/skillstests/practicematerials/ict/practicematerial.aspx Alternatively you could read the following publications: Johnson (2003) Ferrigan (2004) Patmore (2004)

| Q17 | Know how to use skills in literacy, numeracy and ICT to support their teaching and wider professional activities. | Lesson planning, evaluations, observation feedback. Records of pupils' progress – mark sheets. Use of the internet, digital cameras, PowerPoint presentations, interactive whiteboard. Use of ICT for reports and progress checks. Contribution to school intranet (units of work, homework, for pupils to access). Preparation of appropriate resources using literacy and/or numeracy skills. Database work – use of spreadsheets. | The TDA are again looking for a range of evidence here. You need, therefore, to select evidence from each of the three elements described in the standard: literacy, numeracy and ICT. |

Achievement and diversity

| Q18 | Understand how children and young people develop and that the progress and well-being of learners are affected by a range of developmental, social, religious, ethnic, cultural and linguistic influences. | Lesson planning, observation feedback, evaluations, logs of tutor meetings. Selection of relevant topics for lesson content. Contact with form tutors, heads of year (HoY) about pupils with social/emotional difficulties and evidence of pupils with social or emotional problems being catered for. Notes from discussion with SENCO about, e.g., autism, ADHD, dyslexia, Asperger's syndrome. Example of IEP and its implications. Awareness of issues facing children from a variety of backgrounds and/cultures – English as an Additional Language (EAL) policy, working with EAL co-ordinators, differentiated objectives, worksheets, etc. Research assignments. Annotated handouts from EAL training session. | To realize Q18 you simply need to demonstrate that you have an understanding of how the learning of pupils is affected by the various elements described in the standard. This is also the place to link your 'learning theories' work to your work in the classroom. You can do this by identifying the potential implications of this knowledge on your practice and/or by describing your professional experiences. |

| Q19 | Know how to make effective personalized provision for those they teach, including those for whom English is an additional language or who have special educational needs or disabilities, and how to take practical account of diversity and promote equality and inclusion in their teaching. | Lesson planning, observation feedback, evaluations, logs of tutor meetings. Examples of differentiated tasks and resources and evaluations of their use. Evaluation of use of supportive techniques, e.g. writing frames, etc. Notes from meetings with EAL coordinator and reflection/ implications. Multi-cultural displays. Examples of pupils' work. Completed tasks or notes from EAL training sessions. Evidence of differentiation by task, resource and/or outcome. Use of TAs and support teachers in lessons. Use of prior attainment and SEN data. Assignments Notes from discussion with SENCO about autism, ADHD, dyslexia, Asperger's syndrome, etc. Testimonial from appropriate staff. Example of Individual Education Plan (IEP) and its implications. | Again, the TDA is looking for a range of evidence here. Take each element described in the standard and present at least one separate piece of evidence for each. |
| Q20 | Know and understand the roles of colleagues with specific responsibilities, including those with responsibility for learners with special educational needs and disabilities and other individual learning needs. | Notes from discussion with SENCO, annotated SEN code of practice and SEN policy. Notes from discussion with cover supervisor. Evidence of working with TAs, HLTAs, EAL coordinator. Assignments. | Whenever you go to a new school it is vital to find out what people in the school actually do. Select a few core staff and make it your business to interview them with a view to finding out how their roles impact upon your professional practice. |

Health and well-being

| Q21 (a) | Be aware of current legal requirements, national policies and guidance on the safeguarding and promotion of the well-being of children and young people. | Certificate from child protection/safeguarding training. School child protection documentation – annotated with implications for own practice. Accident reports, issues of disclosure and reflections. Restraint issues, medication issues. Out of school trip organizations procedure. Personalized annotations of sections of the Bristol Guide. Personalized annotations of the Every Child Matters agenda. Personalized annotations of the Children's Act. | This is a difficult standard to meet as there are so many national-, county- and school-based policies relating to the safeguarding and promotion of well-being of children and young people. It is extremely important that you demonstrate an awareness of any developments made in this field at a national, LA and/or school level. You will note that the standard stresses your need to 'be aware' of the current legal requirements, etc. You can show this by annotating and, wherever possible, linking the information provided to your own professional experiences, or by outlining the potential implications of this new-found knowledge for your professional practice. |

| Q21 (b) | Know how to identify and support children and young people whose progress, development or well-being is affected by changes or difficulties in their personal circumstances, and when to refer them to colleagues for specialist support. | Evidence of contact with form tutors, HoDs, HoYs, SENCO, parents about pupils.

Notes from form tutors, HOY about pupils with emotional and/or social difficulties.

Use of TAs and support teachers in lessons.

Use of SEN data for individual pupils.

Evidence of working with TAs, HLTAs, contact with social workers, educational welfare officers, school nurse, educational psychologist and other children's services professionals.

Personalized annotations of the Every Child Matters agenda

Personalized annotations of the Children's Act. | In order to realize this particular standard you need to show that you are aware of the procedural protocol required to support your pupils in the circumstances described. You also need to provide first-hand evidence to show that you have carried out some of these procedures. |

3. Professional skills

Those recommended for the award of QTS should:

	QTS standards	Source of portfolio evidence	Supporting notes where appropriate
Q22	Plan for progression across the age and ability range for which they are trained, designing effective learning sequences within lessons and across series of lessons and demonstrating secure subject/curriculum knowledge.	Lesson planning, observation feedback, evaluations, logs of tutor meetings. Target setting for pupils. Schemes/units of work – medium-term plans. Assignments. Planning includes detailed and relevant differentiated learning objectives and evidence of differentiated tasks. Use of prior attainment and SEN data for planning lessons. Annotated National Curriculum for KS2, KS3, KS4 showing progression within a topic/area and reflection about implications for teaching.	You should be able to provide evidence for this standard with your day-to-day planning and teaching.

Q23	Design opportunities for learners to develop their literacy, numeracy and ICT skills.	Lesson planning, observation feedback, evaluations, logs of tutor meetings. Schemes/units of work – medium-term plans Resources and reflection. Assignments. Examples of marked pupils' work and evaluation of effectiveness of activity. Internet research tasks.	Again, the TDA is looking for a range of evidence here. Provide at least one piece of evidence to cater for each of the elements described in the Standard.
Q24	Plan homework or other out-of-class work to sustain learners' progress and to extend and consolidate their learning.	Lesson planning, observation feedback, evaluations, logs of tutor meetings. Evidence of extension work for pupils, e.g. research tasks and evaluation. Fieldwork tasks and evaluation. Examples of marked homework tasks and evaluation of effectiveness of activity.	
Q25	Teach lessons and sequences of lessons across the age and ability range for which they are trained in which they:		
Q25 (a)	Use a range of teaching strategies and resources, including e-learning, taking practical account of diversity and promoting equality and inclusion.	Lesson planning, observation feedback, evaluations, logs of tutor meetings. Evidence of differentiation by task, resource and/or outcome. Use of prior attainment and SEN data. Evidence of variety of teaching strategies in lessons. Evidence of pace and purpose in lessons. Effective and safe use of resources. Effective use of ICT by pupils. Completed task or notes from EAL training session. Use of SAM Learning (software asset management), Yacapaca, etc. (or other e-learning activities) by pupils.	In order to realize this standard you need to make overt and explicit provision for the EAL and SEN pupils in your teaching groups. You also need to provide evidence of having differentiated your activities by outcome, task and/or resource.

Q25 (b)	Build on prior knowledge, develop concepts and processes, enable learners to apply new knowledge, understanding and skills, and meet learning objectives;	Lesson planning, observation feedback, evaluations, logs of tutor meetings. Notes from talk with teacher responsible for liaison with feeder primary schools and reflection. Use of prior attainment data in planning. Evidence of appropriate activities to allow pupils to apply what they have learned. Starter activities. The context section of a newly created scheme of work.	This standard has links with Q13 and you could cross-reference some of the evidence from this standard.
Q25(c)	Adapt their language to suit the learners they teach, introducing new ideas and concepts clearly, and using explanations, questions, discussions and plenaries effectively.	Lesson planning, observation feedback, evaluations, logs of tutor meetings. Observation feedback and evaluations highlighting effective communication with pupils. Observation feedback and evaluations highlighting effective use of questioning. Observation feedback and evaluations highlighting effective use of plenary session.	
Q25(d)	Manage the learning of individuals, groups and whole classes, modifying their teaching to suit the stage of the lesson.	Lesson planning, observation feedback, evaluations, logs of tutor meetings. Effective use of group work, pair work and a variety of teaching strategies. Use of individual and group research tasks. Evidence of pace and purpose in lessons. Effective use of behavioural management strategies.	You would be advised to make group work the focus of a lesson observation.

Assessing, monitoring and giving feedback

| Q26 (a) | Make effective use of a range of assessment, monitoring and recording strategies. | Lesson planning, observation feedback, evaluations, logs of tutor meetings. Formative marking of pupils' work. Evidence of oral assessment and feedback. Coursework marking and moderation. Marked tests and feedback. Peer-assessment tasks and evaluation. Target setting. Evidence of effective use of questioning. Examples of pupil self-assessment sheets. Use of plenary session. Annotated GCSE assessment grids. Testimonial from subject tutor HoD to verify standard of marking. Mark-book. Contributions to report-writing and progress checks. | This standard is explicably linked with Q11 and Q12 and, if you have previously provided evidence to show how you have implemented your newly discovered knowledge of assessment strategies, you may be able to cross-reference these in order to meet this standard. |

| Q26 (b) | Assess the learning needs of those they teach in order to set challenging learning objectives. | Lesson planning, observation feedback, evaluations, logs of tutor meetings. Evaluations which specifically link the assessment of pupils' learning with learning objectives for future lessons. Formative marking of pupils' work with reflections about implications for future lesson planning. Target setting. Pupil self-assessment sheets and reflections about implications for future lesson planning. Effective use of plenary sessions. Examples of pupils using meta-cognitive processes. Use of knowledge of pupils' learning styles to set differentiated and challenging work. Assignments. | The main purpose of this standard is to get you to use your own assessment data to inform your planning. In order to realize this Standard you need to make the links between your assessment and planning absolutely transparent. |
| Q27 | Provide timely, accurate and constructive feedback on learners' attainment, progress and areas for development. | Lesson observation feedback, evaluations, logs of tutor meetings Formative marking of pupils' work. Contributions to progress checks. Communications with other professionals on these issues, e.g. round robin sheets issued by HoYs to ascertain current pupil progress. | The TDA is again looking for a range of evidence to support this standard. |

| Q28 | Support and guide learners to reflect on their learning, identify the progress they have made and identify their emerging learning needs. | Lesson observation feedback, evaluations, logs of tutor meetings

Effective use of questioning.

Pupils' evaluative work.

Pupil self-assessment sheets.

Use of plenary sessions.

Examples of pupils using meta-cognitive processes.

Assignments.

Evidence of pupils using their own learning logs. | There is no reason why you cannot employ a reflective strategy similar to the one described to you later on in this chapter. The formula is appropriate and transferable to all levels of education. |

Reviewing teaching and learning

| Q29 | Evaluate the impact of their teaching on the progress of all learners, and modify their planning and classroom practice where necessary. | Lesson evaluations, observation feedback, logs of tutor meetings.

Reflective journal.

Notes and reflections from discussions with colleagues.

Pupil questionnaires.

Logs of tutor meeting showing responses to feedback.

Assignments. | |

Learning environment

Q30	Establish a purposeful and safe learning environment conducive to learning and identify opportunities for learners to learn in out of school contexts.	Lesson planning, observation feedback, evaluations, logs of tutor meetings. Evidence of teaching assertively, with pace and purpose, good use of body language and voice tone, effective use of praise, selection of appropriate tasks. Evidence of good working relationships with pupils. Evidence of implementation of school behavioural policy. Evidence of use of effective pupil grouping strategies. Individual behaviour plans. Pupil seating plans with evaluation and justification. Assignments. Academic trips – evidence of assisting with these and associated reflections. Social trips – evidence of assisting with these and reflections. Work experience. Evidence of having created a can-do culture through classroom displays.	Most of the evidence for this standard will come from lesson observations. You are also advised to log your contributions to the out of school context scenarios and ask your colleagues to comment on and sign to verify this input.
Q31	Establish a clear framework for classroom discipline to manage learners' behaviour constructively and promote their self-control and independence.	Lesson planning, observation feedbacks, evaluations, logs of tutor meetings. Evidence of good working relationships with pupils. Evidence of implementation of school behavioural policy. Rules and routines posters for classes. Personalized behaviour plans. Evidence of dealing with individual pupils. Reflective journal. Assignments.	Bearing in mind that full competence in this standard can take a lifetime to achieve; this should be one of the last standards to get signed off.

Team working and collaboration			
Q32	Work as a team member and identify opportunities for working with colleagues, sharing the development of effective practice with them.	Observation feedback for lessons with TA, HLTA, language assistant or technician support. Written communication with TA, HLTA, language assistant or technician. Testimonial from support staff. Evidence of corporate planning, team teaching and contribution to departmental meetings. Contribution to working parties. Working with colleagues in PD/INSET sessions. Use of librarian.	
Q33	Ensure that colleagues working with them are appropriately involved in supporting learning and understand the roles they are expected to fulfil.	Observation feedback for lessons with TA, HLTA, language assistant or technician support. Written communications with TA, HLTA, language assistant or technician. Evidence from lesson plans. Testimonial from support staff. Evidence of effective deployment of TA, HLTA, language assistant or technician. Assignments.	The notion behind insisting that you gain competence in this Standard is to pressurize you into being proactive in establishing and maintaining effective working relationships with colleagues. Include your colleagues in the planning and evaluation stages of your lessons.

Professional Standards for the Awards of Qualified Teacher Status (Secondary)

By the end of the course trainees must provide evidence to demonstrate that they have met all the Standards.

Figure 12.2 Portfolio guidance

13 Becoming a reflective practitioner

The term reflective practice, introduced by Donald Schön in his book *The Reflective Practitioner* (1983), lies at the very heart of every teacher training course. According to Schön, reflective practice is the process of thoughtfully considering one's own experiences in applying knowledge to practice while being coached by professionals in the discipline. In education, it refers to the process of the educator studying his/her own teaching methods and determining what works best for the pupils. At a later stage in your career you may be interested in exploring the numerous interpretations of the notion of reflective practice. However, for the time being, I am going to focus my attention on the work of Schön and use this to help you explore this issue. My rationale for focusing on Schön's work is that his ideas have been extremely influential in initial teacher training in Britain in recent years.

Schön (1983) cited in Furlong and Maynard (1995), emphasizes that teachers have to cope with the fact that no two groups of pupils are alike and that even with pupils with whom they are familiar, they are constantly having to present new material to them. This inevitably creates its own unique problems in terms of explanation and understanding. The teacher has to constantly reflect upon, and react to, the ever-changing scenarios that occur in his/her classroom in such a way that the process appears to be seamless to the pupils. Schön called this process 'reflection-*in*-action'. Reflection-*in*-action occurs when a practitioner faces an unknown situation. In these circumstances, the practitioner is able to bring certain aspects of his/her work to his/her level of consciousness, reflect upon it and reshape it without interrupting the flow of proceedings. It is fair to say that many experienced teachers do this quite naturally and intuitively, without giving the process a great deal of thought. However, to beginning teachers, be they a trainee or an NQT, this process does not come naturally and they tend to become somewhat flustered when new scenarios are presented to them, and in situations when things don't quite go according to plan. My message to you as trainees is not to worry too much about this at the moment

– things will get better with experience. Some of the unpredictable and untoward things that are likely to throw you off track in the initial stages of your teaching will be of little or no consequence as you become more used to the role. Having said this, you still need to practise the skill of flexibility in your lessons and this requirement is demonstrated in the necessity for you to realize QTS 29:

> Evaluate the impact of their teaching on the progress of all learners, and modify their planning and classroom practice where necessary. (QTS 29)

Reflection-*in*-action largely involves 'situated knowledge' and is a process that we often go through without necessarily being able to say exactly what we are doing. Reflecting on, and articulating our thoughts about our teaching *after* the lesson has happened, is called 'reflection-*on*-action' and it is something that many teachers find challenging. They find it difficult to articulate all the things they do intuitively in the classroom to produce a good lesson. I am in agreement with Schön who believed passionately that reflection-*on*-action is a key process in learning how to teach. In Schön (1983), he argues that no matter how inadequate a beginning teacher's verbal reconstruction of events, it is only by constantly bringing the ways in which they are framing their teaching situations to their level of consciousness, that they will eventually gain control of their own teaching. The following quote from Schön (1987) cited in Furlong and Maynard (1995), makes the point clearly.

> As I think back on my experience ... I may consolidate my understanding of the problem or invent a better or more general solution to it. If I do, my present reflection on my earlier reflection-in-action begins a dialogue of thinking and doing through which I become more skilful.

All ITT providers will encourage reflection-*in*-action and in order to help you to move towards gaining competence in Q29, will highlight this as an area for development in your classroom practice. They will also insist that some kind of reflection-*on*-action takes place in the form of a reflective journal or series of lesson evaluations. Using this 'reflection-*on*-action' process as a model I have worked with a colleague to create a reflective formula which is currently used by trainees in two ITT programmes. I have presented the general principles underlying the formula in Figure 13.1 and have also provided four extracts from the reflective logs of some of my trainees. In order to support the diagram presented in Figure 13.1, I will briefly take you through the process as described in the formula.

You are first required simply to *describe* the professional scenario presented to you. This could be something that happened in the classroom, an incident in the school corridor or your observations of interactions between colleagues and/or pupils. At this point in the reflective process, there is no evaluative input whatsoever – you merely need to describe the scenario. Having done this, you now need to describe the perceived consequences of what you have just experienced; in other words, what happened because of what happened. For example, you may have noticed that in one of your lesson observations that a science teacher failed to establish his/her expectations, rules and sanctions before he/she allowed the pupils to carry out an experiment. The consequences of him/her not doing this might have been that the pupils behaved in an unruly fashion thus disrupting learning in the lesson. Another consequence could be that laboratory health and safety rules were breached and an accident occurred. I call these crucial decision-making factors in a lesson 'watershed moments' because they represent specific points in lessons where teachers' actions or inactions can lead to varying and sometimes adverse consequences (Dixie, 2007). As part of the induction process in my school, I ask trainees to carry out lesson observations that require them to identify these watershed moments in lessons, and to then describe the subsequent consequences arising from these. You will also note from the diagram that this is also the place to describe your emotional responses to the scenarios presented to you. In Dixie (2005, 2007) I give a high profile to the importance of exploring the emotional side of teaching. I feel strongly that recognizing and dealing with your emotional responses to teaching is an important part of the reflective process.

Experience shows me that most trainees are quite adept at describing professional scenarios but are far less skilled at recognizing watershed moments and/or the potential consequences of them. In most cases, this is where their reflective practice usually ends. Unless pressurized, most trainees do not take the process any further. They neither identify the implications of their teaching experiences nor do they show how they have modified or altered their practice in the light of their reflections. If the reflective cycle illustrated in Figure 13.1 is to be successfully realized then the third and fourth requirements need to be fulfilled. Having responded to your reflections by taking the appropriate action, the whole reflective process starts over again. This document does not have to be completed electronically nor does it have to be completed in the column form presented in Figure 13.1. It is, however, very important that the criteria in all four stages are met if you want to demonstrate your skill as a reflective practitioner and realize the following standards:

Q7(a) Reflect on and improve their practice, and take responsibility for identifying and meeting their developing professional needs.

Q8 Have a creative and constructively critical approach towards innovation, being prepared to adapt their practice where benefits and improvements are identified.

Q9 Act upon advice and feedback and be open to coaching and mentoring.

I have provided exemplars of three reflective logs to support theoretical diagrams shown in Figure 13.1.

Figure 13.1: The reflective cycle

Reflective formula

Identification/description of professional scenarios.

- Lesson observation
- Out-of-classroom scenarios
- Interaction with colleague(s)
- Interaction with parents/carers

What happened?

What are the perceived consequences of these behaviours

- Identify teaching and learning consequences by looking for watershed moments.
- Identify the emotional consequences for you as a teacher. Did the incident make you feel proud, angry, disappointed, disempowered, etc.?

Implications and targets for professional practice

- How will you use this to inform your professional practice?
- What targets will you set yourself?
- What strategies will you use?
- How are you going to use these emotions to inform your future practice?

Provide evidence showing how you have used this experience to develop your professional practice. Make overt reference to a professional standard.

How do you know whether you have been successful?

e.g. planning lessons with pupils' learning styles in mind.

e.g. dealing with a challenging situation in a non-confrontational manner.

e.g. being proactive in seeking advice and guidance from colleagues.

e.g. evidence of using knowledge of pupils' background to inform planning.

Trainee X: Extract from reflective journal

Identification/description of professional scenarios

In a recent Year 8 drama lesson I had planned to use a starter activity that involved pupils throwing a ball to each other.

The learning objective required the pupils to understand the concept of the 'naturalistic performance'. The idea behind the starter was that pupils would have to throw the ball to one another. Having caught the ball, each pupil would have to act out a particular emotion and then throw the ball to another pupil in the room for him/her to do the same.

In this particular lesson I made the mistake of not prefacing the activity with my expectations and/or my health and safety rules.

I also made the mistake of allowing the pupils to carry out the starter activity while I was still writing the learning objective on the board.

Perceived consequences of these behaviours

As I was writing the learning objective on the board, several of the boys saw this as an ideal opportunity to throw the ball as hard as they could at the walls of the classroom and/or at their fellow pupils. My failure to set up clear 'ground rules' provided many of the pupils with the 'go ahead' to behave inappropriately.

Many of the pupils simply saw this as a 'throwing and catching' exercise. The net result of this was that no real learning took place and the purpose of the starter was not realized.

Although majority of pupils *do* know how to behave in my drama lessons, introducing the 'ball throwing' activity to this starter somehow made it seem more like a PE lesson. This was a new experience for my pupils which some of them found difficult to cope with. I should have done more to set this activity in context.

Implications and targets for professional practice

If I had to do this kind of starter activity again, I would make sure that I give the pupils a 'settling down' task to do while I write the learning objectives on the board.

I would then launch the activity in a more robust manner making sure that my expectations had been made transparent and that the pupils fully understood the health and safety rules.

Provide evidence showing how you have used this experience to develop your professional practice. How do know whether you have been successful?

I have since tried this activity again but this time I provided the pupils with the rationale for the activity and issued the class with a series of detailed task instructions. I also established my rules and expectations for the session in a robust and transparent manner.

On this occasion, the starter activity was highly successful in the sense that it served its purpose of introducing naturalism via a kinesthetic approach. I was also pleased with the behaviour of the pupils during this phase of the lesson.

Trainee Y: Extract from reflective journal

Identification/description of professional scenarios.

This week I conducted a pupil trail with the purpose of observing a range of teachers in a variety of settings and subjects. The focus of these observations was effective classroom management.

Perceived consequences of these behaviours

Having made my observations, I then identified common strategies for good classroom management. I was quite surprised to see that so many pupils in these observed classes were clear about what was expected of them in terms of their behaviour. This was noticeable even when the pupils entered the classroom. Having discussed this issue with the host teachers, I am certain that their good behaviour was as a result of the rules and consequences being established and reinforced so early on. In situations where the school's behaviour policy was used, teachers were only successful in gaining discipline in their classes, when this was supported by assertive body language, tone of voice and a consistent approach towards the offences. Pupils also behaved well in classes where teacher praise was abundant and where a 'can-do' climate had been established.

Implications and targets for professional practice

When I begin teaching next week I will ensure that I start all my lessons by outlining my expectations to my pupils and by making my rules, rewards and consequences transparent. I will supply each pupil with a class contract that outlines my expectations of their behaviour and work ethic in lessons. I will then ask them to sign this agreement and stick the rules into the front of their books for future reference.

Provide evidence showing how you have used this experience to develop your professional practice

I have already taken over four classes from my host teacher. I have introduced my expectations to these pupils in an assertive and robust manner. I have my rules clearly displayed on laminated sheets at the front of the room. We have discussed the class rules and the pupils have glued these into their books.

Although the behaviour of the pupils in my lessons has not been perfect, I am generally pleased with the way my lessons have gone. I have found that, despite this still being 'early days', I have already had to reinforce my expectations, rules, routines, sanctions and rewards and have had to keep some pupils behind to talk to them about their behaviour.

Trainee Z: Extract from reflective journal

Identification/description of professional scenarios

12/1/SO1– all five lessons taught by me.

- This is a big group consisting of 22 pupils.
- There are no real problems with group dynamic to date.
- Due to the size of the group, and the fact that I am taking them for all of their sociology lessons, getting the group organized and keeping them motivated, has been somewhat problematic.
- The main issue I have with this group is their total lack of preparation for their lessons. Many of them are now turning up to lessons without a pen, without their folders and often without their homework.
- I found that this week I had to keep hold of some of the students' work as they didn't have folders with them. I also had to remind them which topic we would be studying on the specific days of the week.

Perceived consequences of these behaviours

I feel that if this situation isn't 'nipped in the bud', these students will not develop as independent learners. I am really concerned that, unless I am very careful and extremely proactive, these lessons could end up with me simply 'spoon-feeding' information to these pupils. Doing this would be totally contrary to my teaching philosophy.

One of the major consequences of these pupils not taking full responsibility for their learning is that I have to constantly 'nag' them about their failure to adopt a responsible attitude towards their learning. This is not what I came into teaching for.

Implications and targets for professional practice

This is what I intend to do:

- Reinforce my expectations of these pupils in terms of their attitude and work ethic.
- In order to keep my relationships with these pupils on an 'even keel' I will add an element of 'playful' embarrassment to proceedings in order to combat the pupils' forgetfulness; e.g. I intend to get some giant pens to hand out to pupils. I am rather hoping that by doing this, these pupils will understand the point I am trying to make.
- I will design and produce a sociology planner page for the front of their folders so that the pupils are always aware of what they are studying and when.
- I will develop a series of gradated sanctions designed to deal with those pupils who fail to hand their work in on time.

> **Provide evidence showing how you have used this experience to develop your professional practice. How do know whether you have been successful?**
>
> I have created and distributed colour-coordinated front sheets for the pupils' folders that display a timetable of the topics being studied on any one day. Some of the pupils have told me how useful these are.
>
> I have also ordered some 'giant stationery' that I will issue when people have not got the correct equipment with them. Hopefully having to use a 30cm pen will dissuade people from being unprepared.
>
> Having reflected on this issue, I gave notice of a potential new sanction that would be imposed upon pupils who failed to hand in their work on time or to bring the correct equipment to lessons. In order to provide some ownership of the issue I negotiated with the class that this system would be trialled until Christmas.

How to get the most out of attending lectures, presentations and workshops

14

Although all ITT programmes contain elements of theory in their training, the degree to which this occurs depends very much on the nature of the programme and on the specific requirements of the training provider. Although many of you will be simply itching to get to work in the classroom, do not underestimate the importance of knowing about, understanding and being able to apply educational theory to your practice. Most of this theoretical input will be formally offered to you in lectures, presentations and workshops, and it is vital that you recognize the importance of these opportunities in helping to support your pedagogic practice. The best trainees/teachers are those who successfully link the theory of teaching to their everyday practice. In addition to providing you with a theoretical perspective to your teaching, these sessions will also be an important conduit for disseminating practical and logistical information about the requirements of the course. Tempting as it may be to absent yourself from these sessions, I would strongly urge you to attend and take full advantage of what is being offered to you. Failure to do so could have serious effects on the quality of your work and on the assessment process. Following is a range of advice to help you to get the most out of these sessions:

- Always approach your training sessions with an open mind. Some of us become very entrenched in our views, so try to be receptive to new ideas and prepared to try these out in the classroom. If these are not immediately successful, do not simply dismiss them out of hand – it could be that you are not quite ready for these strategies to work yet.
- Lecturers and trainers hold their own value systems which may be at odds with your own. Make sure that you critically evaluate what is being presented to you and be prepared to justify your opinions of the issues being discussed.

- It is often tempting to switch off during training sessions – especially after lunch and/or when the room is hot and stuffy. One way you can stop doing this is to take as many opportunities as you can to interact with the lecturer/trainer and/or your peers during group-work sessions.

- Believe it or not, lecturers/trainers are human and they depend heavily on your making a contribution to their sessions. Do not be afraid to ask questions, challenge their assertions in an appropriate manner and/or relate the content of the discussion to your own professional experiences.

- If you know that there are people on your course who do not have the same passion for learning as you, then it is quite simple – do not sit near them. By taking this course of action, you will not become distracted and you will not be negatively labelled by your trainer/lecturer.

- Remember that the information gathered is only useful if it is easily available to you when you want to access it. Make detailed notes and store them appropriately because you never know when you will need them. Using ring binders with dividers to organize your work can save you a lot of time in the long run.

Essays and assignments 15

It will probably be no surprise to hear that many trainees do not like writing essays/assignments. They often cite the process as being a waste of time because it supposedly takes their attention away from their work in the classroom. Not only is this response likely to appear extremely arrogant to programme organizers, lecturers and mentors, but these trainees are also likely to miss out on opportunities to make good links between theory and practice. Failure to complete your assignments to the best of your ability will mean that you will miss out on the chance to develop your professional practice. I have known of teachers in their second and third years who, having just been awarded a post of responsibility, revisit their assignments in an effort to understand the theory underpinning their new roles. Having to draw your own conclusions from your primary and/or secondary research will help you to formulate your own views and ideas with more confidence.

You are likely to have to produce a range of essays/assignments during your training year, some of which will be prescribed to you and some where you will be given a choice of topic. The difference between essays and assignments is that the latter require you to carry out primary research to support your secondary data. This primary research could take the form of questionnaires, experiments and observations, from which you would be expected to record the results, analyse your findings and draw conclusions. Some essays/assignments may be subject-based, while others may take on a whole-school or generic slant. Here are some general topic areas for you to consider for your non-prescribed essay/assignments:

- behaviour management
- differentiation
- learning styles
- learning theories
- inclusion
- Assessment for Learning
- schemes of work.

Essay/assignment writing is not usually too much of a problem for those trainees who have taken a traditional route through education via sixth form and university before starting their teacher training course. However, for those trainees who have had an extended time away from the educational system, even thinking about writing an essay/assignment can be a traumatic event. With this in mind, I have provided a number of tips which I hope will support those of you for whom academic work does not come easy:

- In situations where you have a choice, select a topic that interests you.
- Carry out a portfolio check to see which Standards you are struggling to meet, and target your assignment accordingly. If, for example, you have been placed in a school with a predominantly white middle-class catchment area, then you may struggle to find evidence to meet Q18, Q19 and Q25a, which relate to the issue of culture, ethnicity and social background. You might, therefore, like to consider producing an assignment on ethnic diversity and inclusion/achievement.
- Don't prevaricate! Start reading around the topic as soon as you can after receiving the assignment instructions. Leaving things until the last minute never works.
- Discuss your essay topic and title with your tutors and with your fellow trainees. Doing so can provide you with different perspectives, help you to get your own thoughts in order, and provide you with greater focus.
- Make sure that you fully understand and meet the assessment criteria. Do not do what I have seen so many trainees do, which is to ignore the assessment requirements and then regret it when they receive their grades.
- Essay/assignment deadlines have been set for a reason. Although there is no doubt that these deadlines have been imposed to aid the smooth running of the assessment process, they are also there to help you. We all know that it is human nature to prevaricate and these deadlines have been imposed to avoid a 'log jam' of work for you at the end of the course.

For those of you for whom essay/assignment writing is a problem, I have provided further detailed guidance for you below. I am hoping that the somewhat formulaic approach offered will provide sufficient support to allow you find a stress-free route through the academic elements of your course.

Producing an essay or an assignment

The first thing I need to make absolutely clear, is that there is no one definitive method for writing an essay or assignment. However, although lecturers, trainers and tutors all have their different styles, they will still be looking to see whether you have adhered to the general principles of writing an academic paper. Most academics would, therefore, accept that there are four main stages involved in developing an assignment: the research stage; the planning stage; the reading and organization stage; and the writing stage.

Research stage

In this stage you need to find out the essential information required for the assignment. Whether you have a choice about the assignment topic, or whether the focus is compulsory, the title or question should provide you with a clue as to the context and content of the paper. Ensure that you read widely around the subject, and that you support your work with a balance of texts and websites. Make sure that you select sources that are contemporary, especially when you are writing about issues and topics where scenarios and viewpoints are constantly changing. Support your work with a range of literature on the topic, and do not over-rely on specific texts. DfCSF documents, educational newspapers and magazines will all provide alternative viewpoints for you to consider. It is fine to use the internet to source your paper, but make sure that you only use reputable websites. Wikipedia, for example, is not recognized as an acceptable source for academic assignments. You are strongly advised to keep organized and efficient notes to support your reading. Using a highlighter pen to identify relevant sections of your notes is an effective way to identify information for your paper.

Planning stage

It is very important not to underestimate the value of planning your paper. Bearing in mind your heavy workload, I can understand you simply wanting to get your assignment out of the way as quickly as possible. However, rushing the process will only result in you having to redo your work at a later stage. Hopefully, if your planning is of a good standard, it will provide you with a transparent and painless journey through the writing process. Giving yourself adequate planning time will help you to organize the key aspects of your assignment and then to break these down into sub-categories. At this stage, you need to draft out any specific arguments and debates you want to discuss, and make a note as to how you are going to support these with potential texts or references. You are highly likely to be given a word limit for the assignment, so you need to consider a word count for each of the sections. You also need to give some consideration to the time you intend to allocate to each section and to the essay in general.

Reading and organization stage

You need to remember that not everything you have read will be relevant to your title, so make sure that you are ruthless in selecting those areas of text which reflect the content of your assignment. When trawling through literature, it is often a good idea to put sticky notes on those sections that you think might prove to be relevant later on. For those trainees who find it difficult to organize their material in a coherent manner, I usually suggest the following strategy. I get them to photocopy various sections of text and then to cut these up and place them into one of three sections: introduction, core, conclusion. Although this may appear to be a rather long-winded approach, it does cater for the kinesthetic and visual learners who need to physically produce a framework for their assignment before they start writing.

Writing stage

It is at this stage that you need to prepare a first draft of your paper. However, you must remember that this is only a first effort, and that it is inevitable that you will have to review and revise it. You may need to be quite ruthless, especially if you are significantly over your word count. When editing your work, cut or revise long-winded passages, avoid clichés and slang and don't waffle. The message is simple; if the text does not relate to essay/assignment title in some way then 'ditch it'.

I cannot stress the importance of the proofreading process. This too needs to be carried out in stages. I would strongly suggest that you check your assignment through very carefully by reading your work out loud as though to a public audience. By doing this, you will be able recognize where to put commas and full stops. You also need to check very carefully for poor punctuation, grammar and spelling. When checking for spellings, do not rely entirely on a computer spellchecker as it may not pick up typos, e.g. 'form' instead of 'from'. You need to bear in mind that an assignment which is poorly written, and which contains spelling and grammatical errors, is likely to receive poor marks even if your ideas are excellent. The other question you need to ask yourself is 'does your work flow?' Does it follow a logical sequence, or have you jumped from one idea to another? In hindsight, do you think that everything has been adequately explained? Finally, check your conclusion through to see whether you have inadvertently slipped any new ideas into this section.

The second stage requires you to get someone else to read through your assignment. I would suggest that you ask your professional tutor to do this, as he/she is likely to be well versed in current educational issues and have probably had a great deal of experience in proofreading and editing trainee assignments.

There are certain elements that can be found in any good assignment. The Suffolk and Norfolk SCITT programme provide their trainees with excellent guidance, some of which I have summarized below:

- clear structure
- appropriate style
- good presentation
- arguments or ideas that are supported by evidence.

(Remember that it is vital to refer constantly to the marking guidance for each assignment in order to ensure that you have addressed all the criteria.)

1. Clear structure

Structure refers to whether the approach will be 'descriptive' or 'argumentative' or, indeed, a bit of both.

Descriptive passages usually reproduce information or facts which give you an opportunity to demonstrate your understanding of the topic. They do not provide scope for analysis and evaluation.

Argumentative passages express particular points of view and use information to support or contradict these. Using argumentative passages will provide you with an opportunity to demonstrate your extensive reading around the subject and allow you to compare and contrast other authors' views and opinions.

Providing 'structure' to your assignment requires you to provide your paper with an introduction, core and a conclusion. I explore these elements in more detail below.

Introductory section

This is your opportunity to provide a contextual background to your assignment and to set the scene. You need to explain the purpose of your assignment, e.g. what you are going to be discussing and/or debating, and the specific areas of interest. This introductory section is also the place to outline your assignment journey.

Within this section you should also include information about your research methodology. Essentially this tells the reader where you obtained your information, how you accessed this and how you processed your findings. For example, you may have compiled a questionnaire – so how many people did you send it to? How many replied? Was this a representative sample? You also need to explain how you made use of the relevant resources to inform your assignment in an attempt to identify specific models, examples, ideologies, philosophies, etc., from key texts you have read.

In this introductory section, you may also want to consider ethical principles and procedures, such as confidentiality, anonymization, professional codes of conduct, access to colleagues/staff or to documents that are not within the public domain, sensitivity of data, etc.

The core

Essentially, this is where you carry out your aims as set out in the introduction. Try not to wander off the main point or get sidetracked. Use appropriate examples and illustrations to support your points, as doing so gives credibility and weight to your arguments. However, you must make sure that you reference your citations properly using the Harvard protocol described later in this chapter. Avoid generalizations and bear in mind that different people have varying ideas which may be informed/influenced by their culture, background, experiences, etc. It is therefore important to acknowledge this diversity.

Conclusion

The important point to remember about the conclusion is that you should not introduce any new material into this section. It is at this stage that you need to draw together all the threads discussed in the core. The conclusion is a useful place to offer your own perspective on the issue, and to provide a rationale to support your views. It is also an opportunity to evaluate the information you have included in your assignment. A summary is helpful in longer assignments, because it can remind the reader about the main points covered within the paper. Sometimes you may also be able to make recommendations. These could relate to further research or some future action.

2. Appropriate style

If you are unclear as to what style you should adopt when writing your essays/assignments, you could reflect on the work of other authors and analyse their styles. Some providers require you to write your paper in the first person, so make sure that you check on this before you start. It is very important to give some consideration to the tone of voice conveyed in your text. Make sure that you do not sound patronizing, pompous or arrogant. Try to view your audience as people with intelligence who have a reasonable grasp of the subject matter but who are not necessarily experts. Don't make assumptions and try to make your points as explicit as possible.

3. Good presentation

Each training provider will have its own protocol in terms of the way you are expected to present your essays/assignments. However, as a rule these are usually expected to be word processed with the final draft in double-line spacing. All pages should be numbered appropriately and you should make good use of headers and footers.

I would strongly suggest that your work be presented in an appropriate plastic presentational folder rather than in a lever-arch file, which can be bulky. You could present your work using the following layout:

- a front sheet which specifies your assignment title, your name, the date and word count
- the assignment
- bibliography
- appendices, if relevant.

4. Arguments or ideas that are supported by evidence

When writing your essay/assignment, you need to be very cautious with your assertions. It is very important that you write with clarity and relevance, and that you only make claims which you can substantiate either with quotations or other evidence. The aim of your paper will be to produce and present a series of coherent arguments that offer alternative viewpoints on the issue in question. When giving the for/against, pros/cons, strengths/weaknesses of the issue, you need to identify and use relevant texts to support these viewpoints. Of course, you can express your own views but you need to support these by citing the work of published authors who share your premise. Academic writing should take on an exploratory stance, should be open-minded and should recognize that there will always be people who do not share your particular viewpoint on the issues in question.

Referencing your essays/assignments

Having reached a postgraduate level of education, you should be able to reference your work in accordance with the Harvard protocol. However, if you are a little rusty, you may appreciate the guidance offered below. This guidance has also been reproduced with the kind permission of the Norfolk and Suffolk SCITT training provider.

Harvard Referencing Guide

Referencing is important because it helps those people who read or mark your work to identify, locate and read the sources you have used. The Harvard referencing system is one of the main methods used for this purpose.

References should be cited twice in your assignment: first, at the point at which the source is referred to in your text; second, in an alphabetical reference list at the end of your assignment.

Additional reading that you have not directly quoted from may also be incorporated into the references, in which case it becomes a bibliography.

Using references within the text of your paper

You should incorporate cited publications into the body of your assignment as follows:

- In a recent article, Smithson (1998) reports that …
- According to James *et al.* (1993) … (Note the use of *et al.*, an abbreviation of the Latin *et alii*, meaning 'and others', when there are three or more authors.)

Quotations

Avoid excessive use of word-for-word quotations. If it is no more than three lines, it may be incorporated in the body of the text in quotation marks, e.g. Burnard (1992) asserts that 'As people begin to disclose themselves to other people, their rate of talking often speeds up. Thoughts run into one another and are made into sentences.'

If the quotation is longer, it must be entered as a separate paragraph and indented from the main text. It is not necessary to use quotation marks, but you must add page references, e.g. Dixie (2007, p. 106) states that:

> It is your role as a teacher to educate children to take responsibility for their own behaviour in your classes. Any attempt to 'over control' pupils in the classroom without giving them an opportunity to take responsibility for their

actions, is simply doomed to fail. If you exercise authoritarian control over your pupils without giving them the opportunity to make, and learn from their mistakes, then you are well on course for conflict with your classes.

Summarizing in your own words

If you summarize in your own words what someone else has said, you should acknowledge the original author and provide the date of the publication in the text of your work, e.g. 'As a group, females tend to be more successful than males (Argyle, 1988) and this …'. Please note that it may not be possible to supply a page reference if you are summarizing a chapter or larger section of the work.

Citing secondary sources

Sometimes you may wish to cite a secondary source that refers to the original work (primary source) but which you may not have actually seen. Secondary sources should be cited in the following way:

> Those perceptions, which enter with most force and violence, we may name *impressions* … By ideas I mean the faint images of these in thinking and reasoning … (Hume, 1941, cited in Sartre, 1972, p. 2)

Edited works

When the quotation comes from an edited work, where each chapter has a separate author, you should give details in your text of the author of the chapter, the publication date of the whole book and the page number(s) on which the quotation appears, e.g.:

> Nursing scientists in general are either interested in or pressurised into 'testing' theories empirically rather than 'evaluating' or 'reflecting' on what theories are being produced or how they are being produced. (Kim, 1989, p. 106)

This example is a quotation from a chapter written by Kim, but which appears in a book edited by J. A. Akinsanya. In the bibliography at the end of your assignment this would appear thus:

- Kim, H.S. (1989) The theoretical thinking in nursing: problems and prospects, in Akinsanya, J.A. *Theories and Models of Nursing*. Edinburgh, Churchill Livingstone.

The Bibliography at the end of your assignment

At the end of your assignment you should organize your references alphabetically in one sequence by authors' surnames following the formats below:

Book references

To reference a book you need to note:

- the author/editor(s) surname(s) and initial(s)
- the date of publication of that edition (no reprint dates)
- title and subtitle of the work in italics
- edition of the book other than the first
- volume number if it is part of a multi-volume set
- publisher and place of publication (first named place only).

Examples

- Arts Council (1995) *Excellence in Schools*. London, HMSO.
- Knot, G. and Waites, N. (1988) *Computer Studies*, 4th ed. Sunderland, Business Education Publishers. [Include both authors when there are only two]
- Feldstein, R. *et al.* (eds) (1996) *Reading Seminars I and II: Lacan's Return to Freud*. New York, State University of New York. [Use *et al.* when there are three or more authors.]

Journal references

To reference a journal you need to know the following:

- author(s) surname and initial(s)
- year article was published
- title of the article
- title of the journal (in italics) containing the article
- volume number
- part number (in brackets). If the journal is a weekly publication, the actual date of the issue may be added
- page extent.

Examples

- Cunningham, M. (1999) Saying sorry: the politics of apology. *Political Quarterly* 70 (30), 285–293.
- Berry, M. J. and Vishnick, C. (1994) Counselling practice. *Nursing Standard* 9 (9), 33–6

Internet references

As internet references are of an ephemeral nature, it is good practice to include a copy of the source of reference as an appendix to your assignment. You need to include the following:

- author/editor(s)
- year
- title of article in italics
- [online]
- [edition]
- place of publication
- publisher (if known)
- available from: use web address
- [date accessed]

Examples

- Parra, L. (1999) *Information ownership* [online] Available from: http://humanism.org/~/ucas/ip/short.html [accessed 19 February 1999]
- *Student grants and loans: a brief guide for higher education students* [online] Available from: www.open.gov.uk/dfee/loans/loans.htm [accessed 19 September 1998]

Online journal article references

The citation order is as follows:

- author(s)
- year
- title of article
- title of journal (in italics) containing the article
- [online]
- volume (issue)
- pagination
- available from: use web address
- [date accessed].

Example

- Haggard, P. (2001) The psychology of action. *British Journal of Psychology* [online], 92 (1), pp.113–28, Available from: http://barbarina.catchword.com/vl=8356867/d=30/nw=1/rpsv/catchword [accessed 21 July 2001]

Email references

The citation order is as follows:

- sender
- (sender's email address)
- day, month, year
- subject of message (in italics)
- email to recipient
- (recipient's email address)

Example

- Smith, A. (Asmith@hotmail.com) 7 August 2000. *RE: Canadian Rainfall*. Email to M. James (Mjames@suffolk.ac.uk)

Improving your subject knowledge for teaching

16

My conversations with current and past trainees inform me that one of the biggest areas of concern for beginning teachers is their perceived vulnerability as far as their level of subject knowledge is concerned. This is particularly the case for trainees who qualified with a joint degree and/or for those who have been away from the world of academia for some time. The main question that they tend to ask themselves is – is my subject knowledge good enough to support the learning of my pupils effectively? What most trainees do not realize in the early stages of their training is that a knowledge one's subject is not sufficient on its own; you need to know how to deliver this knowledge in an accessible manner to your pupils, hence your need to also gain a secure knowledge of relevant pedagogy. When discussing the QTS standards earlier in the book, I provided you with guidance on how to find relevant portfolio evidence to support those standards relating to your professional knowledge and understanding (Q10–Q21). You will have noted that these standards cover a wide range of topics that relate to your subject knowledge and understanding, e.g.:

- teaching, learning and behaviour management strategies
- assessment
- subject knowledge for teaching
- understanding the relevant statutory and non-statutory curricula
- use of literacy, numeracy and ICT to support your teaching and wider professional activities.

However, in this part of the book I intend to focus on the Q14 and Q15 Standards because of the concerns shown by trainees with these aspects of their training, and also because of the great emphasis placed on subject knowledge and pedagogy by the TDA. I have presented the first of these standards below.

Q14 Have a secure knowledge and understanding of their subjects/curriculum areas and related pedagogy to enable them to teach effectively across the age and ability range for which they are trained.

You will note that there are two requirements of the standard – you need to demonstrate a secure subject knowledge *and* related pedagogy. In other words, you are not only required to prove that you have a solid fund of subject knowledge, but you also need to show that you know how to deliver this in an accessible manner to pupils across the age ranges and within the two key stages. As a trainee, you will need to prove that you have a sufficiently secure grasp of the concepts, ideas and principles relevant to your subject. You can show this secure subject and pedagogical knowledge by demonstrating your ability to:

- plan individual lessons in an effective and challenging manner;
- plan effective and challenging sequences of lessons and schemes of work;
- set challenging teaching and learning objectives;
- assess pupils' progress towards these objectives;
- set subject-related targets for individuals and groups of pupils;
- react confidently and accurately to pupils' questions;
- successfully break down ideas and concepts and sequence them logically to support the development of pupils' knowledge and understanding;
- recognize and respond to pupils' common misconceptions;
- make effective interventions to construct and scaffold pupils' learning;
- analyse pupils' progress and make accurate assessments of their learning and achievement;
- critically reflect upon issues relating to this Standard;
- hold informed discussion with your tutors and colleagues;
- produce effective essays and/or assignments on related issues.

QTS standard Q15 requires you to gain a secure knowledge of the curricula frameworks within which you will be working. In effect, this means that most of you will need to demonstrate a knowledge and understanding of the relevant aspects of the National Curriculum, as set out in the *National Curriculum Handbook*. You will need to demonstrate that you fully understand the three principles of inclusion: the need to set suitable learning challenges; the need to respond to pupils' diverse needs; and the need to find ways to overcome barriers to learning and assessment for individuals and groups. You will need to reflect your understanding of these principles in your lesson planning and teaching. You are also required to know about and understand the principles and approaches to teaching underpinning the National Strategy relevant to the age range you are training to teach. If relevant to your subject, you will also be expected to have a knowledge and understanding of the

National Curriculum programmes of study. You will also be expected to hold and demonstrate a secure knowledge of the examination syllabus of the subject(s) you are teaching. If you are teaching a vocational subject in the 14–19 phase, you will need to demonstrate a secure knowledge and understanding of your subject and show that you are familiar with the Secondary National Strategy.

Although you may not actually teach PSHE, you will nevertheless be expected to demonstrate your familiarity with the National Curriculum guidance on this subject relevant to the age ranges you are training to teach. You need to be aware that the 14–19 curriculum is subject to continuous change and you are expected to keep up to date with these developments. The Standard is presented below:

> Q15 Know and understand the relevant statutory and non-statutory curricula, frameworks, including those provided through the National Strategies, for their subjects/curriculum areas, and other relevant initiatives applicable to the age and ability range for which they are trained.

You can show your competence in this area by demonstrating your ability to:

- make reference to the relevant curricula, frameworks and initiatives in your planning;
- plan for, and practise inclusion in your lessons;
- show your knowledge and understanding of National Strategy approaches in your planning and teaching;
- critically reflect upon issues relating to this standard;
- hold informed discussion with your tutors and colleagues;
- produce effective essays and/or assignments on related issues.

Just as you would expect to monitor the progress and achievement of the pupils in your classes, so the TDA requires its training providers to monitor your subject and pedagogical knowledge over the training year. Although all of you will have entered the profession at degree level, it would be totally unfair and unrealistic to expect you to hold sufficient subject and pedagogical knowledge to be able to teach confidently a range of topics to pupils across the age ranges you are being trained to teach. It is with this in mind that training providers have been asked to audit your subject/pedagogical knowledge at the beginning of the course, and to monitor your progress in this field throughout the training year. It is up to you, therefore, to make sure that you provide evidence to illustrate this progress. Different training providers use different methods to do this and I have described some of these below.

Some training providers require their trainees to 'traffic light' their subject knowledge at the beginning of the course. Trainees are asked to highlight the various elements of the National Curriculum or examination syllabuses in one of three colours: green to show their *confidence in being able to teach* this element of subject knowledge; amber, if they are only partially confident *in their ability to deliver* this aspect of the curriculum; and red if their subject knowledge is rusty or non-existent and if they *do not feel confident in being able to deliver* this to their pupils. This highlighted document is then presented to the mentor/tutor before the trainee starts to teach. Please note the emphasis being placed on your confidence levels in *being able to teach* the specific elements of the curriculum. Simply knowing your subject is not enough; you must be able to deliver this content effectively to your pupils. How this subject knowledge is tracked varies across providers. Some providers issue these audits on a regular basis and ask trainees to complete these periodically; in this way progress can be plotted. Other providers are quite happy for trainees to simply add annotated notes alongside the highlighted text.

Some providers require their trainees to keep a weekly subject knowledge for teaching audit tracking sheet, on which they are required to log all the things they have done to improve this aspect of their teaching. This log is then verified by the subject tutor and/or the professional tutor on a regular basis. Trainees are required to make reference to any new subject knowledge they have picked up while on courses, when researching for and planning for their lessons, when observing colleagues and while researching for essays and assignments.

If your training provider has not been prescriptive in how you demonstrate your progress in these two standards, then you need to come up with your own strategies for plotting your journey. As a GT mentor one of the questions I ask every time I meet with my trainees is – what evidence do you have to show that you have developed your subject and pedagogical knowledge since the time of my last visit? If they cannot demonstrate progress here, I will not sign these Standards off. If you have not been given guidance on how to plot your progress with subject knowledge for teaching, Figure 16.1 may help you to do this.

Task/experience	How this has supported my subject knowledge for teaching
I have purchased and read the Letts' Geography revision guide. I have obtained and read through the Chief Examiner's report for last year's GCSE paper and have identified and highlighted common misconceptions and errors made by pupils in their examinations. I have video-taped and watched the GCSE Geography Bitesize programmes shown on BBC2. Topics included: • population and resources • urban and rural environments • plate tectonics • rivers and water management • glaciation • coastal regions • managing ecosystems. I have familiarized myself with the BBC Geography Bitesize website: www.bbc.co.uk/schools/gcsebitesize/geography/ I have read through the geography department's scheme of work for GCSE revision. I have attended a geography subject day on revision techniques and have annotated my handouts. I have read through and annotated the examination papers for the past 5 years. Using all of the above research I have produced and used my own PowerPoint revision presentation during a planned sequence of lessons.	I have been team teaching a Year 11 class with my subject tutor. As we have now come to the end of the course, he would like me to use the pupils' remaining lessons to support their revision. With this in mind, and using the findings of my research shown in this table, I have designed a one-lesson-a-week revision programme for the class. The experience has been invaluable to me because it has allowed me to become fully intimate with the requirements of the examination board, because it has highlighted for me the common misconceptions of examination candidates and provided me with a fund of interesting ways to revise familiar topics. I have placed my PowerPoint presentation and lesson plans in my portfolio and provided reflective and evaluative comments in my reflective log. The whole process has been successful in helping me to go some way to realizing Q14 and Q15.

Figure 16.1 An effective way to record your subject knowledge for teaching

Bearing in mind the large number of ITT providers in the country, it has obviously not been possible to provide you with programme-specific guidance on the issue of subject knowledge for teaching. If you require this level of detail, you will need to explore the literature and website pages of the relevant ITT provider/programme. However, I hope you feel that the advice proffered in this chapter has gone some way to helping you to meet the generalized requirements that would be expected in any ITT course.

Part 6
UNDERSTANDING YOUR SCHOOL PRACTICES

Different types of school practices **17**

Let's face it, this is probably the moment you have all been waiting for. Walking through the gates of your first teaching practice school is something you probably envisaged from the time you first started to think about teaching as a potential career. There is also no doubt about the momentous nature of the occasion, as your experiences in your practice schools are likely to impact heavily upon you as a person and as a professional for the rest of your life. It is also no exaggeration to say that the experiences you are about to embark upon represent an extremely steep learning curve, and that there will be times when you are bound to feel that you are simply not up to the job. This chapter has been written with a full understanding of the intricacies of this journey and as a means of guiding you through the complex and challenging process of learning to teach. Although I have provided you with a pretty comprehensive set of guidance and advice on how to succeed as a trainee teacher, there really is no substitute for learning from your mistakes. Please use the guidance offered to you in an honest and reflective manner and try to find a path that best suits your experience and personality.

Different types of teaching practice

The nature of your practice depends upon the length of the course you are undertaking, the college/university you are attending and/or the requirements of your specific recommending body. I have furnished you with a brief exploration of the costs and benefits of each type of practice below.

The BEd course

BEd trainees spend more time in school, although each practice is of a shorter duration. The obvious benefit to this arrangement is that you are less likely to experience burn-out during this intense period of training. The downside of this practice format is that you will be less likely to make an impact upon the pupils in your classes and on the school in general. Because of the transient nature of your visit, it is often difficult to forge and maintain good working relationships with the pupils in your classes. The situation will be exacerbated if you are in a school where staff turnover is high. Convincing many of the pupils of the long-term benefits of establishing relationships with you will be significantly more difficult than if you were teaching in a one- or two-term block. Flexibility will be a key issue for you on the BEd course. Each school has its own distinct culture and ethos and it takes a considerable time to understand and adjust to the nuances of each institution. Establishing good professional relationships with colleagues is also more difficult when undergoing the short BEd practices. Teachers in these practice schools are so used to such a large turnover of trainees that they are less likely to make the effort to get to know you. Bearing in mind that good working relationships with pupils and colleagues lie at the heart of effective teaching, leaving a school after a four-week practice block could be likened to having to rush away leaving a half-eaten meal on the table.

Postgraduate courses

In some postgraduate courses you start your training year by spending two days a week in school and three days in college or university. Again, there are obvious benefits of getting into school quickly and in gaining hands-on experience so early on. However, as with any training scenario, there are negative aspects for you to consider. Many trainees complain that this system leads to the lack of continuity so essential to forging good relationships and to good learning. You must try not to worry about this too much because as the PGCE year progresses you will be sent to other schools for extended periods of time, thus increasing your opportunity to make a real impact on your pupils.

In addition to the university/college-based PGCE courses, there are of course other teacher training programmes. The LA-based SCITT programmes offer a similar training model to the PGCE described above, but there will be variations in terms of the time spent in schools and in the type of academic work set. My local SCITT programme, for example, requires trainees to undertake a week's intensive training before spending their first term in their Practice A school. After Easter, the trainees are moved on to their Practice B schools in which they spend a further two terms. These periods in school are punctuated by both generic and subject-based training days where the trainees are provided with full opportunities to gain a theoretical perspective to their practice.

As you are already aware from reading Chapter 2, the GT programme is an employment-based route into teaching and, apart from one relatively brief second practice, all of your time will be spent in one school. There are obvious advantages to this in terms of establishing and maintaining relationships with pupils and colleagues, but the big disadvantage is that you will have to learn to live with those early mistakes for almost an entire academic year.

18 Acclimatizing yourself to the school

Once you know the name of your first practice school you need to do everything you can to prepare for your experience. One of the first things I would suggest you do is to phone the school and ask them to send you a school prospectus. Reading through this will provide you with an understanding of how your training fits into a specific school context. The prospectus will provide contextual information on the demographic, socio-economic and academic make-up of the school and will help to prepare you for the type of children you will be teaching. To support this process, I would also advise you to log on to the school website and access as much information as possible. Often a brief drive around the school's catchment area will give you a rough idea of the type of youngsters you can expect to be teaching.

Most websites and brochures contain abridged versions of the latest Ofsted Report, which you can use to identify the strengths and weaknesses of the school. Logging on to the website will also inform you whether the school has gained specialist status in such fields as science, technology, sport or PE, etc. In addition to this, you will be able to identify the nature of the extra-curricular activities being offered and also see how proactive the school is in the local community. You could also gain an excellent flavour of the ethos and culture of the school by reading through the various school policy documents relating to such issues as behaviour management, equal opportunities, assessment and ICT. Doing this before you visit your practice school will give you a head start and save you a great deal of time later on when you become fully immersed in teaching.

A cautionary note

Before you start your school practice you need to be well aware of the health and safety issues that are likely to confront you during your training. In short, you need to know how to protect yourself.

It is common practice in all schools to forbid teachers from leaving pupils unsupervised by an adult. However, you will find that what actually happens in practice in our schools is often far removed from this underlying principle. Therefore, I am advising you to play this by the book because if you do leave pupils unsupervised and something untoward happens, you may be sued by parents for compensation. If you have broken the rules it makes it very difficult for your union solicitors to defend you in court. Of course, this depends entirely whether you have actually joined a union in the first place. My advice to you would be to join the students' section of a teachers' union or professional association and extend this when you enter the profession as an NQT. Usually membership is free to trainees and some unions will even give you a reduced membership rate when you start your induction year.

Although it is highly unlikely, you do need to know that it is possible that a child could make an accusation of abuse against you while you are on teaching practice. The advice is simple; avoid being alone with a pupil. If you have to talk to a pupil privately, inform a nearby colleague and leave the door open so that you are both in full view. There are limited circumstances when appropriate physical restraint may be used with pupils, but make sure you understand fully what your individual school's policy is in this area. As a general rule, physical contact with pupils is to be avoided.

Many of you will be fortunate enough to be placed in schools with one or more fellow trainees. I use the term fortunate, because your colleagues can prove to be an invaluable form of moral and practical support. You need to milk every opportunity to share resources, to explore ideas and to share your vulnerabilities. I also need to stress that this is not the time to be competitive – there is room for more than one brilliant trainee in the school.

19 Preparing yourself psychologically for your practice

Be prepared for periods of extreme self-doubt during your teaching practices. However, whenever you simply feel like giving up, remember that you will either be moving practice schools soon, or starting as an NQT at some point in the near future. Take it from me it does not get any harder than when you are on your teaching practices. Having to meet the many and varied demands of the school and the training programme, while at the same time planning meaningful and stimulating lessons for your pupils, is a difficult ask. It would therefore, be extremely surprising if you did not question whether you really want to teach and/or whether you are any good at the job. Try to remind yourself that when you are in your own school with your own classes, it *will* become easier. You also need to hold on to the fact that every teacher trainee across the country is feeling, or has felt, the same as you at some point during his/her training year. This is why it is so important to talk openly to fellow trainees about some of the issues troubling you.

Do not throw a sickie just because things get tough. Running away from your problems will not solve anything. However, if you feel that the pressures of meeting your training and teaching demands are beginning to have an adverse effect on your health and on your ability to make sound judgements, you need to speak to your subject or external tutor about this.

Dealing with stress

You will have gathered from reading the above text that stress is likely to be a major issue while you are on your teaching practices. We all need a degree of stress in order to perform well but there is a limit to how much we can tolerate. You are highly likely to find yourself feeling stressed in school-based situations where you are:

- unable to meet your assignment deadlines;
- anxious about meeting the required standards of the course;

- worried about teaching a particularly challenging class;
- in a school that does not provide you with enough support;
- struggling to keep up with the workload.

When asked about what causes stress, many people put this down to simply having too much work to do. I do not think it is as simple as this. I do not necessarily feel that stress is caused by the amount of work we have got to do, but that it is more down to a lack of control and ownership of the tasks being given to us. It is important that you make yourself fully aware of the potential signs of stress so that you can nip them early in the bud. Signs of stress could include:

- frequent headaches
- exhaustion
- insomnia
- a feel of powerlessness and lack of control
- panic attacks
- crying at inappropriate times
- feeling inadequate and depressed.

If you will accept the premise that stress is caused by a feeling of impotence and a lack of control over your workload, then you will be receptive to the fact that there will be things you can do to improve your situation. I offer the following suggestions:

- Improving your personal organization is absolutely crucial. If you have an essay or an assignment to do, you need to consult your calendar in order to give yourself plenty of time to plan and complete your paper. It is worth aiming to hand in your work 1 week early because as Murphy's law states, 'if something can go wrong it will go wrong' and doing this will afford you a degree of leeway. Starting your assignments before everybody else will also give you a head start when it comes to finding books and journals in the library.
- You also need to build checking and amending time into your planning. I would always suggest that you give your work to someone reliable to check. It is only reasonable that you give them at least a couple of days to do this.
- Before you leave school each day make sure that you have a pretty good idea of what you will be teaching the next day.
- Plan out your week carefully. If you are a morning person, go to bed early, get a good night's sleep, get into school early and do the main bulk of your preparation and/or marking then. Conversely, if you work better at the end of the day, stay on at school and get your work done.
- Make sure that you plan some leisure time activities into your week.

- You cannot possibly do everything perfectly. Learn to prioritize and don't get diverted by interesting but futile side issues.
- If you feel that you are suffering from stress, you need to seek medical help and inform your subject mentor and/or your external tutor/mentor/ supervisor. They would prefer to know early on if you are feeling under the weather rather than hear about you experiencing significant difficulties which might call into question your ability to finish the course.
- Treat the feedback you receive during your school practices as preparation for your teaching, and not merely as a means to gain a good teaching practice grade. Be prepared to experiment. If things go wrong it really doesn't really matter as no one will be expecting you to get everything right. Trainees who have never received an unsatisfactory grade for a lesson will have probably resorted to playing safe rather than having really challenged themselves. Even if a lesson goes completely awry, with the right approach you will be able to learn something from the experience. Adopting a more sanguine approach to making mistakes will go a long way in helping to reduce your stress levels.
- Be both proactive and reflective in your training. Your subject mentor will really appreciate your coming to the table with a balanced evaluation of your progress and/or lesson. By doing this you will be able to exercise some control over the feedback process.

Understanding your development as a trainee

20

One of the things that can help you to take a balanced and informed view of your teaching practice experiences, is to understand your development as a teacher trainee over the year. Numerous studies carried out into ITT/induction issues reveal that there is a high degree of predictability in the attitudes, emotions and behaviours exhibited by trainees at specific points along the training continuum. As you can see from the following model (Furlong and Maynard, 1995) most trainees enter their training year with a fairly idealistic view of teaching. They firmly believe that, provided they treat their pupils with reasonableness and respect, this approach will be immediately reciprocated. However, what these trainees initially fail to understand is that teaching and learning relationships are far more complex than this and that there is a great deal of hard work to do in order to win over the trust of their pupils. Once they understand this, they recognize the need for a more robust approach towards their behaviour management and begin to search for the strategies that will help them simply to survive in the classroom. You need to understand that, because this realization has the effect of stripping away some of your ideals, this can be an extremely emotional part of your training year. Some trainees, once their behaviour management and planning is of a reasonable standard, take their foot off the gas and start to coast for the rest of their practice. You will see from the following model that the role of the subject mentor also changes in response to the changing needs of the trainee. Any mentor worth his/her salt, who recognizes that you are not making the progress you should be making, will simply do everything they can to move you off the plateau. Be prepared for this to be an uncomfortable experience.

I have presented you with the following developmental model to show that many of the feelings and emotions experienced at specific points in your training year are predictable and will pass (Figure 20.1) This is not to say that all of you will progress at exactly the same pace. Some of you, for example, will spend far longer in the survival stage than others.

However, it is worth noting that the training journey is fairly predictable and that you will get through it.

Early idealism	Survival	Hitting a plateau	Moving on
I'm a reasonable and caring person – I am sure that if I show this side of me, my pupils will respect me. On this basis I am confident that I can get through to them.	Help! I'm going under! On its own this approach is not working. I now realize that I need to be stronger in establishing, maintaining and reinforcing my expectations, rules, rewards and sanctions in a warm, caring, but nevertheless assertive and consistent manner.	Generally speaking I've got my behaviour management sorted. The kids aren't rioting so I can relax now knowing that I have got this teaching thing taped. I'll start pushing myself in my NQT year.	My subject mentor seems to want blood! He doesn't seem to be happy with what I am doing at the moment and is constantly setting me targets.

T R A I N E R → C R I T I C A L F R I E N D → CO-ENQUIRER

Note the changing role of the subject mentor as you progress through the year.

Figure 20.1 Understanding the developmental nature of your training year (adapted from Furlong and Maynard, 1995)

Understanding the roles of those supporting the training process

21

The external tutor/mentor/supervisor

Each trainee will be assigned an external mentor and link tutor/supervisor who will liaise with the trainee, school and the Accredited Body. The external mentor/tutor/supervisor understands the organization and content of their specific ITT programme and, when visiting you in school, should offer you and the ITT tutor/school mentor the support you need to realize your QTS standards. The external mentor/tutor/supervisor has been given responsibility to oversee the delivery of the programme on behalf of the Accredited Body.

The external mentor/tutor/supervisor also meets with the ITT tutor in the school to ensure that all parties have the necessary support required for them to meet their training responsibilities. It is also their responsibility to check that the training programme is being properly implemented by the school, and to make sure that trainees are receiving the support they need from relevant training staff.

The school

Before you start your teaching practices you need to understand that your school will play a major role in your training and in your assessment against the Standards for QTS. This process will be overseen by an ITT tutor or professional tutor who you may or may not get to see on a regular basis. The school will also assign you to a subject mentor who will have responsibility for working closely with you and who will guide you on issues relating to your planning, assessment, teaching and learning. This subject mentor will have ultimate responsibility for the classes you teach and should meet with you regularly (at least once a week) in a designated time slot to review your progress. The subject mentor will also support you in maintaining a Training File or School

Practice folder and in compiling your Portfolio of Evidence. Along with other class teachers, your subject mentor will undertake regular formal observations and provide you with verbal and written feedback identifying both your strengths and areas for improvement. Through the medium of meaningful discussion, he/she will provide opportunities for you to learn and improve your professional practice.

When supporting you, your subject mentor should make continuous reference to the Standards for Qualified Teacher Status and help you to achieve competence in these and identify evidence which demonstrates exactly how these standards are being met.

ITT tutor

This is not the place to offer a full-blown job description of the role of your ITT tutor and/or your subject mentor/tutor but it would be helpful for you to you have an understanding of his/her part in the training process. To this end, I have produced a list of entitlements that you should receive from the school. You should expect your ITT tutor to:

- provide you with a planned and structured induction into the school;
- oversee your training programme and timetable commitments;
- make sure that your subject mentor/tutor has been given protected time to hold a weekly meeting with you;
- monitor the quality of the mentoring you are receiving;
- ensure that training opportunities are offered to you;
- provide you with access to the school's CPD programme;
- facilitate your release from the school so that you can attend courses run/sponsored by your training provider;
- ensure that your progress is monitored and assessed through observations and effective written and verbal feedback, and that written reports are produced.

Subject mentor

You should expect your subject mentor/tutor to:

- provide opportunities for you to improve your subject knowledge for teaching;
- offer you advice and guidance on how to develop your planning, assessment, teaching and classroom management skills;
- hold regular weekly meetings with you and ensure that the agreed key points and targets in the meeting are recorded;

- support you in completing the specific documentation required by your training provider;
- provide a suitable teaching timetable in accordance with the requirements of your training provider;
- make regular lesson observations and provide you with verbal and written feedback;
- assess your professional practice against the Standards for QTS and moderate this assessment with both your ITT tutor and external mentor/tutor;
- complete the relevant assessment paperwork required by your training provider.

When you undertake your first practice you might find it difficult to be objective about your experiences. In other words, you simply don't know what you don't know. By providing you with a list of your training entitlements I hope that you will be able to ascertain whether any aspects of your training are missing. If, having read this chapter, you feel that you have cause for complaint then you need make contact with your external mentor/tutor and/or the training provider in order to discuss the situation.

Interacting positively with other members of staff

Teaching is very much a team game and there is absolutely no place for the lone wolf. It is vital to establish and cultivate good professional relationships with all of your colleagues if you are going to do the very best for your pupils. Knowing how to act in a professional manner and how to cultivate good collaborative relationships, are deemed to be very important by the TDA who devote specific QTS standards to this issue. I have outlined these below:

- Q4 Communicate effectively with children, young people, colleagues, parents and carers.
- Q5 Recognize and respect the contribution that colleagues, parents and carers can make to the development and well-being of children and young people and to raising their achievement.
- Q20 Know and understand the roles of colleagues with specific responsibilities, including those with responsibility for learners with special educational needs or disabilities and other learning needs.
- Q32 Work as team member and identify opportunities for working with colleagues, sharing the development of effective practice with them.

- Q33 Ensure that colleagues working with them are appropriately involved in supporting learning and understand the roles they are expected to fulfil.

As imperative as it is for you to gain competence in these standards as a means of obtaining your QTS award, they are fundamentally much more important than this. The quality of your relationships lie at the very heart of your interaction with the people you work with on a daily basis, and your competence in realizing these standards can often be displayed through the quality of your verbal and non-verbal communication. I have provided a brief guide below to help you to get off on the right foot with those working closest with you.

Working with your link tutor/mentor/supervisor

- Try to remember that irrespective of his/her seniority in the training 'pecking order', this person is a guest in the school and, as such, should be treated with courtesy and respect. Find him/her an appropriate space in which to meet with you and/ your subject tutor/mentor and get him/her a cup of tea or coffee. Do not forget that he/she is probably unfamiliar with your school's timetable so furnish him/her with an itinerary.
- If there is a mismatch between the requirements of the training provider and the needs of the school, then take the opportunity to discuss this with your tutor/mentor/supervisor. Whatever happens, do not try to solve the issue all by yourself.
- If your tutor/mentor/supervisor intends to observe you, then make sure that you provide him/her with a detailed lesson plan and a context sheet outlining details of any teaching/learning-related issues that may inform the observation. Be extremely receptive to the feedback offered and ask for ways in which you can put this advice into practice.
- If you feel that you are getting a bad deal as far as your allocation of challenging classes is concerned, or if you feel that you are not getting enough experiences of two key stages, then you need to discuss this with your external tutor/mentor/supervisor.
- Make sure that you are fully organized and prepared for his/her visit. Have all the relevant paperwork to hand. As a GT mentor, I can assure you that there is nothing more off-putting than having a trainee frantically searching for his/her paperwork while the clock is ticking away.

Working with your departmental colleagues

- Try to engender really positive relationships with your head of department. Difficult as it will be at times, endeavour to stay cheerful and offer to help them with extra tasks in the department. However, you need to be very wary that you are not bombarded with unrealistic tasks. Be up front in saying that you simply haven't got the time to take on extra responsibilities, but that you are prepared to offer some help when needed.
- Arrive early at the school on a daily basis – not only does this show the department that you are keen, but it gives you time to deal with any unforeseen circumstances that may arise.
- If you are not sure about anything, don't leave it – ask.
- If you feel you really cannot manage a challenging class without the subject teacher's or head of department's help, then say so.
- Get involved with parents' evenings by sitting in on the interviews. In case you are invited to make a contribution, have a few notes on each pupil already prepared.

Working with your subject mentor

- Your subject mentor is the most important person in your school life so it is worth doing everything you can to cultivate and maintain a good professional relationship with him/her. Remember that first impressions are very difficult to change. Arrive for your meeting on time, have your paperwork ready. Show willingness to learn and enthusiasm for your subject and for teaching in general, and demonstrate an understanding and empathy for their demanding workload.
- Be proactive in finding out about the department and the school in general. Ask about the practical issues such as photocopying and stockroom protocol. Find out whether you are expected to attend the various school/departmental meetings, school INSET sessions and/or assemblies. Identify the specific customs of your school. Who do you have to pay for tea, coffee and lunches? Make sure you find out about, and adhere to, the staff dress code.
- It is very important to remember that the role of subject mentor is voluntary and that, although some of them might receive a non-contact period to carry out their role, they are never fully compensated for all their hard work. However, they have committed themselves to certain responsibilities as far as your training is concerned, so they may need a gentle nudge from time to time.

Working with other colleagues

- Offer to do break time and/or lunchtime duties.
- Attend extra-curricular activities such as educational, fund-raising or social events. Not only will this impress your fellow colleagues but it will certainly get your pupils on board.
- Although honesty is usually deemed to be the best policy, there will be times when you may have to curb your tongue. Even if it is obvious to you that your views and ideas are likely to improve the smooth running of the school and/or department, you need to remember that you have only just started your teaching career and that this is a time when you need to show some humility. There will plenty of time for you to share your ideas once you have established yourself at the school.
- *Never* allow yourself to be embroiled in staffroom politics. Rest assured that any indiscreet slip of the tongue you make, will spread like wildfire across the school and you will spend a lot of time and energy trying to put things right.

Making effective use of classroom teaching assistants

22

It is highly likely that, at some point during your teaching practices, you will be working with a TA (teaching assistant), LSA (learning support assistant) or CTA (classroom teaching assistant). For the purposes of this publication I will refer to this additional adult in the classroom as a teaching assistant. Bearing in mind that many of these colleagues are likely to have a far greater knowledge of the pupils and of the workings of the school in general than you, it is understandable that this might appear to be a potentially intimidating experience. Please note that I have used the term 'might appear' in the above sentence because, at a time when your anxiety levels are probably quite high and your confidence levels quite low, it is easy to forget that these colleagues are there to support the learning of your pupils. They are not simply there to judge you. In order to make the most out of this working relationship and to rid this working arrangement of any ambiguities, it is important that you take control of the situation. To this end I have provided you with a range of guidance that has been designed to give you a higher degree of autonomy as to how you can make full use of these colleagues.

Make sure that you know exactly why the teaching assistant is in the classroom. Is he/she there to support one or two pupils or is he/she there to provide more generalized support? Ascertain exactly what type of support he/she will be offering the pupil(s). The following advice could cover a range of scenarios. Depending upon their specific remit, you could use your TA in the following ways:

- ask him/her to read through the teaching resources prior to the lesson;
- scribe on the board while you are talking to the class;
- act as timer and/or point scorer when you are running quizzes;
- check and sign homework diaries;
- use an observation checklist to monitor his/her pupil's participation;
- help pupils to use the learning resources and equipment;
- ensure that pupils fully understand instructions;

- encourage pupil participation by using the prompts and questions issued by the teacher;
- rehearse answers with pupils ready for the plenary session;
- remind pupils of set targets and help them to assess their own progress;
- work with small groups and/or individual pupils;
- extend and support the more able pupils in the class.

Raise the status of your teaching assistant by ensuring that your pupils understand that you and your teaching assistant will be working as a team. It is important for you to show the pupils a united front and that you will not tolerate rudeness or lack of cooperation towards your colleague.

- Make it clear to your teaching assistant whether you are happy for him/her to correct any mistakes you might make during the lesson, e.g. making a spelling mistake when writing on the board.
- Ensure that your teaching assistant knows of your classroom expectations, rules and routines, as well as the rationale behind them.
- Clarify what you expect of your teaching assistant as far as disciplining the pupils is concerned. Ascertain which sanctions and rewards you are happy for him/her to use.
- Where possible, share learning objectives with your teaching assistant in advance. If you cannot do this, have a quick word with him/her before the lesson starts.
- Try to meet with your teaching assistant on a regular basis to evaluate your professional relationship and its effect on the pupils' learning.

Working with parents 23

It is highly unlikely that in your initial teaching practice(s) you will be expected to play a dominant role in the parents' consultation process. At this stage of your teaching career, unless your host teacher is absent, your contribution will probably be reduced to a 'shadowing' and/or supportive role. However, by the time you reach your final practice, you could very well be asked to make a significant contribution to proceedings and even lead the meetings with selected parents. I know, from having discussed this issue with many trainees, that this can be a time of potential anxiety.

It may sound an obvious thing, but you really do need to clarify in your own mind the exact purpose of these evenings. They are not solely there for you to demonstrate your excellent interactive skills and/or your ability to realize QTS standards Q4 and Q5, although of course they will provide opportunities for you to do so. The purpose of consulting with parents is to nurture the home/school partnership and use these relationships to ultimately improve pupil performance.

Following are some top tips for parents' evenings:

1 Preparation is all!
   - Find out exactly who is coming to see you. Bearing in mind the high rate of marriage breakdowns, it is almost inevitable that you will be meeting partners, step parents, grandparents and other relatives.
   - Find out from more experienced staff if any of the parents you are seeing can be difficult – and the best way to deal with them.
   - Prepare notes on each of the children you teach and support this with their prior attainment data.
   - If possible check back to the pupil's previous report – it is embarrassing if your comments are very different from what has gone before – unless you have firm evidence to support this change of stance.
   - Post a list of appointment times in a visible place. If parents are aware that there are others waiting, they will be more ready to stick to the schedule. Even if parents are late make sure you stick to the order

displayed on the appointment sheet. They may have been held up in other parts of the school and their lateness is probably not their fault.

- See if you can predict the issues that might arise and prepare some answers.
- Try to look confident even if you don't feel it. Remember, most parents will be nervous too.

2 Suggested structure

Introduction: 'Hello you must be X's mum' or 'You've come to talk about X' (don't use a surname unless you are sure of it, can pronounce it and know the person's title).

Headline: e.g. 'X has settled in well and is making good progress.'

Strengths (social and academic): 'I'm particularly pleased with … (have a clear example to illustrate your point).

Areas for improvement (social and academic): However, X still needs to work on … (again, have some illustrations).

Parents' views: How do you feel that things are going in this subject? Do you have any worries? (Make a note of their concerns.) If this discussion goes on for too long, say something like 'Can I suggest that we make another appointment to discuss this? I'm afraid there are a lot of people waiting.' If you are worried about the possible nature of this further meeting, discuss your concerns with your head of department or head of year, who will be able to offer you advice and support.

Parental help: 'Could you make sure that X practises …'

Conclusion: Look at your watch, smile, stand up and offer a handshake. 'Well thank you very much for coming, it was good to meet you.'

3 Further tips

- Remember that parents want to know that you care about their child. Put their minds at ease by saying something positive about the pupil.
- Always try to be objective. Make sure you separate the work ethic and/ or behaviour from the child's personality. Do not use an acerbic tone of voice to make a point about the pupil. You are more likely to get somewhere if you offer your criticism in a warm and affirming manner.
- Have a programme of appointments with you – this will prevent you getting confused and talking about the wrong child! (It has happened!)
- Keep a clock or watch on the table – try to be politely ruthless; a slight delay with some pupils may lead to massive backlogs!
- Have a notebook in which to record the things you said you would do. If you have promised to follow up on an issue then make sure that you do it.
- Do not be afraid to ask for advice or support from colleagues during the evening if you need it.
- Celebrate your success when it's over!

4 Dealing with difficult parents

There is a big difference between challenging parents and difficult parents. The former may put you on the spot by asking challenging and searching questions about their children's progress, but do so in a spirit of collaboration and cooperation. Difficult parents, however, are those who usually come to the meetings simply 'spoiling for a fight'. At this stage of your career, it is unwise to deal directly with these parents – get a more senior member of staff to handle the situation. The guidance that follows has been offered as means of informing your NQT year and beyond.

- Refer any complaints to your head of department or a senior member of staff and ask them to deal with the situation without you in the room.
- If you have made a mistake then simply admit it and then allow your head of department to sort this out for you.
- Develop your listening skills by allowing parents to have their full say. Many problems arise because of parents' frustrations that they are simply not being listened to. Do not get defensive and do not bear a grudge. You have to show them that you are better than this!
- Make sure that you are clear in your own mind about the reasons behind your actions and behaviour. This will allow you to convey your perspective to the parents.
- Stay calm and do not get drawn into arguments. Repeat your own version of events and justify this in a professional manner. Avoid confrontation wherever possible but know when it is important to repeat your position in an assertive manner. If parents become aggressive or raise their voices, make full eye contact with them and say calmly and authoritatively, 'I am not prepared to conduct this interview under these conditions. If you feel that you cannot talk to me in a civilized manner, I will have to terminate proceedings'. If they do not calm down, stand up and open the door. If they still refuse to go, leave the room and find your head of department or mentor.
- Try to understand alternative perspectives even if you do not agree with them. There is nothing wrong in saying something like, 'I can certainly see where you are coming from, but in my professional opinion …'
- Be the one to rebuild bridges. This is very difficult to do especially if we feel that parents have really got us wrong. As professional people we are often better able to reopen channels of communication after a difficulty.
- Try to end the meeting on a positive note. Make sure that the parents know that you are still interested in their child by saying something like, 'Please don't feel you have to wait for another parents' evening

to discuss X's progress. Just give me a ring and you can come up to the school at any time'.

- Use your experiences in dealing with challenging parents as learning opportunities. If you feel that you did not do yourself justice in your meeting, then ask the simple question, 'What would I do differently next time?'

Getting to grips with your behaviour management

My experience as a teacher trainer convinces me that behaviour management is an absolute priority for the majority of trainees in schools. It is this belief that has led me to writing the two books constantly referred to throughout this book. The first book, *Getting on with Kids in Secondary Schools* (2005), focuses on the relationship side of teaching. The second, *Managing Your Classroom* (2007), provides advice and guidance on how to establish and maintain an effective behaviour management regime in your lessons. Because good behaviour management lies at the heart of effective teaching, it is absolutely vital that you either carry out some background reading into this issue using these books, or those cited in the reading list provided in Chapter 9.

To further support your reading on this issue you should reflect on your pre-course observation data as discussed in Chapter 5. Chapter 10 also provides detailed advice on the link between body language and assertive discipline. So important is behaviour management to the classroom practitioner, that the TDA has allocated a total of four standards to this issue. These are as follows:

Q1 Have high expectations of children and young people including a commitment to ensuring that they can achieve their full educational potential and to establishing fair, respectful, trusting, supportive and constructive relationships with them.

Q10 Have a knowledge and understanding of a range of teaching, learning and behaviour management strategies and know how to use and adapt them, including how to personalize learning and provide opportunities for all learners to achieve their potential.

Q30 Establish a purposeful and safe learning environment conducive to learning and identify opportunities for learners to learn in out of school contexts.

Q31 Establish a clear framework for classroom discipline to manage learners' behaviour constructively and promote their self-control and independence.

If you have been given classes that would seriously challenge even the most senior and experienced teachers, then you need to speak to your external tutor/mentor/supervisor about this. I can assure you that your reluctance to take on classes such as these is not a sign of weakness. It is extremely unrealistic to expect a beginning teacher such as yourself to cope with the more serious behavioural issues that may occur on a regular basis in challenging classes. However, it is fair to say that you are likely to come across some extremely challenging behaviour from time to time in your lessons, so you need to be prepared to deal with it. Although it is unrealistic to expect you to become a proficient behaviour manager overnight, there is a number of things you can do to reduce the opportunities for your pupils to disrupt your lessons. As you will see below I have put this advice into two distinct categories; those relating to 'whole-class' behaviour management planning and those linked to your relationship issues with pupils.

Whole-class behaviour management planning (technical domain)

- Make sure that you outline your expectations, rules, routines, rewards and sanctions with your classes and provide a visual reminder of these. This could be in the form of an A5 sheet which you ask your pupils to stick in their books and/or classroom posters. As a trainee you may find establishing your expectations extremely difficult to do especially when the pupils have been used to the host teacher's way of working. However, doing this is absolutely vital if you are going to establish yourself in an assertive manner. Run through your expectations with the host teacher and ask him/her to support you with this approach.

- Make sure that you constantly revisit your rules, routines, rewards and sanctions with your classes on a regular basis and that you issue your sanctions and rewards in a *consistent* manner. You could do this is the following way: 'We are now going to have a question and answer session. What are my expectations and rules for this kind of work? What sanctions will apply should you shout out or start talking among yourselves?'

- Start your lessons on time and devise and apply sanctions to latecomers. You will have to decide exactly what you mean by the term 'late'. You could find out what the furthest distance one of your pupils has to travel to get to your class and then time how long you take to make the same journey. Again, make sure that you deal with lateness in a fair and consistent manner. Do not interrupt the flow of your lesson by challenging latecomers when they arrive. Simply record their names in your notebook and ask to see them at the end of the lesson. If you are not happy with the reasons given to you then you could keep them in at break to tidy the classroom or collect up the resources.

- Ensure that you always prepare extension tasks to keep your pupils fully occupied. Try to engender a climate where these tasks are not merely seen as extra work for the sake of it. Offer a word of challenge to your more able and/or faster workers and reward them for their efforts either through the school's system or, better still, through your own personalized reward system.

- Make sure that the work is set at the appropriate level for each pupil in the class. Provide opportunities for differentiation by task, resource, outcome, questioning and preferred learning styles. Because you will not know the pupils very well in the early stages of your practice, this will be difficult to achieve. However, as you get to know your youngsters you will get to know their strengths and 'areas for development' and it will become much easier to offer them opportunities for personalized learning.

- Use the school's assertive discipline policy consistently but support this early on by using your own set of personalized gradated sanctions. These sanctions should preferably be implemented on the same day. In *Managing Your Classroom* (2007) I discuss the need for teachers to take on the bulk of responsibility for their own classroom discipline. Far too many teachers simply dish out whole-school sanctions like confetti and then wonder why their pupils don't treat them seriously. Issuing your own sanctions at an early point along the sanction continuum, communicates to the pupils that you are fully prepared to do your own dirty work and that you are not simply passing the problem on to someone else. Provided you give the pupils rationale for doing this, they will end up respecting you far more than if you had simply notified another member of staff of their misdemeanours.

- Have a system for gaining your pupils' attention. Some teachers use a countdown system; some teachers use a bell while others simply raise their hands. Again, whatever method you use, do so in a consistent manner and make sure that you have sanctions planned for the occasions when pupils fail to comply with your expectations.

- Get yourself a small notebook in which to record the names of pupils who you feel deserve rewards or for those whose actions you have deemed to be inappropriate and where follow-up action is needed. Doing this will help you to demonstrate the consistency which is absolutely fundamental to good classroom management.

- Where possible share your lesson plan with teaching assistants who will be working with you in your lessons. Make sure that your expectations, rules, rewards and sanctions have been made absolutely transparent to these colleagues and make sure that you fully empower them to support you in your drive towards good pupil behaviour. Make it clear what you want them to do when they spot pupils misbehaving.

- Ensure that all of your resources have been fully prepared, that they are easily accessible and that you have planned how they will be distributed during your lesson. The smooth distribution of resources is one way of avoiding those 'break-in-flow' points that disrupt lessons and which offer pupils full opportunities to become distracted. If you have time, you could lay out the resources on each of the pupils' desks. Alternatively, you could train the pupils into picking these up as a matter of course as they enter the room. Provided you do this early on in your practice, and providing that you are consistent in using this approach, the pupils will soon pick up on the way you work. You also need to make it clear what resources and equipment you expect your pupils to bring with them to the lesson. I have seen the flow of many a lesson interrupted because pupils did not readily have the resources required for their learning.

- Make sure that you include as many elements of your behaviour management in your lesson plans as possible. As you get more experienced, you will not need to do this to the same extent. However, at this early stage of your pedagogic development there is so much for you to remember and writing this into your plan can often help you to maintain or regain focus. The sorts of things that could be included in your plan could be your seating plan arrangements, a list of your personalized gradated sanctions, any arrangements you have made for the removal of challenging pupils, etc.

Interactive and relationship issues (personal and clinical domains)

- Make sure that you learn pupils' names as quickly as possibly. Using a pupil's name establishes a psychological contract between you, and makes it harder for him/her to misbehave.

- Talk to the class teacher and find out about the social and academic background of the pupils in your lessons. Sometimes, finding a point of contact with the pupil can help to resolve potential conflict situations. Finding out from the host teacher what works best for specific pupils can also go a long way to alleviating indiscipline in your lessons.

- Always speak respectfully to the pupils even if you have to admonish them. Make it clear that it is their behaviour that you are unhappy about and that you bear them no grudge as individuals.

- Try to catch pupils doing things well. Take every opportunity to praise them directly or, if you need to use a more subtle and indirect approach, make effective use of 'proximity praise'. This simply involves praising the behaviour of those pupils in direct proximity to the miscreant, in an attempt to influence his/her behaviour in a positive manner. The issue of proximity praise is explored in more detail in Chapter 10 of *Managing Your Classroom* (Dixie, 2007). I thoroughly recommend you giving this further attention.

- Hard as it may be, you are advised not to lose your temper. The message here is simple: if you lose control of yourself, you will lose control of the class. Having said this, there will be occasions when you will need to raise your voice in order to gain the full attention of the class. Having done this, lower the pitch of your voice while still using an assertive and firm tone.

- Never back a pupil into a corner otherwise the pupil is likely to move into 'fight or flight' mode. Always try to give pupils a dignified way out of a tricky situation. They will respect you all the more for not having sought your pound of flesh.

- You may find that pupils get so angry with you that they threaten to bring their parents into school. Do not appear to be fazed about this but simply call their bluff. Use a positive tone of voice, pick up your diary and say something like, 'I think that is a really good idea. It would be really great to meet your parents and then we can work together to help you achieve success.'

- Whatever you do, do not shout over pupils' noise. If you do this you will have established the fact that it is acceptable for them to talk while you are talking. It is important for you to wait until the class is silent before you move on. Ensure that you support this with a firm sanction, otherwise you will simply have to repeat this performance every time you want to get your pupils' attention.

- Be sure not to personalize behavioural issues. Focus on the pupils' behaviour rather than them as individuals. Do not label the class as 'horrible' or 'unteachable', as you will find it difficult to move forward with these pupils. Get to know the backgrounds of the pupils and spend some time talking with some of the more challenging youngsters and finding out what makes them tick. It is amazing what you can find out when you really try. I remember adopting this approach with one really challenging low-ability Year 9 class and finding out that my three challenging pupils (I called them my three musketeers) all led quite disciplined lives outside of school. One pupil set his alarm for six o'clock every morning and carried out two paper rounds. One pupil was a successful ballroom dancer and this involved him practising for hours after school. The other pupil worked in his father's joinery after school and all day Saturday. The process of my taking the trouble to find out about the lives of these three boys, afforded them status and self-esteem, and established a climate of mutual respect. Needless to say, although they were no angels, their behaviour and work rate did improve dramatically for the rest of the year.

- It is human nature to want to be liked, and it is true that if you are liked by the pupils, you are more likely to be able to motivate and encourage them. However, *being liked should be a by-product of being a good teacher, and not an aim*. Provided you approach your role in a sincere, consistent and equitable manner, and providing you show your pupils that you really care, popularity and respect are likely to follow.

- It is very important that you listen to your pupils, even the most challenging of them. If they can see that you are taking the trouble to listen to them, they are more likely to listen to you as a mark of mutual respect.

- If pupils are off task, try to use positive phraseology. Instead of saying something like, 'Stop messing about', you need to adopt a more positive stance by presuming the best of them. You could then say something like, 'Do you need some help with this, Gary?'

- Do not overreact if any of your pupils refuse to carry out your instructions or tell you that they are not going to do the work. Simply adopt a relaxed body stance, smile and say something like, 'No worries, I am in my classroom at break, you can do it then.'

- Where pupils are displaying challenging behaviour, you need to offer them choice direction. Choice direction means giving the pupils alternative scenarios. For example, if a pupil is playing with a mobile phone you could say something like, 'You can either give the phone to me and collect it at the end of the day, or you can put it in your bag.' Given the closed nature of these directions, most pupils will choose the latter option.

- Try to give pupils opportunities to take control of their own behaviour by giving them a chance to improve. You could say something like, 'Your behaviour so far has been unacceptable. If you manage to make a real effort to work and to behave between now and the end of the lesson, you can avoid the half-hour detention I have got planned for you.'

- Don't be frightened to call upon your head of department to support you in dealing with a challenging class. *However*, and this is a big *however*, what is really important is that it is *you* who take control of the situation. Ask a senior member of staff to come along to your lesson and to act as a witness and to hear what you say to your pupils. By doing this, you will keep your integrity and maintain control of the situation. Having this senior member of staff in the room will lend status and kudos to the messages you impart to your pupils, without them having to play a dominant role. Once you have finished speaking to the class, you could invite your senior colleague to support you in the issuing of your sanctions.

25 Lesson planning

All good teaching requires careful planning. As you can see from the box below, planning can occur on three or four levels. Most schools will have the following types of plans for each year group in each subject:

Long-term plans	The yearly plan includes a description of the topics required to be covered and the expected teaching order.
Medium-term plans	This plan is usually produced on a termly basis but it could take the form of a scheme of work for each module/ topic taught.
Weekly plans	Some schools use these as their lesson-planning documents.
Lesson plans	The day-to-day planning of individual lessons

All training providers require their trainees to prepare, and work from, a formal lesson plan for *every* lesson (or part lesson) taught. As outlined in the box, the lesson plan should evolve from the medium-term plan. Although you will initially be required to work on the lesson plan with the close support of the school mentor, you will soon be able to produce these on your own. However, you will probably still need to get them checked over by the school mentor before you deliver your lesson.

The point of a lesson plan is to guide you in organizing yourself and your material with the purpose of helping your students to achieve the intended learning outcomes. Although I provide an example of a lesson plan in Figure 25.1 on page 208 you need to know that there is no single format for successful lesson planning. However, you must be aware that there is a number of key elements that make for good planning. Although you will be required to present your lesson plan to your class teacher, subject mentor and/or your external tutor/ mentor/supervisor, you do need to remember that the main audience for the lesson plan is *you*. Before you start planning your lessons you might like to consider the following prompt questions:

1 What is the purpose of the lesson?
2 What are the objectives for the lesson?
3 What is the best way for the pupils to achieve?
4 What activities or tasks will help them to achieve?
5 What is the minimum amount of time needed for each task or activity?
6 What will happen when different pupils take different amounts of time to do a task?
7 What extension activities can I provide for those pupils who finish their work early?
8 How much time do I set aside to settle the class, take the register, introduce the topic, hand out equipment or books, clear up and dismiss the pupils?
9 What materials and resources will I need to assemble before the lesson?
10 Are the pupils likely to be fully occupied in learning throughout the lesson?
11 Have I planned homework opportunities for pupils?
12 Have I catered for my EAL, SEN and/or G&T pupils?
13 Have I made the learning journey transparent to my teaching assistant?

Although there has been a recent move towards the four-part lesson, I am suggesting that when you plan your lessons you think about the process as having three discrete phases: an introduction, the main body and the conclusion.

Introduction

The introductory phase of the lesson requires you to set out your aims and objectives for the lesson, perhaps using a 'holding' or 'starter' task to launch the main theme. It is also the part of the lesson that requires you to consolidate and review the learning that has occurred in previous lessons and then to make links with new learning scenarios. This phase of the lesson requires you to *introduce* new concepts and content to the pupils and to put these into context using language they are likely to understand. This is also a good time and place to model examples of good practice as a means of raising pupils' expectations of their performances.

Main body

The main phase of the lesson requires you to teach a new body of knowledge or to provide pupils with an in-depth exploration of these concepts, ideas or viewpoints. This is the part of the lesson when you would expect pupils to complete their tasks and activities, in groups, in pairs or on an individual basis. The main body of the lesson should contain a range of activities and should offer opportunities for pupils of different abilities and learning styles to achieve. Assessment for Learning opportunities should also be planned for this phase of the lesson. This is also the phase of the lesson where full teacher monitoring of pupils' learning should take place.

Conclusion

The concluding phase of the lesson requires you to consolidate upon the learning that has just taken place. This could be done through a question/answer session, through class discussion and/or through quizzes and games. Your job as a teacher is to reframe the responses given to you by the pupils, and then summarize the learning that has occurred during the lesson. Although good teachers will constantly monitor and assess pupil learning as they teach, rather than wait until the end of the lesson, most of you will not yet have the skills to do so fully. This makes your plenary session even more important. Your plenary session needs to be designed to assess the degree to which your learning objectives have been realized. The final part of the lesson should see you linking the learning that has just occurred to the content of the next lesson.

What needs to be in your lesson plan?

Contextual information

This part of the plan should give information which provides a background to the lesson and which sets the boundaries or limits of the plan. As an experienced observer I would expect you to include the following contextual information in your lesson plan:

- the name of the subject, unit of work and topic being studied
- the date, time and place of the lesson
- a seating plan
- the gender and ethnic breakdown of the class
- an explanation to show how a member of the support staff is being used

- details of any SEN, EAL and/or G&T pupils
- details of any pupils with social or behavioural problems
- a description of how this lesson fits into the learning sequence. What was learned previously and how will this new learning feed into future lessons?
- the attainment levels you are aiming to cater for? (You need to use National Curriculum, examination board or departmental assessment levels here)
- the prior attainment data for each of the pupils
- an indication of the assessment opportunities provided
- a description of the resources you intend to use
- a description of your relationships with the pupils in the class.

Learning objectives

All lessons need *learning objectives*. You need to make it absolutely transparent what you expect the pupils to know and understand by the end of the lesson. It is very common to confuse the tasks/activities that will be done in the lesson with learning objectives, so be very wary of doing this. Schools will use different systems for setting objectives, but it is expected that pupils will know – by being told or by seeing these displayed on the board – what the learning objectives are. I would strongly advise that pupils copy these learning objectives down into their books so that they can refer to them both during and after the lesson. When setting your learning objectives you could consider the following questions. By the end of this lesson, what should pupils know? What should pupils be able to understand? What should pupils be able to do? These may be expressed using the language of differentiation using the following formula:

- all pupils will …
- most pupils will …
- some pupils will …

Starter activity

All lessons should have a starter activity. The purpose of the starter is to get the pupils fully engaged in the learning process as soon as possible and to engender a sense of pace in the lesson. Starter activities do not have to be directly linked to the main body of the lesson, although they are a good opportunity to use creative strategies to provide that all-important hook. It is very important that your starter does not take too much time and that it doesn't dominate the lesson. The starter activity could take on numerous forms, some of which I have outlined below:

- a brief quiz
- a brief research task using reference books provided
- interpretation of visual or textual material
- responding to questions having heard a music track or having seen a brief video clip
- paired discussion on a relevant topic
- revisiting and improving previous work.

Main activities

When selecting the activities and tasks you intend to use in your lesson, you need to think about the following key questions:

- Will the tasks and activities enable the learning objective(s) to be met?
- How are the tasks and activities going to enthuse and engage pupils of all ability levels?
- How successful will your tasks and activities be in catering for the different types of learners in your lesson?
- How can you use these tasks and activities to monitor and assess learning?

Plenary activity

Many trainees find that, because of their inability to plan effectively, this phase of the lesson often gets squeezed out. However, you do need to know that this is a crucial part of the lesson because, if it is carried out properly, it will provide you and the pupils with an indication as to whether the learning objectives have been met. As with the starter activity, there is a range of different formats for the plenary. The suggestions made below, along with those made for the starter activity, only scratch the surface and you need to carry out more specific and focused research into this aspect of your teaching:

- verbal or written quizzes supported by a follow-up discussion
- question/answer session in which you select pupils from a range of abilities to respond
- providing pupils with new scenarios in which to apply their newly gained knowledge, understanding and/or skills
- asking pupils to refer back to the learning objectives and to provide evidence from the lesson to show how these have been met.

Evaluation and reflection

To a greater or lesser degree, all trainees are expected to evaluate their lessons and reflect upon ways in which to improve their practice. You may find that your training provider has furnished you with a set of questions to be answered or a set of instructions to be followed. Alternatively, you may be left entirely to your own devices. If the latter is the case, I would strongly suggest that you use the reflective formula provided for you in Chapter 13. Whichever method you use to evaluate and reflect upon your performance and on the quality of learning in the lesson, you do need to identify *and act* upon the specific targets identified for your development.

Bearing in mind the vast range of subjects offered within schools today, it has been difficult to provide you with a lesson plan that is fully representative of your needs. Subjects such as PE, science, technology and drama, for example, require some kind of input that relates to health and safety isues, while other subjects very rarely require this consideration. In presenting you with the following exemplar lesson plan, I have included aspects of planning that may not be generally appropriate to your subject but which might, however, be needed for the occasional lesson.

Teacher:	**Teaching group**	Room:
Date:	Time:	LSA:

Learning objectives:

National Curriculum links:

SEN pupils:

Differentiation: By the end of the lesson

All pupils will ....

Most pupils will ...

Some pupils will ...

LSA support will be used to ...

Other means of differentiation:

Context:

Resources (including ICT):

Behaviour management issues:

Health and safety issues:

Lesson structure

Teacher activity	Pupil activity
Starter:	
Main activities:	

Monitoring and assessment

During lesson:

After lesson:

Plenary:

Key learning points to be confirmed:

Questions to ask:

Evaluation:

What went well:

What did not go well:

Changes for next time:

Figure 25.1 Exemplar lesson plan

Having prepared your lesson plan, you will now have to think about preparing the resources to support your pupils' learning. Sometimes this can take the form of a simple but effective worksheet. However, it is crucial that you provide a variety of sources and activities to engage your pupils and that you do not inflict death by worksheet on them. The guidance shown in Figure 25.2 has been adapted from an excellent publication on lesson planning: *Lesson Planning* (2006, p. 55).

Purpose
- What is the purpose of the worksheet?
- What are the learning objectives I want to cover?
- What specific subject knowledge, understanding and skills will the worksheet address (in the NC, GCSE or AS/A2 level)?

Planning
- What resources/materials do I need to construct the worksheet?
- Where are these available (textbooks, Internet, CD-ROM, newspapers, photographs, cartoons, etc.)? Are these resources up-to-date and free from bias?
- Do I have the technical ability to construct and reproduce the worksheets?
- What activities should be included to meet the 'Purpose' outlined above? How will these activities be differentiated according to the abilities of the pupils?
- How will student learning be assessed?

Presentation
- What design do I want for the worksheet – portrait or landscape, font sizes and types, pictures, maps, cartoons, tables, diagrams, graphics, etc.? Will visual images reproduce clearly if the worksheet is to be photocopied?
- Is the text engaging and clearly sequenced for the pupils? Is the text readable and is the amount of technical vocabulary and use of jargon acceptable?
- What headings and labels do I need to include to identify the activities to be undertaken? Is there too much/not enough text?
- Should keywords (and their definitions) be identified in bold type?

Use
- How does the worksheet fit into the lesson plan and its stated learning objectives?
- How will I introduce the worksheet to the pupils? Do I want them to complete it all in the lesson? Are any activities for homework? Are there different sheets and/or activities for different pupils?

Evaluation
- Did the worksheet help me achieve my learning objectives?
- Was the worksheet capable of providing differentiated learning for different abilities?
- Did the pupils find the worksheet interesting, motivating and stimulating to use?
- What might I change about the worksheet, or the way I used it, in future lessons?

Figure 25.2 Lesson planning: producing an effective worksheet

26 Engaging your pupils

There is no doubt that keeping the pupils active and fully engaged in your lessons will have extremely positive knock-on effects in terms of behaviour management and the learning taking place. Therefore, you need to do everything you can to keep your pupils focused, on-task and motivated. In order to help you to do this I have offered you some guidance on a number of relevant issues below.

Giving instructions to classes

Giving instructions to pupils is more difficult than it seems. My observations of both teachers and trainees at work in the classroom have highlighted to me the importance of giving transparent instructions to pupils. Failure to do so can result in pupils losing interest and veering off task. The importance of this is compounded if you are teaching practical lessons where pupils have a degree of freedom to use the resources located at various points in the classroom. When determining the specific instructions you want your pupils to follow, use these guidelines which have been taken from *Managing Your Classroom* (Dixie, 2007).

Keep it simple and choose instructions that are observable

Choose a limited number of instructions for each classroom activity. Do not include vague instructions such as 'behave appropriately'.

Relate your instructions to

- How you want the pupils to participate in the activity or procedure – what you expect them to do?
- How you expect the pupils to behave in order to be successful in the activity. An exemplar set of instructions is given below.

Sample lesson sequence for teaching specific instructions for taking a test

1 Explain the rationale for your instructions
Explain to the pupils the benefits of following your instructions carefully.

On Friday you will have a test. At the beginning of the lesson I will give you instructions. It is very important that you follow these instructions carefully so that you complete the test and do well.

2 Involve pupils by asking questions
Pupils will follow your instructions more readily if you involve them in a discussion that rationally addresses their concerns.

What would happen if we wasted a lot of time getting ready for the test? What are the consequences of pupils not coming to the lesson with the correct equipment?

3 Explain the specific instructions for the test
Teach the specific instructions they will be expected to follow. Remind them that when everyone follows these instructions *all* pupils will have an opportunity to succeed in class.

I want you to clear your desks, except for a pen.

There is to be no talking or getting out of your seat.

When you receive your paper lay it face down on the desk until I tell you to begin.

When I say 'begin', turn your paper right side up, write your name and the date, read the questions carefully.

When you are ready, begin writing.

If you have any questions, put your hand up and wait until I get to you.

When you have finished, check over your answers, come to the front of the class and hand your sheet in. You may take out a book and read quietly until the papers are collected.

Reproduced from Dixie, *Managing Your Classroom*, 2007, by permission of Continuum.

Using an effective questioning technique

Much research has been carried out to show that good questioning techniques lie at the heart of effective classroom control. In the early stages of your career you are advised to produce a list of questions in your lesson plan. It is really important to involve as many pupils as possible in your question/answer and discussion sessions. By doing so, you will provide pupils with a high degree of ownership of the lesson and you will soon note significant and positive effects of this increased involvement on your class control. Ensure that you obtain a gender balance when choosing pupils to answer your questions and make a point of not ignoring those really 'quiet' pupils who can often leave a lesson not having said anything to anybody. It is also very important that you do not allow individuals to dominate. Make sure that you have a word with them privately, thank them for their enthusiasm and commitment, and explain to them the need to let others have a go.

There is a real need for you to establish and maintain an effective climate for question/answer sessions and discussions. I have suggested a number of rules for the really challenging pupil:

- Do not shout out your answers in class.
- You should try to leave the easier questions to other pupils in the class. Your target is to focus on the really challenging questions.
- If you feel you are bursting to answer a question, you must put your hand up and wait for the signal from me.
- If I think the question is too easy for you, I will simply put my thumb up and draw an invisible line with my hand under this signal.
- When I am about to ask a particularly challenging question, I will let the class know beforehand.
- This is where you come in. Again, do not shout out your answer but wait until I am ready for you to respond. You need to understand that, even at this point, I may still seek a response from someone else in the class. However, I will come back to you to see whether you agree with the response or whether you have anything else to add.

There is, however, a substantial number of pupils who are extremely reluctant to make a verbal contribution to lessons. Often it is those very same pupils who become distracted and miss out on the learning experiences offered to them. It is not all down to the ability levels of the pupils involved. (I discuss this in more detail in *Managing Your Classroom*.) Often it is the brighter pupils who find it most difficult to speak up in class. I have come up with a number of suggestions as to why this is the case.

My first suggestion relates to the pupils' perception of the *value* of actually participating verbally in class in the first place. Why should pupils take risks and put themselves on the line by volunteering answers in class? Your job as a teacher is to clarify the value of such a contribution. Second, we are talking about young people at a stage in their lives where their confidence is often quite low. Speaking out in class is simply a non-starter for many of them. Getting things wrong in front of their peers is seen as a major humiliation by many pupils of this age. The third reason behind the non-participation of many pupils is because they don't want to be labelled as boffs by their peers. The important thing to remember here is that it is their *perception* of the situation that affects their behaviour and which ultimately hinders their verbal contribution to lessons. It is also fair to say that many pupils perceive the working culture of the classroom to be focused on the individual and to be competitive and threatening. This then leads them to opt out of the lesson and subsequently to become prone to distraction and misbehaviour. It is highly likely that there will be pupils in your lessons who fail to fully engage in your question/answer sessions and, as a result of this, miss out on the learning that should be taking place. This is something that an inclusive questioning technique can help to rectify.

Creating a more collaborative and non-threatening climate within the classroom can go a long way to fully involving even the most marginalized of pupils. You are strongly advised to inform your pupils that a wrong answer in class should not invite ridicule or be dismissed by fellow pupils, but should be seen as an important step in the journey towards achieving the objectives of that specific lesson. Stress the importance of pupils getting involved in the process rather than merely providing the final answer.

Some useful strategies for increasing collaborative learning in lessons

Getting the pupils to see the value of verbal participation in class

It is important that pupils understand the value of making a verbal contribution to their learning. In Dixie (2007) I state that:

> … the processes of absorbing information from written or verbal stimuli, of synthesising this material, of formulating a hypothesis and organising one's thoughts into a coherent language form, provides ownership of the concept/issue being addressed and fully commits the pupil to the learning process. (p. 73)

If you provide the pupil with an easy way out by not challenging him/her to verbalize his/her responses, you will decrease the opportunities for him/her to take ownership of his/her learning.

- One of the things you could do to involve your pupils in your question/answer sessions is to give your questions a *currency*. Tell the class that you expect every pupil to answer a question during the lesson, but that the earlier questions are going to be that little bit easier. By doing this, the more reluctant and/or less able pupils are more likely to respond in the early part of the lesson. You could insist that the more able and dominant pupils select their questions from the harder category.
- Before you start the lesson, explain to the class that you will be asking a number of pupils questions relating to the information just delivered in the introductory phase. This is likely to have the effect of gaining the full attention of the pupils during that all-important launching phase of the lesson and is an excellent tool for testing comprehension.
- In order to encourage less successful pupils to participate in front of their more articulate peers, you need to adopt a strategy to keep them involved and valued. *Target specific questions* at these pupils, but ensure they are of a *low level nature*. Hopefully, a correct answer will be forthcoming or at least a response which may provide a starting point for further discussion.
- It is absolutely *vital* that you recognize the verbal contribution of those pupils who are reluctant participants. A quick word of praise, a telephone call home or the issuing of community credits are just some of the ways their contributions can be acknowledged. Discuss the issue with individual pupils and set them targets. If possible, take the opportunity to discuss these with their form teachers. Let the pupils know that what you are asking them to do in class should be transferable across the curriculum, i.e. what they can do in your lesson, they can do in other subjects.

Using ICT to support your professional practice

There is no doubt that the use of ICT helps to increase pupils' motivation, confidence and self-esteem. Effective use of ICT enhances pupils' social and cooperative skills and helps to improve overall academic achievement. ICT is deemed to be such an important ingredient in the teacher trainee's repertoire, that it has three QTS standards, partially or wholly dedicated to this aspect of your pedagogic practice. These are:

Q16 have passed the professional skills test in numeracy, literacy and information and communication technology.

Q17 know how to use skills in literacy, numeracy and ICT to support their teaching and wider professional activities.

Q23 design opportunities for learners to develop their literacy, numeracy and ICT skills.

The drive towards an increased use of ICT has been initiated by the TDA which has funded e-learning projects for teacher training providers on a national basis. In the words of the TDA:

We share the view expressed by the ITT community that the ability to work experimentally helps to create a culture of innovation and change which is central to developing activity and quality in initial teacher training. (www. tda.gov.uk/partners/quality/ict/supportforictinitt.aspx)

In 2006–7, in an effort to introduce innovation, the TDA targeted the following eight areas:

- video conferencing
- video capture and analysis
- PDAs
- laptops for trainees/tablet PCs for trainers

- innovative work in ICT
- interactive whiteboards
- subject-specific software
- ICT-driven subject-specific hardware, e.g. CAD-CAM and data loggers.

The TDA's big push towards using innovative ICT techniques in the classroom, has led to training providers being required to audit and monitor the ICT skills of their trainees. So how exactly does this affect you? In the initial stages of your training year, you will be asked to complete an audit of your ICT skills and of your knowledge and understanding of the role of ICT in the classroom. Having completed your audit, you will need to identify specific areas for development to work on. You will be expected to be competent in using ICT in your professional role, so that you are able to operate the ICT systems used in different schools and adapt to change and innovation. In the early stages of your training year, you are expected to be competent in the programs/skills presented to you in the list below.

Word processing e.g. using tables, inserting pictures and graphs, creating page layouts, adding text boxes and speech bubbles, adding page numbers, adjusting margins and layouts, using the Drawing toolbar, using headers and footers.

Spreadsheets Creating a spreadsheet, using a spreadsheet as a database, drawing graphs, making calculations per cell, using pre-defined functions such as MIN, MAX, AVERAGE, sorting data, organizing data on multiple worksheets.

PowerPoint Making presentation slides, adding images to slides, adding videos and sound files to slides, changing fonts and background colours, inserting hyperlinks, running a slide show in a classroom, printing handouts.

Desktop publishing Showing some familiarity with what these packages can do. Investigate the use of desktop publishing software such as Microsoft Publisher to create classroom displays and banners.

Use of the internet Being able to use a web browser effectively (typing website address in address bar, amending the address book). Being able to use search engines effectively to search for web pages or pictures, downloading material from the internet or from an attachment; retrieving information in different formats (text, picture, video) from the internet to reuse in a different piece of software, etc.).

Email Being able to send and receive emails, reply and forward emails, send files as attachments, send hyperlinked web pages, save and sort emails into sub-folders.

IWB technology Being confident in using interactive whiteboard effectively and efficiently.

Saving documents Saving to school network/intranet to CD; saving to a USB portable drive, memory stick. Being able to transfer files from one computer to another (i.e. using a USB key), being able to take a backup of existing files, being able to organize files in folders and subfolders and rename/delete/move/duplicate files and folders.

Admin Using school reporting system, accessing pupil data from school system.

VLE/intranet Showing some familiarity with how Virtual Learning Environment (VLE) can be used within a school. Show a willingness to see how the school is using a VLE or intranet.

You are also recommended to read your school's ICT policy document carefully and to become intimate with expected protocol. The ICT policy document should make some firm recommendations as to how to make appropriate use of ICT in the classroom as well as in other areas of your professional career. You also need to be aware of certain data protection issues when using ICT within schools. To this end, I offer guidance on some of the key security issues below.

Use personal data sensibly: be very cautious when accessing, saving and communicating pupils' personal data electronically (i.e. through emails, intranet, Virtual Learning Environment (VLE), as some of the data are very sensitive and confidential and should be kept safely. This information should then be removed from the ICT system when it is no longer required.

Security risks: viruses: be aware that 'Trojan Horse' spyware is potentially dangerous to any network system or indeed to your own PC or laptop. Identity theft and hacking are real risks that can result in sensitive data being stolen, altered or deleted. You need to be aware of the risks and to develop the following strategies to minimize these:

- Keep your password safe. Update your password on a regular basis; do not open email attachments from unknown sources.
- Do not browse or download from inappropriate websites.
- Avoid using USB keys on other computers outside the school.

You need to be aware that your training providers will need you to provide evidence to show how you have continued to develop your application of ICT in the classroom and in other aspects of your professional practice. Although the exact format of these audits will differ according to each specific training provider, I feel it is apposite to present you with an exemplar version in Figure 27.1.

First name		Surname	
Specialism		ITT course	

Do you have access to a computer at home? (tick your answer)			
No		Yes, but without internet access	
Yes, with dial-up internet access		Yes, with broadband internet access	

Use this key for the following questions:

3 = I can do this with confidence and could teach someone else how to do it.

2 = I know what this is, but I would need a hint or a reminder to show me how to do it.

1 = I do not know what this is and/or I will not be able to do it without being shown step by step.

Please try to be as truthful with your answers as possible. If you are uncertain which answer to select, choose the lower number.

Managing information (My Documents)			
Create a new folder in My Documents	3	2	1
Rename a folder	3	2	1
Copy files and paste them into a different folder	3	2	1
Select all the files in a folder	3	2	1
Transfer files to a pen drive	3	2	1
Tidy up your folders, then burn a backup CD of all your work	3	2	1

Gathering information on the internet (Internet Explorer)			
Use a search engine to find information on a specific issue	3	2	1
Use an image search to find a specific picture	3	2	1
Use an advanced search to narrow down the number of search results	3	2	1
Add a website to your internet favourites list	3	2	1
Create your own webpage and upload it onto the internet	3	2	1
Subscribe to a site using a RSS feed for updates	3	2	1

Create an online survey	3	2	1
Send and receive emails, insert file attachments and update a contact list	3	2	1
Have a live text chat with another person using MSN or equivalent	3	2	1
Download a podcast	3	2	1
Use a webcam to talk to another person	3	2	1
Research useful information for a honeymoon safari in Kenya	3	2	1

Analysing and processing information (Microsoft Excel)			
Input data into a spreadsheet model	3	2	1
Sort the data alphabetically by surname	3	2	1
Use autosum to add up the data in one column	3	2	1
Use a formula to multiply two cells together	3	2	1
Use a formula to find the mean (average) of one column of data	3	2	1
Use a formula to find out the highest value in one column of data	3	2	1
Use the fill handle to transfer a formula into other cells	3	2	1
Create charts (bar, pie, line, etc.) and know which one to use when	3	2	1
Import a .csv file of data into a spreadsheet	3	2	1
Analyse survey data on recycling and create charts to show results	3	2	1

Word processing information (Microsoft Word)			
Touch type	3	2	1
Format text to resize, change font, make bold	3	2	1
Use the align centre and align right buttons	3	2	1
Insert a clipart image and resize	3	2	1
Wordwrap text around an image	3	2	1
Crop an image	3	2	1
Insert the draw toolbar	3	2	1
Insert a table	3	2	1
Merge two cells in a table	3	2	1
Create a formal letter to a headteacher re: a job application	3	2	1

Presenting information (Microsoft PowerPoint)			
Format the background using Fill Effects	3	2	1
Insert an AutoShape callout	3	2	1
Create a WordArt title	3	2	1
Animate an object on the slide	3	2	1
Insert images found from a website	3	2	1
Insert action buttons to link pages	3	2	1
Insert a hyperlink to website	3	2	1
Deliver a PowerPoint presentation to a group of people	3	2	1
Create a presentation about Mount St Helens Volcano to a class of Y8	3	2	1

Digital media (Microsoft Movie Maker and PhotoShop Elements)			
Use a digital stills camera and upload the images to a computer	3	2	1
Use a digital video camera and upload the footage to a computer	3	2	1
Use a microphone to record a narration as an audio file on the computer	3	2	1
Enhance a digital image by changing contrast, colour saturation, etc.	3	2	1
Compress an image to make it a smaller file size	3	2	1
Edit video footage and create a finished video	3	2	1
Create a digital video about life in the trenches during the First World War	3	2	1

What other ICT skills do you have that were not mentioned in the survey?

What other ICT skills would you like to learn that were not mentioned in the survey?

Figure 27.1 ICT audit (reproduced by kind permission of Alex Savage, Notre Dame High School, Norwich)

Understanding the issue of inclusion 28

If you hope to fully engage all your pupils in the learning process, then you need to be fully aware of what is meant by the term 'inclusion'. This is a term you will come across on a regular basis during your training year and beyond. According to the Centre of Studies in Inclusive Education website (http://inclusion.uwe.ac.uk/csie/csiefaqs.htm) inclusion in education involves:

- valuing all pupils and staff equally;
- increasing the participation of pupils in, and reducing their exclusion from, the cultures, curricula and communities of local schools;
- restructuring the cultures, policies and practices in schools so that they respond to the diversity of pupils in the locality;
- reducing barriers to learning and participation for all pupils, not just those with impairments or those who are categorized as `having special educational needs';
- learning from attempts to overcome barriers to the access and participation of particular pupils to make changes for the benefit of pupils more widely;
- viewing the difference between pupils as resources to support learning, rather than as problems to be overcome;
- acknowledging the right of pupils to an education in their locality;
- improving schools for staff as well as for pupils;
- emphasizing the role of schools in building community and developing values, as well as in increasing achievement;
- fostering mutually sustaining relationships between schools and communities.

What this means in practice is that disabled and non-disabled children and young people should now be able to learn together in all educational establishments and be provided with appropriate networks of support. Inclusion means enabling pupils to participate in the life and work of mainstream institutions to the best of their abilities, whatever their needs. As you can see from QTS Standard Q19, presented below, you need to be extremely proactive in your teaching practices in making sure that you cater for the needs of pupils for whom English is an additional language (EAL) and/or for those with special educational needs (SEN).

> Q19 know how to make effective personalized provision for those they teach, including those for whom English is an additional language or who have special educational needs or disabilities, and how to take practical account of diversity and promote equality and inclusion in their teaching.

Working with SEN pupils

It is absolutely crucial that you keep up to date with the changes that regularly occur to the SEN Code of Practice. You can find a copy of this document at the following web address: www.teachernet.gov.uk/docbank/index.cfm?id=3724

The school is highly likely to have used this document to inform its own special SEN policy, but there will be individual nuances that you need to make yourself familiar with. You also need to be extremely proactive at the beginning of each of your school practices in making sure that you meet with the special needs coordinator (SENCO) to discuss the characteristics of each of your SEN pupils. Some schools allocate their SEN pupils a code that highlights the individual pupil's general areas of need. Separate codes are often given for such conditions as autism, dyslexia, dyspraxia, ADHD, diabetes, asthma, epilepsy and serious food allergies. Although it is very important to enter the code into your mark book, do not rely on the code alone. Although pupils may have similar conditions, they often engage in very different types of behaviour. You therefore need to gain first-hand knowledge of the expected behaviour patterns of your own individual SEN pupils. You also need to seek the advice of the SENCO as to the best ways to simplify the work for these pupils. Bearing in mind the vast array of special educational needs, it is not possible here to offer specific strategies to cater for each of these conditions. However, what I do offer below is a list of generalized guidance that may help to support the learning and inclusion of the SEN pupils in your classes. You can make use of these strategies until such time as when you can seek advice on how to deal with the specific SEN cases in your lessons.

Some top tips for teaching SEN pupils

- Make sure that you have read the pupils' Individual Education Plans (IEPs).
- Set differentiated learning objectives to allow these pupils to succeed.

- Make sure that you provide a strong context for the learning. SEN pupils, more than most, need to see the relevance of the learning.
- Provide your SEN pupils with a lot of one-to-one contact, either with you or your teaching assistant(s).
- Provide non-threatening but nevertheless challenging tasks and activities.
- Provide your SEN pupils with short, structured tasks.
- Provide clear written instructions in bullet point fashion.
- Make sure that you demonstrate or model your learning outcomes. SEN pupils need to know exactly what they are expected to do.
- Ensure frequent repetition of keywords, subject content or concepts.
- Make sure that new vocabulary is recorded and tested on a regular basis.
- Get your worksheets checked for readability by your SEN coordinator.
- Always support your text with visual images such as pictures or video clips.
- Make full use interactive ICT as this helps them to re-draft their work and produce work that looks presentable.
- Provide a range of opportunities for these pupils to demonstrate what they know and what they can do. This could be through the mediums of: drama, artwork, poetry, storyboards, cartoons, flow diagrams, bullet point lists, word association, diagrams, zones of relevance diagrams, puzzles, true/false quizzes, games, etc.
- Provide continuity but avoid 'run-over' lessons – this only confuses these pupils.
- Make sure that the assessment reflects the pupils' learning and does not discriminate by structure or language.
- Promote high self-esteem by overtly valuing every pupil's contribution.
- Liaise with the form tutors of your SEN pupils on pastoral matters.

Working with pupils for whom English is an additional language

In the true spirit of inclusive education, you need to provide appropriate learning opportunities for those pupils for whom the English language is not their mother tongue. It is, therefore, absolutely vital that you familiarize yourself with your school's EAL policy and that you use this newly acquired knowledge and understanding to inform your lesson planning.

Speak to the EAL coordinator and discuss the level descriptors for English provided for you in Appendix 2. In the early stages of your practice, try to involve them in the planning of opportunities for these pupils in your lessons. Don't be frightened to ask whether they have any ideas or resources you can use. After all, their job is to raise the standard of achievement among EAL pupils across the school, and they are not going to get territorial about this. It is important that when you come to record pupils' current levels of achievement, you include an additional column in your mark book for their specific levels of English. You need to use your regular meetings with your mentor to clarify any issues you are not certain about. Make sure that you record the general flavour of your conversation in your meeting logs as this will provide firm evidence for a QTS standard that many trainees find difficulty in realizing.

Just as all English-speaking pupils are different and have their own individual learning needs, so too is the case with EAL pupils. It is crucial that you remember that the fluency of EAL pupils in speaking, reading and writing English does not necessarily reflect their cognitive ability. Do not be seduced into the 'one size fits all' model of provision for these pupils. Having said this, it is fair to say that there are certain generalized principles involved in the teaching of EAL pupils and, to this end, I have outlined a number of strategies:

- Make sure that you carry out some basic research into the cultural and personal backgrounds of the EAL pupils in your classes.
- Ensure that these pupils are comfortable in the classroom. Have them seated in front of you so that they can easily access pictures and texts and where it is easier for you to make regular eye contact with them.
- As far as possible allow each EAL pupil to sit next to a reliable pupil who can act as a translator.
- Identify any cultural content that may be unfamiliar to your EAL pupils and be prepared to explain this, perhaps drawing parallels with other cultures.
- Ensure that you start each lesson by explaining the key vocabulary. Make sure you provide your EAL pupils with a visual version of the glossary of terms to put into their books.
- Make sure that you repeat and summarize instructions and requests, but be very careful not to vary your language too much when you repeat yourself, which might result in the pupil spending unnecessary time working out if there is a differences between the two messages. Moderate your speed of delivery to meet the needs of these pupils.
- Wherever possible, give practical demonstrations to your EAL pupils. Supporting your words with actions is a highly effective way of conveying a message to them. However, you do need to be highly sensitive to the fact that body language and gestures vary in meaning between cultures. In many cultures children are taught to avoid making

eye contact with their elders. A thumbs-up gesture in Britain, for example, symbolizes encouragement. In Bangladesh it is the equivalent of the two-finger sign.

- If you are a trainee who is teaching English, use dual textbooks where possible.
- If there is a bilingual teacher in the school who can help you, get him/her to produce worksheets in the pupil's own language.
- Do not over-correct the mistakes of your EAL pupils as this will soon cause them to become de-motivated. Have a specific focus when assessing pupils' work and when setting targets.
- When you are correcting the written work of your EAL pupil, use the same colour as the pupil has used.
- When providing work for EAL pupils make sure that you differentiate. For example, single-word answers are acceptable from a pupil who is new to English but, with increasing experience, pupils must be encouraged to expand their answers and use full sentences.
- Encourage risk-taking within a safe and secure environment. Create a can-do culture within the classroom and have high expectations of your EAL pupils. Expect them to succeed.
- Where possible, find opportunities to use role play and drama.
- Make use of writing frames but only if pupils have had the opportunity to talk through their work prior to the written task.

29 Gaining form tutor experience

You will note that, although that some aspects of the following QTS standards are broadly related to the pastoral and legal roles of the secondary school subject teacher, they do not directly relate to the role of the form tutor.

Q3a be aware of the professional duties of teachers and the statutory framework within which they work.

Q3b be aware of the policies and practices of the workplace and share in collective responsibility for their implementation.

Q4 communicate effectively with children, young people, colleagues, parents and carers.

Q5 recognize and respect the contribution that colleagues, parents and carers can make to the development and well-being of children and young people and to raising their levels of attainment.

Although there is no TDA requirement for you to carry out a form tutor role during your training year, I would strongly advise you to find time in your busy schedule to explore this absolutely crucial element of school life. However, some schools will attach you to a form group simply as a matter of course. You may find that you are given some responsibility for the tutor group, either by supporting the class tutor or by taking sole charge. Inexperienced as you are, I am sure that you have already begun to realize what a demanding role being a form tutor is. The purpose of this chapter is briefly to explore the role of the form tutor, which I believe to be one of the most difficult and complex jobs in the school. The rationale is twofold: first, to fully prepare you in your role of supporting your host form tutor and, second, to prepare you for your NQT interview when the issue of pastoral education is bound to arise.

As an experienced teacher even I find it difficult to quantify everything I do as a form tutor. There is no doubt in my mind that a good form tutor needs to be multi-skilled, flexible, and physically and mentally robust. All I know is that, having carried out a mountain of tasks in such a short space of time, I very often come out of registration sessions and PSHE lessons absolutely exhausted. To furnish you with a realistic view of the form tutor role, I have come up with a number of broad job descriptional categories which I have placed in order of importance. However, I need to say that the status of each individual category can vary according to the perspective of the school's headteacher.

The roles of the form tutor

- To provide formal and informal opportunities for the personal and social development of pupils.
- To provide an infrastructure to support the school's ethos on behaviour and attitudes. (This is an answer very rarely offered by trainees at interview.)
- To support pupils' academic progress.
- To act as a conduit for communications between school and home.
- To provide formal and informal opportunities for the personal and social development of your pupils.

I feel that the overriding aim of the form tutor should be to create well-balanced, socially and morally competent pupils, who are able to realize their full learning potential and lead happy lives.

Figure 29.1 shows how this can be done. Although this may sound rather idealistic, my premise is that if you begin your career with this view in mind, you will at least start off on the right track. You are unlikely to get it right all the time, but at least you will be clear about the route you wish to take with your pupils.

Although you may be fortunate enough to be afforded some individual responsibility for a tutor group during your teaching practices, it is more likely that you will be asked to adopt a more supportive pastoral and administrative role. However, if you are given the opportunity to take the register or to run some group work sessions within PSHE, then accept these with relish and learn from your experiences. In the same way that the quality of subject teachers is variable across the board, the same principle applies to form tutors. Some form tutors recognize their position as a privilege and are able to demonstrate a full understanding of the complexities of their roles. At the other extreme there will be those teachers who are resentful of the way in which this role impinges on what they believe they are there to do – which is to teach their subject. Because of this variability in the commitment and performances of form tutors, it is difficult to predict the quality of learning experience you will receive from your form tutor attachment. Some form tutors will be highly proactive in guiding you through the process as it should be, while

Supporting academic progress
- Checking homework diaries
- Rewarding academic achievement
- Checking and reporting on academic progress
- Contacting parents on academic matters
- Target setting
- Supporting subject tutors
- Contacting parents about academic matters

Aiding communication between school and home
- Distributing letters to go home to parents
- Collecting reply slips
- Passing on information to pupils

Supporting the personal and social development of the pupils
- Teaching personal and health education
- Organizing form trips and events
- Chairing form meetings
- Collecting monies for charity events

Supporting the school's stance on attitudes and behaviour
- Acting as a mouthpiece for the school's behaviour and attitude policy. Clarifying and implementing school rules
- Supporting school's policy on punctuality, attendance and uniform
- Rewarding good behaviour through credit system
- Imposing sanctions on pupils who contravene school rules, e.g. giving detentions, contacting parents

Supporting the child on an individual basis
- Counselling pupils experiencing difficulties
- Helping to 'move pupils on'
- Referring pupils to other people/ organizations

Figure 29.1 The role of the form tutor (reproduced from Dixie, 2005)

others will probably offer you the bare minimum in terms of instruction and advice. Bearing in mind that at this stage of your teaching career you simply don't know what you don't know, Figure 29.2 is a list of prompt questions to help you to make the most of this experience. You will notice that I have categorized these questions using the same headings as used in Figure 29.1, and these categories cover the range of skills, qualities and duties required by a successful form tutor.

Supporting academic progress

- How often are homework diaries checked?
- What happens if pupils do not complete them and/or fail to get them signed by parents?
- Does the form tutor monitor and reward his/her pupils' academic achievement? If so, does he/she use his/her own personalized system of rewards to support the school system?
- Does the form tutor monitor and report on his/her pupils' academic progress?
- Is this done entirely through the formal school system or does the form tutor have his/her own system for checking on this?
- Apart from the formal parents' consultation evenings, does the form tutor contact parents on academic matters? Is this done on the telephone or on a one-to-one basis?
- Does the form tutor set the pupils in his/her tutor group specific academic targets in addition to those set in the school's subject-based target-setting system?
- Does the form tutor support those subject teachers of the pupils in his/her classes? If so how?

Aiding communication between school and home

- Does the form tutor make sure that all the pupils in his/her class receive those letters intended to go home to parents? If so, what system do they have in place to ensure that this happens?
- Does the form tutor have a rigorous system for collecting and monitoring the return of reply slips? If so, what system does he/she have in place to do this?
- Does the form tutor make sure that all of the pupils in his/her class receive school-based information on a daily basis? If so, what system does he/she have in place to ensure that this happens?

Supporting the school's stance on attitudes and behaviour

- Does the form tutor act as a mouthpiece for the school's behaviour and attitude policy? How successful is he/she in clarifying and implementing school rules on such things as expected work ethic, attendance, punctuality and manners? Are registrations carried out in accordance with the expectations of the school?
- Does the form tutor overtly support the school's policy on uniform? Do they carry out uniform checks? What happens to pupils who are not in full uniform?
- Does the form tutor reward good behaviour through the school's credit system? Does he/she use his/her own personalized system to reward good behaviour?
- Does the form tutor impose school and/or personalized sanctions on pupils who contravene school rules? (E.g. giving detentions, contacting parents.)

Supporting the personal and social development of the pupils

- Does the form tutor teach personal and health education with enthusiasm and passion? If so, how is this demonstrated?
- Does the form tutor organize form trips and events?
- Does the form tutor provide a conduit through which pupils can express their corporate concerns? Does he/she hold and chair tutor group meetings?
- Does the form tutor organize charity events or collect monies from the pupils for charity?

Supporting the child on an individual basis

- Does the form tutor counsel pupils experiencing difficulties on an individual basis?
- Does the form tutor set personal targets for pupils to help them move on?
- Does the form tutor refer pupils with difficulties or issues to other people/ organizations? What mechanism has been put into place to ensure this happens?

Figure 29.2 Supporting a form tutor – prompt questions

Ofsted inspections 30

The Office for Standards in Education (Ofsted) sends inspectors into schools to examine all aspects of school life. The inspection could focus on the quality of teaching and learning, the effectiveness of school management and budgeting systems, as well as on issues such as health and safety and the quality of the school environment. At the heart of every Ofsted inspection should be the academic and social welfare of the children.

As trainees, you need to be fully aware of the stressful nature of an Ofsted inspection. Although you are highly unlikely to be personally involved in the process, you need to know that there will be implications for you during this period. The three days given to schools as notice of an inspection are usually spent in a frenetic manner by the headteacher, management teams, the administration and financial teams, HODs, HoYs, main-scale teachers, and cleaning and caretaking staff alike. The prime aim for these staff over the three days will be to get their paperwork up-to-date, to make the school look as attractive as possible and produce imaginative and enjoyable lessons for the pupils. Whatever your views on the efficacy and/or morality of what you see going on around you, you do need to be aware that this is a very vulnerable time for most teaching and non-teaching staff. Be prepared to receive less personal help prior to and during the inspection period. It is possible that your regular weekly meetings and observations will be cancelled by your subject tutor. Although there is not really much you can do about this, you are advised to let your external tutor/mentor/supervisor and/or training provider know about the situation. Try to remember that teaching is very much a team game and make it your business to offer to help the members of your department in getting ready for the inspection. It is this willingness to collaborate with colleagues that can go a long way to you securing a job at your practice school.

I am confident that the information, guidance and advice proffered to you within this section will go a long way to support you in your teaching practices. Although I fully understand that, in a competitive world, it is tempting to focus your efforts on gaining a good teaching practice grade, I am asking you to take a much broader view of the process than this. Although I hope you achieve the grades you feel to be commensurate with your worth, it is more important for you to treat your teaching practice experiences in the spirit in which they have been designed – as practice for a life-long career in teaching.

Part Seven
LOOKING AHEAD TO YOUR INDUCTION YEAR

Your first appointment 31

Although many of the anxieties about starting at your practice schools will soon disappear as you become acclimatized to your new environments, it is likely that you will then start to worry about looking for a job for next year. Although this will be a time of great uncertainty, you do need to be careful that this anxiety and insecurity do not lead you to make rash decisions and to accept a job that you will regret for some time.

In their drive to fill their teaching vacancies, many of you will be offered jobs by your practice schools. I have two pieces of advice for you to consider. Never accept a job simply because you feel flattered to be offered the position. If the job is not right for you, then once the novelty of having your ego massaged has worn off, you will soon regret making this decision. Second, do not accept a job in a practice school simply because you are used to, and are relatively comfortable with, the school systems. If the culture and ethos of the school fail to match your expectations then the message is simple – seek a post elsewhere. However, in offering this advice, I am fully aware that, if you still have not acquired a post as the year draws towards its climax, you will probably not be able to adopt such a balanced approach towards the decision-making process.

It is, nevertheless, often the case that many trainees who have done a good job in their practice schools and who have been happy in these placements, are offered and accept teaching posts in these schools. Although I suggest that there is a case for advertising your desire to work at the school, you need to do this in a subtle manner. Do everything you can to cultivate positive working relationships with the members of your department and with your other school colleagues. Make it known that you would like to put your name forward as a candidate for any future post but do not under any circumstances overtly curry favour with the decision makers in the school. Doing so will create the opposite effect to that intended.

You also need to be aware of the market forces that are prevalent even within the teaching profession. These changes in market forces can be caused by rising and falling birth rates, TDA recruitment drives and/or the salary levels offered by the government of the time. At times, when there is a teacher surplus, even teacher trainees with top grades are often turned down, whereas in times of teacher shortage schools will unashamedly clamber for your services. The same principle applies within subject areas. For example, if you are a maths or physics trainee, then it is highly likely that you will be courted by numerous schools keen to snap you up as soon as possible. Many schools are starting to recruit trainees in these subjects as early as the December of your training year.

Geographical location and type of school can also influence the availability of vacant teaching posts. There is no doubt that, although extremely rewarding, it is often far more difficult to teach in a school situated in a deprived inner-city area than it is in a middle-class rural comprehensive. The desirability of a teaching post is, therefore, mirrored by the number of applications made to any particular school. However, if you are an ambitious person you may be prepared to accept a post in a challenging school where staff turnover is high, and where opportunities for promotion are more likely to be presented.

Another major factor that will certainly affect the job market is the ever-changing nature of the school curriculum. With the current trends towards the inclusion of citizenship and post-16 vocational education in the school curriculum, there are likely to be opportunities in abundance in these areas over the next few years.

The decision as to where to apply for your first teaching post may be influenced by your personal, social, cultural and/or religious background. For some of you, your choice of area will be dramatically reduced because you will not want to leave friends and family. For others, however, geographical mobility will simply not be an issue. It is also fair to say that your own philosophy towards education can be an important factor when deciding where to apply for jobs. Your beliefs are likely to come into play, for example, when deciding whether to apply to a state or independent school, whether to choose a successful school in an affluent area or whether to opt for a challenging, failing school.

Although we live in an increasingly secular society you may be positively or negatively influenced by religious issues when selecting a school to apply to. If you are a practising Roman Catholic or Muslim, for example, then you stand a better chance of finding a faith school of your choice. On the other hand, if during the course of your life you have rejected a specific religion and you would feel uncomfortable in teaching within this environment, it is highly unlikely that you will apply for a post in a faith school. A dilemma may arise, however, where you like the behaviour and work ethic of a particular school but where you are uncomfortable with the religious aspect of the school's ethos. This is when hard decisions have to be made.

So, why is making the right choice of school so important? After all, can't you simply move on at the end of the year? To address these questions, I need to furnish you with some vital information about your induction year. It is extremely important to find a supportive school because, if you do fail your induction year, you are not given a second chance to qualify as a teacher. On rare occasions and in specific circumstances, your induction year can be extended but this is not the norm. This make or break situation makes your choice of school all the more important. Ensure you log on to the school's website and note the quality of induction provision offered by the school. If you know NQTs in the school, talk to them and ask them about the quality of support offered to beginning teachers. You need to be aware that you are entitled to the following level of support from *all* schools as a matter of course:

- a reduced timetable – you should not teach any more than 90 per cent of a main-scale teacher's timetable;
- an induction tutor;
- a planned induction programme;
- the right to observe experienced colleagues teaching;
- the right to attend local authority-run courses;
- the right to be observed and receive verbal and written feedback.

Another indicator of a suitable school is the Investors in People award which is conferred on schools that treat their staff with professional and personal respect. If this award has been given to a school then it is highly likely that you will be offered numerous opportunities for professional development.

One of the most important sources of information about the quality of a school can be found in the latest Ofsted report published on the school website and on the government website at www.oftsed.gov.uk. Close inspection of this data will inform you about: the behaviour of the pupils, the level of pastoral care and the quality of teaching and learning within the school. However, be extremely cautious when exploring these Ofsted reports. So much depends upon the socio-economic status of the parents living in the school's catchment area. A satisfactory Ofsted grade for a school in a deprived area could compare extremely favourably with a good grade awarded to a school in an affluent middle-class area. You can use the Ofsted report to inform your decision in two ways: you can apply to a school which has obtained a successful report and capitalize upon all the good work that has gone on beforehand; or you could apply to a failing school knowing that you will relish meeting the challenges.

Writing letters of application **32**

The importance of writing a good letter of application cannot be underestimated. This is particularly true in situations where there is an excess of demand over supply. Even in situations where only one or two candidates have applied for a post, I have heard stories of headteachers who have ripped up poor letters of application and thrown them into the bin. It would seem that many of them would prefer to wait until the right person comes along for the job rather than make an inappropriate appointment. Because this is going to be your first full-time teaching job, you will not be expected to write a long letter. As long as you have crafted your letter in an effective and efficient manner, keeping to a couple of sides of A4 should be sufficient. You need to be aware that there is a great deal of variation in terms of the paperwork required to make a job application. Some schools will also ask you to complete an application form in addition to a letter of application. Other schools will require a CV to support both of these. All the advice and guidance offered to you in Chapter 3 about completing application forms applies to this situation.

There are some general principles to consider when writing a letter of application for your first teaching job:

- It is absolutely vital that you make specific mention of what you have been asked to include in your letter.
- You need to include your particular academic interests, achievements, personal qualities and skills, and make them relevant to the advertised position.
- State clearly what you can bring to the role for which you are applying.
- Without pontificating too much about this, you need to describe the educational principles that inform your teaching.
- Make it clear what *additional things* you can bring to the school. You may have particular sporting or drama skills which you will be able to offer. It could be that you used skills in your previous employment that

are transferable to a number of school scenarios. In a highly competitive climate, schools will be looking for that little bit extra.

- It is important to get the tone of your letter right. Make sure that you are enthusiastic about the possibility of teaching at the school, about this specific post and about teaching in general. A good letter of application will be successful in conveying your values, beliefs, skills, qualities and personality to a headteacher, and in giving an indication as to whether the school might possibly want to work with you.

Using the correct protocol

Although it is vital that letters of application show individuality and independence of thought, it is also very important that the correct protocol is followed. Failure to do so could seriously jeopardize your chance of an interview. With this is in mind, I have provided an indication of the expected etiquette when writing letters of application for a teaching post:

- Word-process your letter unless specifically asked not to. In order to avoid a cramped presentational style use one-and-half line spacing. You are also advised to think carefully about using an appropriate font style. I would recommend that you use either Times New Roman or Arial.
- Make sure that your name and contact details have been included at the top of your letter of application (address, phone numbers, email address).
- Ensure that you have addressed the headteacher properly (check on his/ her status).
- Check through your letter thoroughly for grammatical and spelling mistakes, and make sure that your letter reads fluently. Get your professional tutor or an English teacher to read through it.
- Write in paragraphs and remember that each new idea should form a new paragraph.
- Ensure that your letter of application arrives on time even if you have to deliver it by hand.

Providing a structure and content to your letter

When constructing your letter of application you need to think very carefully about the nature of your target audience. Be aware that headteachers and senior managers are extremely busy people and that they will not respond well to having to read and reread a poorly written letter of application. A good letter of application will tell the reader a lot about you. If your letter has a clear and transparent structure, has been written with a real sense of flow and contains no grammatical or spelling errors, it will convey the message that you care about the job you are applying for. It will also emphasize that you are likely to approach your professional tasks and dilemmas in a structured, logical and considered fashion. In short, it will show your ability to demonstrate joined-up thinking. Conversely, if your letter of application is permeated with mistakes, and is muddled in its presentation and style then a very different message will be conveyed to the reader; that you are highly likely to adopt a muddled and unfocused approach to the professional scenarios presented to you. Therefore guidance on how to structure your letter of application is presented below.

Introductory paragraph

- Start your letter by referring to the post for which you are applying and by making reference to where and when the post was advertised. You also need to describe the nature of your university degree and state at which college or university you are currently studying.

Core

- In your second paragraph, make it clear why you want to work in this particular school. You need to impress upon the reader that you have carried out some research into the aims, ethos and academic performances of the school. Be specific in mentioning such sources as school web pages, Ofsted reports, LA documents, etc. Make it clear to the reader that you have read the contextual information sent to you by the school. You could do this by quoting from the documents, by paraphrasing areas of text and then by making links between these and your experiences, qualities, skills and academic interests.
- Although it is important not to adopt a sycophantic tenor in your letter, you do need to convey to the reader that the information gleaned from your research has greatly impressed you and that it has made you excited about the possibility of working at this particular school. When applying to a good school, introduce the phrase 'I would enjoy the challenge of working in a school with such high standards' into your text. That is all very well and good if you are applying to a successful school. However, which approach should you adopt if you are applying to a school that is well down the league table? My advice here would be to display a recognition and understanding of the external factors that can affect a child's performance at school and to say how much you

would relish working towards raising the standards of those pupils from disadvantaged backgrounds.

- In your third paragraph, you need to highlight your particular academic strengths, interests and personal qualities. However, remember to link these strongly with the requirements of the advertised post. For example, if the post requires the successful candidate to teach twentieth-century European history then this would be the place to mention the fact that this is your degree speciality and your dissertation is on the 'Causes and Effects of the Cold War'. If, for example, you have recognized from your research that the motivation and achievement of boys in your subject is a big school issue, then you need to capitalize upon this in your application. You could do this by describing how your personal qualities and skills could help to improve the academic performances and behaviour of these pupils, and how you could help to raise standards in the school. This is also the place to outline your teaching philosophy and make strong links between this and the advertised post. For example, if you have noted that the school has a well-developed and successful pupil and staff mentoring programme, you could write something like, 'I believe that to be an effective teacher one must also be an effective learner, which is why I continue to develop and challenge myself.' Continue in this vein to discuss how your teaching is informed by your beliefs and/or by theoretical approaches towards your subject. An example of how you could do this is:

One of the most motivating ways to engage boys is through the appropriate use of ICT in the classroom. As this is a particular interest of mine, I would aim to work with my departmental colleagues to develop opportunities to integrate ICT into the geography schemes of work and to ensure that educational technology becomes part of our everyday pedagogic toolkit.

- In paragraph four, you need to convey to the reader that you are more than just a subject teacher. At this point, indicate the extra-curricular activities you could offer the school. If you can identify links between the advertised post and your outside interests then do so. For example, if you are a science teacher, you could write about your willingness to set up an after-school science club for the gifted and talented; if you have contacts from your previous jobs in business you could offer to bring in outside speakers to talk to business studies pupils at lunchtime. If you've got other strings to your bow – sports, music, etc. – then explain how you currently (or could in the future) run extra-curricular sessions. Have a look at the extra-curricular programme of the school to which you are applying and identify whether there are any gaps which you could fill.

- Paragraph five could see you describing your pre-training experiences with children and/or the particular areas of success within your training year. Again, I need to stress that it is absolutely vital to link these with the advertised post and not simply present a list. If these experiences have helped to develop your organizational skills or your ability to interact with pupils then describe the positive impact this could have for you in the school, should your application be successful. Remember to stress how much you enjoy working with young people and to describe the satisfaction you gain from helping to move them on.

Concluding paragraph

- If your letter is not accompanied by an application form, then furnish the school with the names and contact details of your referees. You need to end your letter with a concluding sentence that leaves the reader with a positive feeling about your application. Conclude your letter by writing something like:

Example 1

I see the advertised post as being a stimulating and challenging opportunity to develop my pedagogic and subject-based skills. Should my application be successful, I would relish working within a department which has such a good team spirit and within a school which has so many opportunities for professional development.

Example 2

In conclusion, Mr X, I would hope to add to the pool of expertise and excellent reputation of Y school through my leadership skills, innovative teaching and infectious enthusiasm. I would look forward to teaching in a school in which Ofsted has described pupil behaviour as being 'very good' and where achievement is both recognized and rewarded. I believe I can capitalize upon this already successful culture and feel that I can make a real difference.

Example 3

In conclusion, I believe that my experience, energy and drive make me an excellent candidate for the post being offered. I look forward to being given the opportunity to work with the headteacher, staff and pupils at X school to turn our vision of a truly excellent school into a reality.

Mailshot letters

Although I fully anticipate that the advice and guidance proffered will stand you in excellent stead when making your applications, there will inevitably be a number of you who will not have been offered jobs by the end of the second term. You are strongly advised to adopt a proactive approach towards the application process. In other words, write to a selected number of schools, furnishing them with relevant details and informing them of your current availability. At this time of the year, schools will be starting to think about the timetable for the next year and it is possible that your letter of application and curriculum vitae might arrive at precisely the right time. I have known quite a few successful teachers who gained their first teaching post by carrying out a mail-shot of local schools and who responded to the headteacher's invitation to come in to have a chat.

Many of the rules that apply when completing a general letter of application are similar to those required when responding to specifically advertised posts. However, in addition to furnishing the school with details of your subject expertise, you need to stress your flexibility and your willingness to get involved in other areas of school life. If you feel competent enough to teach an alternative subject, even if it is only in Key Stage 3, then say so. Very often schools are looking for teachers who are willing to teach a combination of subjects and the arrival of your application in the post could be the answer to all their prayers.

The benefits of being so proactive in the application process are twofold. Providing your letter of application and CV are faultless, headteachers are highly likely to be extremely impressed by your ability to display drive and initiative. Second, at a time when increasing anxiety about not having a job is likely to affect the quality of your teaching, self-esteem and your interaction with staff and pupils, this is a good way of gaining some psychological control over your professional life. I furnish you with an example of a mailshot letter of application in Figure 32.1.

Mr Dai Lemmer
5 Employment Chase
Barking
UB 40
Tel: 07984 321789

Mrs I. M. Hopeful
Headteacher
Hardknocks High School
Tillett
Herts
IM1 4IT

12 January 2008

Mr Dai Lemmer – PGCE Trainee in History
University of Bradfield

Dear Mrs Hopeful

I am a teacher trainee currently in the third term of my PGCE course at Bradfield University and am now beginning to seek employment for my induction year and beyond. Rather than simply waiting for opportunities to arise, I felt that it would be apposite to make a general application to your school in the hope that you may have a suitable vacancy.

I have looked at your school website and carried out some research into the academic and social aspects of life at Hardknocks High School. My research indicates that the high degree of academic success enjoyed by the school is the result of a combination of excellent subject expertise and an extremely caring and proactive pastoral staff. The chance to work in a school that enjoys such a superb reputation among parents and in a Local Authority which offers excellent support has provided the motivation for this application. The location is perfect for me as my partner has already secured a teaching post for 2009 in a neighbouring school.

You will note from my CV that should an NQT post in history arise, I would be well qualified to make an application. I am particularly proud of the 2:1 I achieved in my degree from Bradfield University. In addition to history, I studied English to subsidiary level and I would be willing to teach this subject at Key Stage 3 level should the opportunity be made available to me. I am confident that my keen interest in drama would also allow me to teach this at Key Stage 3 level. Although I have not yet finished my PGCE course, I have provided my good teaching practice reports for my previous two practices and I am confident that, should you require evidence of my capabilities, these will show that I am making very good progress. I fully anticipate securing QTS status (with the associated PGCE qualification) in June.

I have been fully committed to the idea of teaching for a number of years. My experience of working with young people, in three different practice schools, has strengthened my determination to teach. I enjoy the challenge of motivating reluctant learners alongside those who are gifted and highly motivated. My first teaching placement allowed me to work with a number of pupils who exhibited a range of behavioural problems. In observing experienced colleagues, I soon recognized the importance of teaching with a sense of humour and with a degree of flexibility. While working with these youngsters, I also realized the importance of giving rewards as well as applying sanctions. I know that pupils will work for you if you exhibit warmth and commitment to them. In my current placement, I was pleased to be asked to work with a small number of pupils who exhibit significant gifts and talents. I found this to be particularly rewarding as it challenged me intellectually. In working with these students, I quickly appreciated the pressures that they work under, not least from their parents. I am enthusiastic about taking on the role of a tutor alongside my subject commitments as I am in no doubt that young people, no matter what their academic level, are in need of pastoral guidance to support their academic growth.

Those who know me well recognize a steely determination to succeed alongside a willingness to be part of a team. Although I may lack experience, I am committed and enthusiastic. I would work hard to recruit sixth form students to take English at AS and A2 level as I know that success in this area brings kudos to the subject area and a high profile with parents.

I note that Hardknocks High School has a reputation for the quality of its drama productions. While at university, I was an active member of the dramatic society and would be more than willing to offer my services to the Drama Department in school productions.

I hope my enthusiasm for teaching has been communicated. The chance to work in your school is an exciting one. I would be happy to expand on my aspirations in an interview, should you decide to offer me this opportunity.

Yours sincerely

Dai Lemmer

Figure 32.1 Mailshot letter

Preparing for your NQT selection day 33

On the assumption that at least one of your letters has hit the spot and that you have been called to interview, I would like to offer you some guidance on how to prepare for the selection day. You will note that I have again used the term 'selection day' rather than 'interview day' because, as was the case with your training provider selection day, the interview itself will only form one part of the selection process. It is highly likely that you will have to teach either a full lesson or at least a part lesson and that you will be expected to meet and interact with a group of staff and/or pupils. The main message I want to convey to you at this point is that the selection procedure is very much a two-way process. Although it is vital for you to do everything you can to make a good impression on the school, the converse applies. The school needs to make an impression on you. If you are fortunate enough to have been called for interview I would strongly advise you to visit the school before your selection day to meet the headteacher and take the opportunity to make a tour of the school. By doing this, both parties will have an opportunity to size each other up.

When you visit the school make sure you dress appropriately. If possible, you gentlemen need to wear a suit or at the very least a smart jacket and trousers. Ladies, you need to wear a suit or a smart dress. Make sure that you know the name of the headteacher before you arrive at the school. Be sure to address members of staff formally unless invited to use their first names.

Bearing in mind that the purpose of your visit is to ascertain whether this is the right headteacher, department and school for you, you need to have a number of questions in mind to ask during the day. In preparation for this visit, I would recommend that you reread the section on the hidden curriculum found in Chapter 4 as this will help you to make a decision as to whether the culture of the school is to your liking. In addition to this input, following is a list of specific questions to ask on the day:

- Is the headteacher friendly and approachable? Does he/she make you feel important and comfortable?
- How well does the headteacher interact with pupils and/or other staff. Does he/she show respect to these people?
- How approachable, helpful and supportive do you think the members of the department are likely to be?
- Do the school staff appear to be friendly and happy in their work?
- Can you identify any specific staff with likeminded views to yours?
- Are there teachers in the school of a similar age to you?
- What is the rate of staff turnover?
- Are most of the pupils generally on task and well behaved in their lessons?
- What is corridor and playground behaviour like?
- How effective is the school's behaviour policy?
- What is the quality of teacher/pupil relationships in the school?
- Would your teaching styles and approaches be welcomed in the school?
- What induction training and professional development opportunities exist for your NQT year and beyond?
- What is the physical environment of the school like?
- What is the uniform policy – how strictly is it adhered to?
- To what extent does the school reflect and respect different cultures?

When making your pre-interview visit I would strongly advise you to take detailed notes so that you can use these to make an informed decision as to whether to go ahead and attend the interview. Ideally, you need to discuss your visit with someone who has experience of teaching in a number of schools, but, if this is not possible, take every opportunity to discuss the situation with a friend or family member. Very often just being able to articulate your thoughts to another person is enough to help you to make your decision.

Do remember that you will be asked a number of subject-related questions during your interview, so you need to do everything you can to prepare for this. If you are training in a National Curriculum subject, then make sure that you have studied the relevant documents in detail before your selection day. If you are a Key Stage 4/5 trainee and you are not teaching a National Curriculum subject, make sure that you have studied the examination syllabuses and specifications carefully. Get your current subject mentor to help you to identify some key questions based around these documents and prepare some short answers ready for your interview. You will be asked about areas of the curriculum that would motivate pupils and which would be easy to teach as well as those topics that might represent more of a challenge. Be prepared to talk about the strategies you might employ when teaching these lessons.

Making an initial impression 34

Whatever the outcome of your interview, you need to hold your head up high in the knowledge that you have done extremely well to get this far. Headteachers are pretty ruthless in weeding out sub-standard application forms/letters, so you must be doing something right if you have been called for interview. You also need to know that failure to land the job of your choice might not simply be down to the quality of your application, your sample lesson, your interaction with staff and pupils, and/or your interview performance. There is no doubt that internal school politics often play a big part in the appointment of new staff. Very often, headteachers and/or heads of departments will already have earmarked specific people for particular jobs. However, because it is a legal requirement to interview, you may have been called in simply to make up the numbers. Although you may feel that the odds are stacked well against you, do not treat this process as being a total *fait accompli*. If you interview well, teach a good lesson and interact well with staff and pupils alike, minds *can* be changed. It is also important for you to do yourself justice at your interview because you never know when another vacancy might arise at the school.

Your assessment basically begins from the time when you first start to meet and greet people. Be fully aware that, no matter how pleasant members of staff are towards you, they will inevitably be making judgements about whether they feel they could work alongside you. To this end, make sure that you follow the same advice offered to you about your pre-interview visits. Some schools ask their pupils to take candidates on a tour of the building and/or to hold a discussion forum. It is highly likely that these pupils will be asked to give their opinions of you as a potential teacher at the school. My advice here is for you to interact as much as possible with these pupils making sure that you not only ask questions about the school, but also about these young people themselves. Having said this, ensure that you are also very careful not to pry and not to dominate the discussions and/or question/answer sessions. You may be unfortunate enough to have a domineering candidate alongside you on the selection day. You know the type: they know best, they have been everywhere; they've done everything; seen everything. Whatever you do, do not try to compete with such people. My advice here would be to keep your dignity, and let them get on with it. Staff and pupils alike are very quick to see through people like this and it is highly likely that they will be weeded out early on in the selection process.

Teaching your specimen lesson 35

It is now common practice for schools to ask prospective NQT candidates to teach either a full lesson, or a part-lesson on the selection/interview day. This lesson is likely to be observed by the head of department, a subject mentor, an advanced skills teacher and/or by a well-respected and experienced practitioner. Their observation reports will be fed back to the interview panel and may provide a focus for discussion. Whether you are successful or not in landing the job, you should expect to receive feedback on how your lesson went.

Although this can be quite a daunting experience, you need to treat this lesson observation as a gateway of opportunity, a chance to show what you can really do. No school is going to give you a really challenging class to teach, so, although you need to remember your classroom management strategies, this should not provide the main focus for your planning. You will note that I have titled this section 'Teaching your specimen lesson' and that is precisely what it is. In a period of between 20 minutes and half an hour you have to do everything you can to convince the school that you have got what it takes to join its teaching staff. You are strongly advised to plan this lesson with military precision and to leave nothing to chance. In order to help you do this I have made a number of suggestions below.

Top tips for teaching your specimen lesson

- Find out about the pupils in the class beforehand. Make a note of those pupils with special educational needs or those for whom English is an additional language.
- If you are given a choice, select a topic which you can make highly relevant to your pupils and choose something that you know they will really care about. If you have been allocated a specific topic to teach, do everything you can to make this relevant to the pupils' experiences.

- Plan your lesson in accordance with the guidance offered in Chapter 7. Ensure that your lesson has a starter, core and a plenary. Although you will not have first-hand knowledge of the pupils, offer opportunities for differentiation by outcome. Bearing in mind the limited time available, make sure that you include timing slots in your plan and that you keep to them. Do not let your lesson overrun as doing so will disadvantage the other candidates and will engender a degree of resentment towards you for doing so.
- Provide a brief context for the lesson. Explain why you have chosen this topic and why you have planned to use the strategies outlined in your plan. Show recognition of your need to include all pupils in the learning process and indicate how you are going to monitor and assess pupil learning both during and at the end of the lesson. This is your chance to demonstrate to the observer that you have a full understanding of the planning process. Find out who will be observing you and provide them with a lesson plan, a context sheet and a copy of your resources.
- Make sure that you launch your lesson by introducing yourself and by giving your pupils a brief outline of your expectations as far as their behaviour and work ethic are concerned. Doing this will raise your status with the class and will indicate to the observer that this is what you routinely practise. Obtain a list of the pupils' names beforehand, and either make up some name cards for them, or get them to do this at the start of the lesson. Being able to refer to pupils by name will provide you with the psychological advantage and will help you to engender good relationships with them.
- Produce a range of resources and activities for the lesson taking account of the need to cater for visual, auditory and kinesthetic learners wherever possible.
- Be sure to carry out some monitoring and assessment of pupils' learning during the lesson and in the plenary session. You could even set up a simple peer-assessment activity. For your plenary session you could use a true/false quiz or you could ask the pupils to spot your deliberate mistakes. If you haven't got time to do all of this, the very least you need to do is to carry out a question and answer session to assess whether the learning objectives have been realized. In the spirit of true inclusivity, make sure that you do everything you can to involve and assess the learning of the less able pupils in the class.
- Be sure to thank the pupils for their attention at the end of the lesson and tell them how much you have enjoyed the experience.

While you are teaching your lesson, make a mental note of what you feel is going well and what you would do differently should you be given the opportunity to teach the same lesson again. You may be asked a question about the quality of your lesson in your interview so be prepared to demonstrate your reflectivity.

The interview 36

Although all schools differ, it is highly likely that your interview panel will consist of the headteacher, head of department, professional tutor and possibly a school governor. Because of the extremely mixed nature of the panel, you can expect a wide range of questions to be asked. In addition to the subject knowledge and pedagogic aspect of the interview, the panel will also be looking very closely at your interpersonal and intrapersonal skills. When you enter the room, smile and greet each member of the interview panel warmly, make eye contact with each person and shake their hands firmly.

Some interviews are conducted in a very formal manner, while others are very relaxed. Be prepared for anything! If the interview follows on from the specimen lesson, be prepared to answer questions that will require you to offer an evaluation of your lesson. Make sure that you also know your application form and letter really well, as you could be asked to expand upon a point you made. Each interviewer will have a specific brief. Depending upon their specific area of expertise, different panel members will ask questions which will have been designed to find out about:

- you as a person
- your views on the purpose of schooling and education
- how enthusiastic you are about teaching in general and about teaching at this specific school
- the level of your subject knowledge and expertise
- the quality of your planning and organization
- the nature and quality of your training
- how you can use your skills and personal qualities to good effect in this post
- how reflective and evaluative you are
- how you are likely to respond to specific circumstances.

Because of the unpredictable nature of the interview process, it is not possible for me to furnish you with a finite list of interview questions. I have been on interview panels where colleagues have occasionally asked some quite bizarre questions. However, my experience of being interviewed and of sitting on these interview panels, leads me to believe that there is a set pattern to the interview process. Therefore, Figure 37.1 explores of some of the questions you could be asked on the big day.

The school governor/Professional tutor

- Why do you want to teach in this school?
- How well do you think your ITT course has prepared you for this post?
- What evidence can you provide to show that you are a reflective practitioner?
- What support will you require in your first year of teaching?
- Where do you see yourself professionally in five years' time?
- How might you include classroom assistants in your lesson planning?
- How would you plan for the inclusion of pupils who have a limited or no command of spoken English?
- How would you deal with challenging behaviour in your class?

The headteacher

- What are the characteristics of a good school?
- What has impressed you about this school and what has disappointed you?
- What is the function of the form tutor?
- What skills and personal qualities do you feel you can bring to this post?
- What evidence do you have to show that you are a team player?
- In addition to your work in the department, what else can you offer the school?

The HoD/subject leader

- Why do you want to teach X (subject).
- What are the characteristics of an excellent lesson?
- Give me an example of a recent lesson that you think has gone well. Explain why.
- Give me an example of a recent lesson that disappointed you. What went wrong and what would you do differently in the future?
- What strategies would you use when teaching X (a challenging topic)?
- What would you say to a pupil who asks you a subject-related question which you are unable to answer?
- We are trying to recruit more pupils to stay on at sixth form to study X (subject). What strategies do you suggest we employ?
- We organize our teaching with mixed-ability groups in Years 7 and 8. How do you feel about this?

Figure 37.1 Potential interview questions

In the pages that follow I intend to explore some of the key interview questions identified above and to offer you some ideas as to how you might respond to them. You will note that I have not provided any exploration or discussion on the questions relating to the use of CTAs, working with EAL pupils or those relating to the role of the form tutor. To prepare responses to questions relating to these aspects of school life, I suggest that you turn to the relevant pages in this book for this information.

Q. Why do you want to teach in this school?

A. Take this opportunity to show the interview panel that you have carried out research into the school and make sure that you pay the school a compliment. You could mention that you have heard good things about the behaviour of the pupils in the school, that you have been impressed by their examination results and/or that you would like to work in an already thriving school community. On the other hand, if you know this to be a challenging school, you could say that you have empathy with underachievers and would relish working with challenging pupils.

Q. How well do you think your ITT course has prepared you for this post?

A. Use the findings from your Ofsted research, the school website and the contextual information supporting your letter of invitation, identify the needs of the school and then temper your answer accordingly. If the underachievement of boys is an issue in the school, talk about the really good training sessions run by your training provider. If behaviour management is an issue, discuss the benefits gained from your behaviour management sessions. If you have a particular area of interest and expertise, for example the 'development of thinking skills', then take an opportunity to link your training experiences to the post.

Q. What evidence can you provide to show that you are a reflective practitioner?

A. Here you need to talk in general terms about the importance of reflective practice in helping teachers to develop their professional qualities and skills. If you can support this with any reading you have done on the issue then so much the better. You need to mention the benefits of carrying out your lesson evaluations on a regular basis, before then talking briefly about the role of your reflective log/diary in helping to improve your pedagogic practice. Finally, you need to discuss one specific example where you have reflected upon a professional scenario, be it a lesson, an interaction with a pupil or a corridor incident, and where you have modified or completely altered your practice as a result of this.

Q. Where do you see yourself professionally in five years' time?

A. What the panel is looking for here is an indication of whether you are the sort of person who seeks challenges and who wants to better themselves.

Although this is not the time to hide your light under a bushel, you do, however, need to offer a realistic response. You could say, for example, that you would like to take on some kind of leadership responsibilities within three years, that you would like to take on a mentoring role or that you would eventually like to move into the pastoral side of education.

Q. How would you deal with challenging behaviour in your class?

A. Bearing in mind the decline in good pupil behaviour in many schools, you *will* be asked a question on this issue. Make sure, therefore, that you have read the publications recommended to you and that you have reflected upon your observed practice and on your own teaching. If you want to impress the interview panel, then talk about your need to pre-empt potential pupil indiscipline by adopting a *proactive* rather than *reactive* approach towards your classroom management. Mention the need to set up firm expectations, rules, routines, rewards and sanctions, and stress the need for consistency when applying these. Show a recognition and understanding of the importance of supporting the school's behaviour policy, but stress the need for you as an individual teacher to take responsibility for what goes on in your own classroom. Explain that you would devise a list of personalized gradated sanctions to support the school sanctions, and that you would try everything possible before you devolved responsibility to the school system. However, do not hesitate to say that, should you need support, you would be more than willing to seek help from colleagues.

Q. What are the characteristics of a good school?

A. Although you need to be fairly brief in your response to this question, you do need to mention a range of positive characteristics. Some of them are listed below:

- high expectations of pupils and staff
- strong leadership team
- good pupil discipline
- effective teaching and learning
- good links between home and school
- good pupil/pupil and teacher/pupil relationships
- effective curriculum design and delivery
- positive classroom climate
- a high degree of pupil involvement and ownership
- reflective and involved staff.

Q. What has impressed you about this school and what has disappointed you?

A. I am sure that you will agree that the initial part of the question is fairly easy to respond to but that the second part of the question might prove to be a little disarming. The trick here is for you to be able to display a high level of critical awareness, while at the same time making sure that you do not insult the school. You need, therefore, to be able to turn a negative into a positive. You could say something like, 'I was a little disappointed to see that the fantastic wall displays of pupils' work found in subject classrooms have not been replicated in the school corridors.' Another response could be, 'One thing that has really struck me today is how friendly the school staff are, so I am rather disappointed to note that they do not all congregate in the staffroom at break time or lunchtime.' A further response could be, 'While I was making my tour of the school I passed the music room and heard the pupils playing some wonderful brass band music. I am therefore a little surprised to see that there is no school orchestra.'

Q. Why do you want to teach X (subject)?

A. Here the panel is not only looking to see whether or not you are passionate about your subject but also whether you would be able to sell the subject to your pupils. Make sure that you do everything you can to extol the virtues of your subject and describe the ways in which you feel it is highly relevant to the lives of the pupils.

Q. What are the characteristics of an excellent lesson?

A. When responding to this question you need to mention a number of components. A lesson could be described as excellent where:

- pupils have a clear understanding of the learning objectives;
- pupils have a clear view of the learning journey;
- a can-do learning atmosphere has been engendered within the classroom, where it is fine for pupils to make mistakes;
- the pupils are well behaved and fully engaged in the learning process;
- the lesson content has been presented in an interesting, stimulating and challenging manner;
- the pupils' dominant learning styles have been identified, catered for, and/or challenged through the activities and tasks presented to them;
- all pupils, irrespective of ability, are challenged to show what they understand and what they can do;
- teacher/pupil and pupil/pupil relationships are positive and supportive;
- pupils have a high degree of ownership of their learning;
- pupils know what to do to improve their performances;
- learning is fun.

Q. Give me an example of a recent lesson that disappointed you. What went wrong and what would you do differently in the future?

A. The interview panel will use a question like this to see how reflective and evaluative you are about your teaching. However, as was mentioned in Chapter 13, it is not good enough to show that you have simply analysed your teaching and that you have identified areas for further development. It is vital to show that you have acted positively upon these implications and that you have used this new knowledge to modify your practice. When responding to a question such as this, make it clear to the panel that you understand the general principle of reflective practice and then give a few further examples of the changes you have made to your teaching as a result of this evaluative process.

Q. What strategies would you use when you teach X (a challenging topic)?

A. The interview panel is seeking to find out whether or not you understand the need to relate the content and concepts covered within a lesson to the pupils' own experiences. They will also want to know whether you understand the need to cater for, and/or challenge pupils' learning styles, and whether you are able to introduce a degree of creativity into your teaching. If the subject tutor does not mention a specific topic area by name, then have an example from your own practice up your sleeve ready to discuss with the panel.

Q. What would you say to a pupil who asks you a subject-related question which you are unable to answer?

A. When answering this question it is important to stress the necessity of having a good subject knowledge base. Go on to say that a poor command of your subject material is likely to have serious knock-on effects on the pupils' faith in you as a teacher, and that this is also likely to impact negatively on your ability to control your classes. However, make the point that it is not possible to know everything and that it is quite healthy occasionally to own up to this in front of the class. Explain to the panel that you would adopt a relaxed and confident pose before saying something like, 'That is a really good question to which I am not sure I have the correct response'. Depending upon the situation you could either say that you will find out the answer and let them know next time you see them or you could challenge the pupils to find out the answer for themselves. It is important that you stress to the panel that you would aim to generate an atmosphere in which pupils feel comfortable in asking questions.

Q. We are trying to recruit more students to stay on at sixth form to study X (subject). What strategies do you suggest we employ?

A. You could suggest some of the following strategies:

- organize an Open Day and run taster sessions;
- appoint subject ambassadors to talk to current Year 11 pupils and issue them with pamphlets giving information about the course;
- put up display boards around the school;
- ask department members to run taster lessons before the Year 11s make their option choices.

Q. We teach with mixed-ability groups in Years 7 and 8. How do you feel about this?

A. What the panel want to know is whether you have a knowledge of the pros and cons of mixed-ability teaching. Although members of the team will be looking for your opinion on this issue, they will appreciate that you will have had very little experience on which to base your judgements. You could argue that, in certain subjects, mixed-ability teaching can work well, whereas in others it is generally less successful. My advice would be get to know the arguments for and against mixed-ability teaching and to express your views on this issue knowing that these will be somewhat limited because of your lack of experience. I have furnished you with some of the key arguments below.

Advantages of teaching mixed-ability classes

- National statistics strongly suggest that underachieving boys perform better in a mixed-ability environment.
- If properly managed, mixed-ability teaching provides more opportunities and challenges for the lower-ability pupils.
- In many schools, top-set pupils perfom just as well in mixed-ability sets as they do in streamed top sets.
- Ultimately, no matter how you set, all classes to some extent are mixed ability.

Disadvantages of teaching mixed-ability classes

- Moving to teaching mixed-abilty classes involves a lot of change, rewriting of SOW and the production of new resources.
- Most textbooks are geared to setting as opposed to mixed ability.
- It may be hard to sell to some of the more traditional members of staff.
- Both higher- and lower-ability pupils may not make the same amount of progress as they have in the past.

As we have already identified earlier in this chapter, it has not been possible to totally second guess an interview panel, or to provide you with a definitive list of questions you will be asked on the day. Nor is it likely that members of the panel will ask their questions using exactly the phraseology presented to you in this chapter. Although I hope that the range of questions provided will go some way to supporting you on the big day, you are nevertheless going to have to be extremely flexible and to think on your feet when responding to questions asked by the panel. What I hope I have done in this chapter is to get you to think about using a response style that is transferable and which is more likely to bring you success than not. There is also great a deal of truth in the phrase that practice makes perfect and I strongly recommend you to ask your professional and/or subject tutors to give you a mock interview before you attend your selection days. If you require further support on the interview process then I highly recommend this website: www. interviewstuff.com/

37 Career entry and development profile

Towards the end of your training year you are highly likely to come across the Career Entry and Development Profile (CEDP) which is designed to help you think about your professional development in the latter stages of your ITT training and throughout your induction year. The profile process has been designed to encourage you to reflect on your own teaching and professional development and is structured around three transition points.

Transition point one

As your initial teacher training course draws to a close, you will be given the opportunity to reflect on your professional development, your strengths and developmental needs, and be encouraged to start thinking about your aspirations for your induction year. Although you will work with your subject tutors on this document, you need to be fully aware that it is your responsibility to record your own responses to the CEDP prompt questions provided.

Transition point two

At the beginning of your induction year, you will be asked to meet with your induction tutor and talk through your priorities for induction. Part of the discussion will focus on how you can build upon the targets you set yourself at the end of your training year, and how your induction tutors can use the CEDP to plan and review your support programme in your NQT year.

Transition point three

Towards the end of your induction year, you will be supported by your induction tutor to look back on your induction period to reflect on your progress during the year and to think about your aspirations for your continuing professional development (CPD).

My underlying purpose in writing this part of the book has been to highlight the need for you to take control of your own professional future. Throughout the part I have constantly urged you not to sit back and wait for opportunities to arise, but adopt a proactive approach towards the application and selection process. We live in a highly competitive world and teaching is a reflection of this. Schools are looking for innovative, proactive trainees who have a clear vision of the future and who are able to show personal initiative and drive. I am confident that this book provides the advice and guidance required to set you on your way.

Conclusion

I am both hopeful and confident that this handbook will have provided you with guidance on most of the issues that are likely to arise during your training year. However, I am sure you would agree that it would be totally unrealistic to expect me to have covered all the professional scenarios that are likely to crop up in every secondary school across the country. Each school differs in its ethos, culture and ways of doing things. Each school has a bank of employees who are unique both in terms of their corporate characteristics and in the individual personalities of those who work there. Having said this, my research has illustrated that there are some relatively predictable similarities in the scenarios presented to trainees during their school practices, and I hope I have managed to cover most of these. The guidance offered in this handbook has generally been presented in a chronological manner in order to make it easy for you to identify your needs at any given point during your training year. In order to add further transparency to the process, I have linked much of the guidance to the relevant QT standards. By doing this I hoped to aid you in gathering the evidence you require to move you towards qualified teacher status.

So, where you go from here? On the assumption that you have acted upon the guidance offered within this handbook, and that you have landed yourself a job for your NQT year, I would like to congratulate you on reaching your initial destination. Enjoy the moment but please be fully aware that you are about to start yet another journey; that of your induction year. Do not forget all you have learned and do not rest on your laurels. Ensure that you seize every opportunity to develop your professional practice. Approach your induction year, and every year thereon, with enthusiasm, diligence and above all, reflectivity. Providing you do this, I am convinced that you will enjoy a long and fruitful career.

'He who dares to teach must never cease to learn.'

Anonymous

Appendix 1

Professional Standards for qualified teacher status

Professional attributes

Relationships with children and young people

Q1 have high expectations of children and young people including a commitment to ensuring that they can achieve their full educational potential and to establishing fair, respectful, trusting, supportive and constructive relationships with them.

Q2 demonstrate the positive values, attitudes and behaviour they expect from children and young people.

Frameworks

Q3(a) be aware of the professional duties of teachers and the statutory framework within which they work.

(b) be aware of the policies and practices of the workplace and share in collective responsibility for their implementation.

Communicating and working with others

Q4 communicate effectively with children, young people, colleagues, parents and carers.

Q5 recognize and respect the contribution that colleagues, parents and carers can make to the development and well-being of children and young people and to raising their levels of attainment.

Q6 have a commitment to collaboration and cooperative working.

Personal professional development

Q7(a) reflect on and improve their practice, and take responsibility for identifying and meeting their developing professional needs.

(b) identify priorities for their early professional development in the context of induction.

Q8 have a creative and constructively critical approach towards innovation, being prepared to adapt their practice where benefits and improvements are identified.

Q9 act upon advice and feedback and be open to coaching and mentoring.

Professional knowledge and understanding

Teaching and learning

Q10 have a knowledge and understanding of a range of teaching, learning and behaviour management strategies and know how to use and adapt them, including how to personalize learning and provide opportunities for all learners to achieve their potential.

Assessment and monitoring

Q11 know the assessment requirements and arrangements for the subjects/ curriculum areas in the age ranges they are trained to teach, including those relating to public examinations and qualifications.

Q12 know a range of approaches to assessment, including the importance of formative assessment.

Q13 know how to use local and national statistical information to evaluate the effectiveness of their teaching, to monitor the progress of those they teach and to raise levels of attainment.

Subjects and curriculum

Q14 have a secure knowledge and understanding of their subjects/curriculum areas and related pedagogy to enable them to teach effectively across the age and ability range for which they are trained.

Q15 know and understand the relevant statutory and non-statutory curricula, frameworks, including those provided through the National Strategies, for their subjects/curriculum areas, and other relevant initiatives applicable to the age and ability range for which they are trained.

Literacy, numeracy and ICT

Q16 have passed the professional skills tests in numeracy, literacy and information and communication technology (ICT).

Q17 know how to use skills in literacy, numeracy and ICT to support their teaching and wider professional activities.

Achievement and diversity

Q18 understand how children and young people develop and that the progress and well-being of learners are affected by a range of developmental, social, religious, ethnic, cultural and linguistic influences.

Q19 know how to make effective personalized provision for those they teach, including those for whom English is an additional language or who have special educational needs or disabilities, and how to take practical account of diversity and promote equality and inclusion in their teaching.

Q20 know and understand the roles of colleagues with specific responsibilities, including those with responsibility for learners with special educational needs and disabilities and other individual learning needs.

Health and well-being

Q21(a) be aware of current legal requirements, national policies and guidance on the safeguarding and promotion of the well-being of children and young people.

(b) know how to identify and support children and young people whose progress, development or well-being is affected by changes or difficulties in their personal circumstances, and when to refer them to colleagues for specialist support.

Professional skills

Planning

Q22 plan for progression across the age and ability range for which they are trained, designing effective learning sequences within lessons and across series of lessons and demonstrating secure subject/curriculum knowledge.

Q23 design opportunities for learners to develop their literacy, numeracy and ICT skills.

Q24 plan homework or other out-of-class work to sustain learners' progress and to extend and consolidate their learning.

Teaching

Q25 teach lessons and sequences of lessons across the age and ability range for which they are trained in which they:

(a) use a range of teaching strategies and resources, including e-learning, taking practical account of diversity and promoting equality and inclusion;

(b) build on prior knowledge, develop concepts and processes, enable learners to apply new knowledge, understanding and skills and meet learning objectives;

(c) adapt their language to suit the learners they teach, introducing new ideas and concepts clearly, and using explanations, questions, discussions and plenaries effectively;

(d) manage the learning of individuals, groups and whole classes, modifying their teaching to suit the stage of the lesson.

Assessing, monitoring and giving feedback

Q26(a) make effective use of a range of assessment, monitoring and recording strategies.

(b) assess the learning needs of those they teach in order to set challenging learning objectives.

Q27 provide timely, accurate and constructive feedback on learners' attainment, progress and areas for development.

Q28 support and guide learners to reflect on their learning, identify the progress they have made and identify their emerging learning needs.

Reviewing teaching and learning

Q29 evaluate the impact of their teaching on the progress of all learners, and modify their planning and classroom practice where necessary.

Learning environment

Q30 establish a purposeful and safe learning environment conducive to learning and identify opportunities for learners to learn in out of school contexts.

Q31 establish a clear framework for classroom discipline to manage learners' behaviour constructively and promote their self-control and independence.

Team working and collaboration

Q32 work as a team member and identify opportunities for working with colleagues, sharing the development of effective practice with them.

Q33 ensure that colleagues working with them are appropriately involved in supporting learning and understand the roles they are expected to fulfil.

Appendix 2

Level descriptors for English

Speaking

QCA Level	QCA/EAL statement	What the pupil can do at this level	Teacher strategies to help pupils move on
Pre Step 1		• may use single words • will gesture or use L1 to convey meaning • likely to be in the 'silent period'	• be welcoming • make eye contact • include pupils in a group • provide visual clues
Step 1	Pupils echo words and expressions drawn from classroom routines and social interactions to communicate meaning. They express some basic needs, using single words or phrases in English.	• understands a little, but could still be in 'silent period' • can respond to familiar questions and instructions using single words, short phrases, gestures or L1 • can ask for help using single words • can name familiar classroom objects and equipment	• include pupil in all activities, but do not try to force the pupil to speak • use natural English in short, simple phrases and sentences • use closed questions with contextual support • give time for answers • allow other pupils who speak the same language to support responses
Step 2	Pupils copy talk that has been modelled. In their speech they show some control of English word order and their pronunciation is generally intelligible.	• can use a small range of familiar phrases to communicate needs and ideas/meaning • beginning to use English in small group setting in classroom activities • shows some control of English word order and pronunciation in short utterances • will use repetition to extend use of English	• model key words and phrases and encourage other pupils to do the same • create opportunities to speak in carefully structured situations

QCA Level	QCA/EAL statement	What the pupil can do at this level	Teacher strategies to help pupils move on
Level 1 Threshold (L1T)	Pupils speak about matters of immediate interest in familiar settings. They convey meaning through talk and gesture and can extend what they say with support. Their speech is sometimes grammatically incomplete at word and phrase level.	• can convey meaning and express needs using two–three-word phrases • with support, will make contributions to group/class discussion • can speak more fluently with friends in everyday situations • is exploring grammatical structures to generate meaningful sentences but, although the meaning is clear, the grammar will sometimes not be appropriate	• respond positively to contributions • model language by 'echoing' the pupil's utterances, using the appropriate grammar • be aware that conversational fluency comes a long time before fluency in academic English

Level 1 Secure (L1S)	Pupils speak about matters of interest to a range of listeners and begin to develop connected utterances. What they say shows some grammatical complexity in expressing relationships between ideas and sequences of events. Pupils convey meaning, sustaining their contributions and listeners' interest.	• is beginning to be able to express the logical relationships between ideas using features of language such as connectives
		• can sustain meaning and keep the listener's interest, often by using voice and gesture
			• opportunities for group and pair discussion
			• encourage pupil to develop spoken ideas by:
			  giving thinking time
			  asking questions
			  suggesting connectives (because, although, etc.)
			• sometimes encourage the use of writing to organize ideas before discussion, e.g. flow charts, grids, mind maps
			• give opportunities for group presentations where individual bilingual pupils can be supported by others

Listening

QCA Level	QCA/EAL statement	What the pupil can do at this level	Teacher strategies to help pupils move on
Pre Step 1		• understands a little • may join in activities • understands and responds in L1 • uses visual clues for meaning • can respond non-verbally to everyday expressions, e.g. greetings • may use gestures to indicate active listening	• be welcoming • make eye contact • include pupils in a group • provide visual clues
Step 1	Pupils listen attentively for a short time. They use non-verbal gestures to respond to greetings and questions about themselves, and they follow simple instructions based on the routines of the classroom.	• relies on visual cues for meaning, with L1 support may join in classroom activities • will respond positively to friendly approaches from peers • participates as a listener in group activities • can name familiar class objects/equipment • can listen attentively for a short time • can understand and follow familiar instructions	• mix activities • keep teacher presentations short • keep to familiar classroom routines • structure lessons to include suitable activities, e.g. matching, labelling • give opportunities for listening in small groups
Step 2	Pupils understand simple conversational English. They listen and respond to the gist of general explanations by the teacher where language is supported by non-verbal cues, including illustrations.	• understands familiar conversational phrases • can follow narrative expressed through spoken and visual material • understands simple ideas or explanations with help of mime gesture or pictures • listens and responds to paired/group discussion	• use visuals/practicals/demonstrations to support teacher talk • allow time for pupil to listen to and question a friend who speaks the same language • refer to key visual while explaining
Level 1 Threshold (L1T)	With support pupils understand and respond appropriately to straightforward comment or instruction addressed to them. They listen attentively to a range of speakers, including teacher presentation to the whole class.	• listens well but needs to discuss new ideas to help understanding • can listen attentively to the class teacher or to other pupils • responds to straightforward instructions	• be aware that attentive listening does not necessarily mean understanding • support for keywords using visuals • list keywords before lesson for support staff or use a bilingual dictionary where appropriate • pre-teach key words (through starters, using support staff, etc.)

QCA Level	QCA/EAL statement	What the pupil can do at this level	Teacher strategies to help pupils move on
Level 1 Secure (L1S)	In familiar contexts, pupils follow what others say about what they are doing and thinking. They listen with understanding to sequences of instructions and usually respond appropriately in conversation.	• can understand most classroom interactions and explanations with visual or other support • will follow familiar instructions and respond appropriately but may not understand unfamiliar words or idiom	• be aware that the pupil will not be familiar with many words that the other pupils know • continue to support keywords using visuals • approach abstract ideas through concrete examples or L1

Reading

NB: these steps and levels apply to pupils who are not securely literate in their first language

QCA Level	QCA/EAL statement	What the pupil can do at this level	Teacher strategies to help pupils move on
Pre Step 1		• not securely literate in the home language and will take more time to learn to read in English because he/she needs knowledge of English to use reading for meaning strategies	• model reading behaviour, e.g. locating title, reading from left to right, using picture clues to predict, etc.
Step 1	Pupils participate in reading activities. They know that, in English, print is read from left to right and from top to bottom. They recognize their names and familiar words and identify some letters of the alphabet by shape and sound.	• may use L1 in accessing English text • will recognize his/her name and some other familiar words, e.g. from advertising • is starting to become familiar with the shape and sound of letters of the alphabet	• encourage use of L1, especially for exploring ideas • pupils will be unfamiliar with the names of letters of the alphabet • use group/shared/paired reading • keep texts short and accessible • introduce and explain using words and pictures, labelling, simple sequencing with visuals
Step 2	Pupils begin to associate with letters in English to predict what the text will be about. They read words and phrases that they have learned in different curriculum areas. With support they can follow a text read aloud.	• makes connections between English sounds and letters • begins to read some simple words/signs/labels around classroom/school • can read simple texts with repeating language and structure • predicts story/events of a text using visual cues/discussion • can read back writing scribed by an adult • may be able to decode more than he/she can understand	• encourage use of contextual and visual clues • support the reading of even very short texts using other pupils, support staff, discussion or L1 • use pupil's own writing as familiar text to read • use talking books

QCA Level	QCA/EAL statement	What the pupil can do at this level	Teacher strategies to help pupils move on
Level 1 Threshold (L1T)	Pupils can read a range of familiar words and identify initial and final sounds in unfamiliar words. With support, they can establish meaning when reading aloud phrases or simple sentences and use contextual clues to gain understanding. They respond to ideas in poems, stories and non-fiction.	• recognizes and knows the sound of most letters of the alphabet • has developed a sight vocabulary of some common words and those used in the curriculum • reads aloud known and predictable texts • decodes unknown words using contextual and pictorial cues • can demonstrate an understanding of what is read • can read and understand simple text with support	• introduce and explain active reading strategies – underlining, colour-coding, transferring words into a grid, annotating pictures, etc. • activate prior knowledge and thinking as a way into a text • use group and paired activities to support reading • avoid silent reading and use talk to support understanding
Level 1 Secure (L1S)	Pupils use their knowledge of letters, sounds and words to establish meaning when reading familiar texts aloud, sometimes with prompting. They comment on events or ideas in poems, stories and non-fiction.	• increased sight vocabulary of commonly used words in different contexts • can read aloud using knowledge of sounds and letter (but may not understand) • can read complex known English texts but needs support with unfamiliar text, idiom and grammar • responds to text expressing personal views, answering factual questions • with support can infer meaning	• make talking books with pupils • always discuss topic before reading • active interaction with text • choose text with visual clues • let pupil know the purpose of the reading task • teach pupils how to navigate non-fiction text (blocks of text, etc.) • explain how to read diagrams, graphs, grids, etc.

Writing

NB: these steps and levels apply to pupils who are not securely literate in their first language

QCA Level	QCA/EAL statement	What the pupil can do at this level	Teacher strategies to help pupils move on
Pre Step 1		• not securely literate in the home language and will take more time to learn to write in English • can use pictures to convey meaning • can understand that written scripts convey meaning • can hold and use a pencil appropriately • can copy recognizable English symbols	• model writing behaviour, e.g. writing from left to right, keeping to the line, shaping letters, and support correct use of pen and pencil • speaking and listening are essential before any writing to give meaning to the task • encourage use of pictures to convey meaning • use picture annotation
Step 1	Pupils use English letter and letter-like forms to convey meaning. They copy or write their names and familiar words and write from left to right.	• can form some letters from memory • can write own name and some other familiar words • can write some initial sounds • can relate some English sounds to the written form	• generate text orally • support writing of single words and short, simple phrases • confine initial writing to lower case • encourage use of L1, especially if L1 is written in Roman script • using single words and phrases in L1 helps to establish the concept of sound/letter relationship
Step 2	Pupils attempt to express meaning through writing supported by oral work or pictures. Generally their writing is intelligible to themselves and a familiar reader and shows some knowledge of sound and letter patterns in English spelling.	• writing stems from oral rehearsal and pictorial support (may also want to practice in L1) • writing is legible to themselves and familiar readers • can write final sounds • will attempt to read back own writing • in discussing own written text, will be able to explain more than he/she can write	• use grids, labelling, captioning, etc. • use shared writing with peer or adult support • encourage pupil to dictate text to scribe and then to reread text with scribe

QCA Level	QCA/EAL statement	What the pupil can do at this level	Teacher strategies to help pupils move on
Level 1 Threshold (L1T)	Pupils produce recognizable letters and words in texts, which convey meaning and show some knowledge of English sentence division and word order. Most commonly used letters are correctly shaped, but may be inconsistent in their size and orientation.	• writes letters and words increasingly legibly • can write independently and convey meaning through recognizable words, phrases and sentences but spelling and sentence structure are irregular	• respond to the meaning of the pupil's writing, not the form • encourage pupils to read own writing aloud and help them self-correct orally • do not over-correct • use sentence starters and simple writing frames to support
Level 1 Secure (L1S)	Pupils use phrases and longer statements to convey ideas to the reader, making use of full stops and capital letters. Some grammatical patterns are irregular and pupils' grasp of English sounds and how they are written is not secure. Letters are usually clearly shaped and correctly orientated.	• begins to use simple punctuation: full stops, capital letters • can write increasingly legibly with letters clearly shaped and correctly orientated, appropriate spacing between words • can spell familiar and consonant-vowel-consonant (CVC) words correctly • writing demonstrates more complex ideas in sequences of events	• scaffold writing with group activities and oral rehearsal • use grids, flow charts, etc. to help structure writing • let pupils read back own writing and discuss the ideas with supporting adult in English or L1 if preferred • model correct grammatical expression in responses to work while still focusing on content before form (this is important at all levels)

Level 2

Skill	QCA/EAL statement	What the pupil can do at this level	Teacher strategies to help pupils move on
Speaking & Listening	Pupils begin to show confidence in talking and listening, particularly where the topic interest them. On occasions, they show awareness of the needs of the listener by including relevant detail. In developing and explaining their ideas they speak clearly and use a growing vocabulary. They usually listen carefully and respond with increasing appropriateness to what others say. They are beginning to be aware that in some situations a more formal vocabulary and tone of voice are used.	• beginning to show confidence in speaking to convey meaning. This could be by using familiar language in new contexts • uses interactions to extend his/her range of speaking styles • in these interactions, shows awareness by responding to both verbal and non-verbal clues • uses a wider range of vocabulary, including subject-specific vocabulary • beginning to use a wider range of strategies, both verbal and non-verbal, for checking understanding • beginning to be aware of change of register in different situations, although social talk will be ahead of talk for learning	• continue to respond positively and constructively • avoid seeming to correct even when grammar and/or vocabulary is not entirely appropriate • responses should include: acknowledging understanding continuing dialogue modelling appropriate language in context • provide opportunities for small group and 1–1 interaction • appropriate register should be made explicit and discussed
Reading	Pupils' reading of simple texts shows understanding and is generally accurate. They express opinions about major events or ideas in stories, poems and non-fiction. They use more than one strategy such as phonic, graphic, syntactic, and contextual, in reading unfamiliar words and establishing meaning.	• beginning to read a variety of fiction and non-fiction without support • can sustain accurate, independent reading over short passages of text • in discussion, gives views on some main points of the text • when subject matter is familiar, can use a variety of strategies to make sense of the text and self-correct	• occasionally discuss methods of reading for understanding, e.g. 'How did you work out what it meant?' • continue to support reading by activating prior knowledge and thinking • continue to support understanding with visuals • continue to use text for a clear purpose (active reading)

Skill	QCA/EAL statement	What the pupil can do at this level	Teacher strategies to help pupils move on
Writing	Pupils' writing communicates meaning in both narrative and non-narrative forms, using appropriate and interesting vocabulary, and showing some awareness of the reader. Ideas are developed in a sequence of sentences, sometimes demarcated by capital letters and full stops. Simple monosyllabic words are usually spelled correctly, and where there are inaccuracies the alternative is phonetically plausible	• can write accurately enough for an outside reader to understand • can write for different purposes, although may produce writing based more on speech than written models • can link ideas together within a text • usually spells simple words correctly and uses phonetically plausible spelling for others • can use capital letters and full stops • can use more complex or lengthy sentences, although grammatical construction may show evidence of EAL • can use a wider vocabulary • will be able to structure a chronologically organized text more easily than other types of text	• teach how to use a simple thesaurus (e.g. *Usborne's Illustrated*) • encourage pupils to use or compile a subject-specific glossary • support pupils in structuring non-narrative text through discussion and use of simple writing frames • make explicit and discuss different forms of writing (e.g. story, report, explanation, instructions, etc.)

Level 3

Skill	QCA/EAL statement	What the pupil can do at this level	Teacher strategies to help pupils move on
Speaking and listening	Pupils talk and listen confidently in different contexts, exploring and communicating ideas. In discussion, they show understanding of the main points. Through relevant comments and questions, they show they have listened carefully. They begin to adapt what they say to the needs of the listener, varying the use of vocabulary and the level of detail. They are beginning to be aware of Standard English and when it is used.	• can understand main points from discussion and respond to them • able to recount the content of a presentation or discussion • use vocabulary appropriate to subject, although it may not be very wide • may try to be adventurous but may misjudge vocabulary choice sometimes • can ask relevant questions and make comments • beginning to know the difference between Standard English and other dialects	• continue to respond positively and constructively • may still need support with new or unfamiliar concepts and vocabulary • be explicit about the contexts in which Standard English and other dialects are used • discuss synonyms and other vocabulary choices looking at differences in use and meaning
Reading	Pupils read a range of texts fluently and accurately. They read independently using strategies appropriately to establish meaning. In responding to fiction and non-fiction they show understanding of the main points and express preferences. They use their knowledge of the alphabet to locate books and find information.	• can read a range of age-appropriate texts and understand most of what they read • can make simple inferences from the text • can choose leisure reading they enjoy and say why • can coordinate a range of reading strategies to read for understanding • can use the alphabet to access reference materials, e.g. indexes and encyclopaedias	• encourage pupils to identify vocabulary, phrases, expressions or idiom which they do not understand • recognize that pupils might wish to read younger repetitive text for pleasure. This is a useful way of developing fluency and understanding. • support all use of references materials by: modelling note-taking limiting the research questions limiting the range of texts used

Skill	QCA/EAL statement	What the pupil can do at this level	Teacher strategies to help pupils move on
Writing	Pupils' writing is often organized, imaginative and clear. The main features of different forms of writing are used appropriately, beginning to be adapted to different readers. Sequences of sentences extend ideas logically and words are chosen for variety and interest. The basic grammatical structure of sentences is usually correct. Spelling is usually accurate, including that of common, polysyllabic words. Punctuation to mark sentences – full stops, capital letters and question marks – is used correctly. Handwriting is joined and legible.	• beginning to compose different forms of writing for different audiences • can structure writing showing a logical progression of ideas • can use some tenses accurately, e.g. simple past and simple present. • beginning to make a conscious choice of different vocabulary • many pupils' work will show minor grammatical errors, e.g. in tense, use of pronouns, use of prepositions • growing sight vocabulary but will spell many words phonetically • handwriting is legible but may not be joined unless this has been explicitly taught	• make good use of scaffolding • help the pupil to structure text cohesively, e.g. through consistent use of pronouns, time sequencing, etc. • embed use of keywords in writing through shared writing • discuss word roots and families • in marking or discussing written work, always respond to the content of the piece before commenting on presentation • do not over-correct, but choose one or two technical issues which are common errors in the writing

Level 4

NB: many more advanced bilingual learners 'plateau' at this level. The overall aim for teachers should be to extend the range of vocabulary and structures across the four skills, e.g. by maximizing opportunities for Language Development through oral and written scaffolding and full, positive response to pupils' work

Skill	QCA/EAL statement	What the pupil can do at this level	Teacher strategies to help pupils move on
Speaking & Listening	Pupils talk and listen with confidence in an increasing range of contexts. Their talk is adapted to the purpose: developing ideas thoughtfully, describing events and conveying their opinions clearly. In discussion, they listen carefully, making contributions and asking questions that are responsive to others' ideas and views. They use appropriately some of the features of Standard English vocabulary and grammar.	• can choose from a range of vocabulary and structures for different purposes and for emphasis • can vary expression and speed of delivery for effect • can follow an extended discussion or presentation but may have difficulty with idiom and cultural nuances • responds to others' ideas and views by expressing alternative and personal opinions	• make the aim of group/pair discussion very clear, i.e. are pupils being asked to persuade, collaborate, debate or advise? • make explicit the forms of language they are being expected to use • use role play and discuss the forms of language used by particular people, e.g. scientist, businessman, farmer and consumer discussing GM crop • use formal debate • use thinking time for response and encourage collaboration for building on answers
Reading	In responding to a range of texts, pupils show understanding of significant ideas, themes, events and characters. They begin to use inference and deduction. They refer to the text when explaining their views. They locate and use ideas and information.	• can read a range of age-appropriate text and understand the important ideas, themes, events and characters • are beginning to interrogate text – agreeing, disagreeing, developing ideas • can show clear reasoning • can show personal interpretation of information or personal voice in narrative • can make links with other texts they have read	• use grids, etc. to help develop ideas from text • teach explicitly to use quotations from text as evidence for an argument • teach explicitly how to summarize particular points from a text • causes and consequences of human actions are culturally based. Pupils need support in understanding the cultural context when they are asked to make inferences and deduction

Skill	QCA/EAL statement	What the pupil can do at this level	Teacher strategies to help pupils move on
Writing	Pupils' writing in a range of forms is lively and thoughtful. Ideas are often sustained and developed in interesting ways and organized appropriately for the purpose of the reader. Vocabulary choices are often adventurous and words used for effect. Pupils are beginning to use grammatically complex sentences, extending meaning. Spelling, including that of polysyllabic words that conform to regular patterns, is generally accurate. Full stops, capital letters and question marks are used correctly, and pupils are beginning to use punctuation within the sentence. Hand-writing style is fluent, joined and legible.	• can use text structure, particularly paragraphing, to suit the purpose of the text • can use a variety of complex sentences, usually correctly • can use a growing number of tenses appropriately and usually correctly. This would include present and past simple, present and past continuous and conditional • spelling of longer words is becoming accurate • basic punctuation is accurate • beginning to use the comma	• gradually introduce a range of different connectives, e.g. so that, although, despite, to help pupils write in complex sentences • model and develop complex sentences in shared writing • discuss purpose of writing before starting shared writing or supporting independent writing • ask pupils to read back writing in appropriate tone of voice • continue to use a thesaurus and discuss the effect of vocabulary choices • model more complicated tense forms in discussion before writing • in marking or discussing written work, continue to focus on content before forms of expression or grammar • take opportunities to explore culturally based interpretations and implications

References

Bennett, H. (2006) *The Trainee Teacher's Survival Guide*, London: Continuum

Butt, G. (2006) *Lesson Planning*, London: Continuum

Dixie, G. (2005) *Getting on with Kids in Secondary Schools*, Dereham: Peter Francis

Dixie, G. (2007) *Managing Your Classroom*, London: Continuum

Ferrigan, C. (2004) *The ICT Skills Test*, Exeter: Learning Matters

Furlong, J. and Maynard, T. (1995) *Mentoring Student Teachers*, London: Routledge

Johnson, J. (2003) *The Literacy Skills Test*, Exeter: Learning Matters

Keddie, N. (1976) *Tinker, Taylor ... the Myth of Cultural Deprivation*, Harmondsworth: Penguin

Leibling, M. and Prior, R. (2005) *The A–Z of Learning*, Abingdon: RoutledgeFalmer

Marland, M. and Rogers, R. (2004) *How to be a Successful Form Tutor*, London: Continuum

Mitzoz, I. and Browne, K. (1998) 'Gender differences in education: the underachievement of boys', *Sociology Review*, September, 27–31

Patmore, M. (2004) *The Numeracy Skills Test*, Exeter: Learning Matters

Rist, R. (1970) 'Student social class and teacher expectations: the self-fulfilling prophecy in ghetto educations', *Harvard Educational Review* 40, 411–50.

Schön, D. (1983) *The Reflective Practitioner*, New York: Basic Books

Schön, D. (1991) *The Reflective Turn*, New York: Teachers College Press

Shaw, S. and Hawes, T. (1998) *Effective Teaching and Learning in the Primary Classroom*, Leicester: Optimal Learning

Zimpher, N. and Howey, K. (1987) Adapting supervisory practices to different orientations of teaching competence, *Journal of Curriculum and Supervision*, Winter, 2, 104–7.

DATE DUE

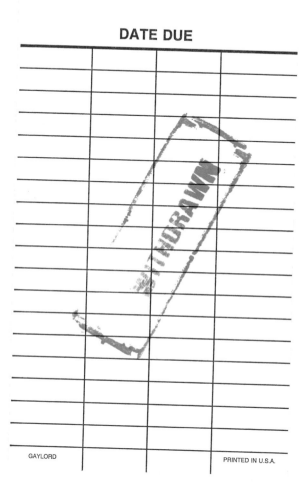

GAYLORD   PRINTED IN U.S.A.

LB 1737 .G7 D59 2009

Dixie, Gererd.

The trainee secondary
  teacher's handbook